The International Baccalaureate Diploma Programme

The International Baccalaureate Diploma Programme (IBDP) is a respected qualification, gaining increasing currency around the world, and has been adopted by a
wide variety of schools, both public and private. In the UK, growing dissatisfaction with the A-level system has led to an intense debate about alternative qualifications, and in many schools IBDP courses have been introduced alongside
conventional A-level courses. The IBDP offers students:

- breadth of study;
- independent research skills;
- rigorous academic standards;
- recognition of achievement in extra-curricular activities.

This accessible introduction to the IBDP takes a balanced look at the pros and
cons of the qualification, and features a wealth of advice from those actually
involved in teaching and implementing it in schools. Providing comparative material on how IBDP courses differ from A-levels, and a subject-by-subject account of
best practice in teaching the IBDP, this book offers a rich source of practical advice
for teachers, school leaders and managers involved in teaching and implementing
the IBDP.

Tim Pound is a Research Fellow at the Westminster Institute of Education,
Oxford Brookes University. His research interests lie in the field of post-compulsory
education, and his publications have focused specifically on qualifications and
curriculum reform.

The International Baccalaureate Diploma Programme

An introduction for teachers and managers

Edited by Tim Pound

Routledge
Taylor & Francis Group

LONDON AND NEW YORK

First published 2006
by Routledge
2 Park Square, Milton Park, Abingdon, Oxon OX14 4RN
Simultaneously published in the USA and Canada
by Routledge
270 Madison Ave, New York, NY 10016

Routledge is an imprint of the Taylor & Francis Group

© 2006 selection and editorial matter, Tim Pound;
individual chapters, the contributors

Typeset in Times New Roman by
Bookcraft Ltd, Stroud, Gloucestershire

Printed and bound in Great Britain by
TJ International Ltd, Padstow, Cornwall

British Library Cataloguing in Publication Data
A catalogue record for this book is available from the British Library

Library of Congress Cataloging in Publication Data
A catalog record has been requested for this book

ISBN10: 0-415-39044-3 (hbk)
ISBN10: 0-415-33537-X (pbk)

ISBN13: 9-78-0-415-39044-6 (hbk)
ISBN13: 9-78-0-415-33537-9 (pbk)

Contents

Figures and tables

Contributors

Peter Allen is Assistant Principal at The Henley College. He introduced the International Baccalaureate Diploma Programme (IBDP) at Henley in 1990, and has been a tutor on the programme as well as subject leader for English A1. He also represents the college on the International Baccalaureate Schools and Colleges Association (IBSCA), which acts as a forum to support schools offering IBDP courses.

Ian Andain has been Head of Broadgreen High School in Liverpool since 1990, and has been associated with the IBDP since 1992. He has contributed articles about the IBDP to *The Head's Legal Guide* and to the research magazine of the International Baccalaureate Organisation (IBO). He is currently chair of the Regional Heads' Representative Committee, and secretary of the International Heads' Representative Committee. He is also treasurer of the IBSCA in the UK.

Sue Austin has been International Baccalaureate (IB) Diploma Coordinator since 1997 at Sevenoaks School, Kent, where she teaches French, Italian and Theory of Knowledge. She is also secretary of the IBSCA.

Michael Coffey is currently working in Spain, having recently completed a Master's degree in Educational Management at the University of Bath. He has taught in schools and colleges in Oman, Uruguay and Mexico as well as the UK. His professional interests include African and South American literature, and marketing education to parents in an international context.

Sharon Dunkley teaches mathematics on the IBDP at Impington Village College, Cambridgeshire, where her colleague **Dave Banham** is Head of Department.

Mary Hayden is Senior Lecturer in the Department of Education at the University of Bath, and Director of the Centre for the Study of Education in an International Context (CEIC), where her teaching and research interests relate to the field of International Education. Between 1982 and 1991 she worked for the IBO in London, Bath and Cardiff as subject officer for mathematics and science, and latterly as research and development officer. She is currently editor of the magazine *IB World*.

David Lepine is Head of History at Dartford Grammar School, Kent, and has been teaching on the IBDP since 1996.

Alex Macfarlane is Head of Science at Impington Village College, and has taught chemistry on the IBDP since it was first introduced in 1991.

Tim Pound is Research Fellow at the Westminster Institute of Education, Oxford Brookes University. His research interests lie in the field of post-compulsory education, and his publications have focused specifically on qualifications and curriculum reform.

Jill Rutherford is Director of IB at Oakham School, Rutland, where she introduced the IBDP. She has taught at schools in the UK and Hong Kong, and has been chief examiner for environmental systems and vice-chair of the IBO. She has also led IBDP teacher-training workshops on environmental systems, and served as an IBDP adviser to a number of UK schools.

Gary Snapper taught in comprehensive schools for 14 years, most recently as Head of English in an 11–18 school with an international sixth form. He is currently at the Institute of Education, University of London, where he is researching the transition between sixth-form and university English. He is editor of the magazine *English Drama Media*, published by the National Association for the Teaching of English (NATE).

Preface

With the future of A levels still hanging in the balance, it is hardly surprising that interest in the International Baccalaureate Diploma Programme (IBDP) has recently intensified. Currently, 65 schools and colleges across the UK offer the IBDP (IBO 2004), a comparatively modest figure, which bears little relation to the degree of attention the IBDP has attracted in both educational circles and the media. The reasons behind this heightened profile are readily discernible. Not only has the IBDP proved to be a compelling alternative to A levels because it guarantees breadth of study, but it also provides opportunities for students to develop their independent research skills through an extended essay; to foster an understanding of the epistemological links across the different subject domains through its Theory of Knowledge (TOK) course; and to gain formal recognition of achievement in extra-curricular activities through its Creativity, Action, Service (CAS) requirement. Moreover, having established an international reputation for rigorous academic standards, it maintains these standards through an assessment pattern that does not stifle the capacity for critical thinking or intellectual enquiry. Expressed in diagrammatic form, the IBDP can thus be seen to present its students with a truly broad and integrated curriculum (Figure 1).

Typically, students take one subject from each of the six subject domains, three at standard level and three at higher level. Thus, all students following the IBDP are required to study their first language and literature; a modern foreign language; mathematics; a science; one subject from the humanities or social sciences; and, finally, one from the arts (or a *second* choice from one of the other five subject domains) – a model of breadth and curricular balance, which stands in stark contrast to the comparatively narrow and fragmented nature of A-level study. Moreover, since each subject is graded on a points scale, with a maximum of 7 points allocated at both higher and standard level, the IBDP has never been tainted with the kind of accusations about grade inflation (or the impossibility of discriminating between the most able candidates) that have recently been levelled at the A-level system following the *Curriculum 2000* reforms. The fact that the IBDP was given a resounding endorsement by higher-education institutions in a recently published enquiry into university perceptions of the IBDP provides further confirmation of its reputation for breadth and rigour (IBO 2003).

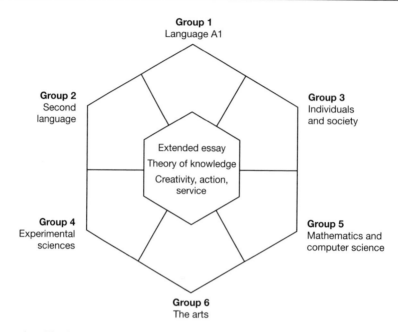

Group 1
Language A1

Group 2
Second
language

Group 3
Individuals
and society

Extended essay
Theory of knowledge
Creativity, action,
service

Group 4
Experimental
sciences

Group 5
Mathematics and
computer science

Group 6
The arts

Figure 1   The hexagon: The IBDP curriculum model

Whether the proposed Diploma framework embodied in the *Final Report* of the Tomlinson Working Group on 14–19 Reform (DfES 2004) would have delivered an equally broad and rigorously-assessed programme of study for students in England seems highly improbable. Although a number of Tomlinson's recommendations for a diploma system at Advanced Level demonstrate a marked indebtedness to the IBDP – for example, the formal recognition of community work or more general employment experience, together with a mandatory 'extended project' – it appears that the principle of encouraging breadth of study was largely overshadowed by the more urgent need to raise participation rates through the achievement of parity of esteem across vocational and academic pathways. While this is an entirely laudable aim, the absence of any degree of prescription governing subject choice would no doubt have meant that, after more than four decades of policy debate and incremental reform, the establishment of breadth, balance and rigour across academic routes would still have remained as elusive as ever.

In the wake of the Government's much-criticised rejection of the Tomlinson recommendations, however, one can only speculate on the likely impact of the proposed reforms on patterns of study at 16+ had they been accepted. What is clear is that A-levels are here for the foreseeable future – at least, that is, until 2008, when a further review of qualifications and the 14–19 curriculum is promised. Yet in its response to the Tomlinson recommendations, while affirming the fact that A-levels would continue to function as one of the 'cornerstones' of the 14–19 qualifications framework (DfES 2005), the Government also acknowledged that in its current form the A-level system intrinsically fails to promote academic breadth. As the authors of the latest White Paper on post-compulsory qualifications and curriculum reform concede:

> We understand and appreciate the argument that we should challenge our A-level students further, by demanding more breadth. But there is no clear consensus amongst pupils, parents, employers or universities on whether and how it should be done.
>
> (DfES 2005: 4)

Those already familiar with the IB Diploma Programme, of course, might well take issue with the point about 'how it should be done' – but for those who are not, this book will hopefully provide a much sharper sense of what it is like *in practice* to teach and manage the IBDP. It is not, however, intended as a practical guide to the implementation of the Diploma Programme, nor does it attempt to present a comprehensive picture of the wide range of subjects which fall within the parameters of the IBDP as a whole. Rather, its subject-specific chapters are broadly grouped around what the IBO has referred to as the 'two great traditions of learning: the humanities and the sciences' (IBO 2004). Moreover, in providing what amounts to a snapshot of contemporary practice, it engages particularly with the theme of how both the teacher and student experiences of the IBDP compare with those of current A-level provision under the *Curriculum 2000* reforms.

Although the focus has been confined to the English experience of the IBDP, the transnational appeal of the Diploma Programme means that the contents of the book should be of equal interest to a prospective international readership as well as to those with more immediate concerns about the future of advanced-level qualifications in a post-Tomlinson era in England. There are, however, a number of reasons for the delimited, anglocentric focus. Firstly, as far as the rest of the UK is concerned, following political devolution in Wales and Scotland – with the Welsh Assembly having sanctioned the piloting of the 'Welsh Baccalaureate' while Scotland continues to develop its historically broader pattern of studies through the incorporation of vocational awards within an integrated qualifications framework – it seems inevitable that the momentum for reform in England is set to intensify. Secondly, despite the Government's controversial rejection of the Tomlinson proposals and its ostensible commitment to A-levels, the question that still begs an answer is how much longer can we tolerate a system which not only fails to encourage students in England to take a broader mix of subjects, but which is inherently powerless to counteract the continuing decline in the demand for key subject areas, most notably modern foreign languages? Finally, on a more general note, given the fact that the Diploma Programme is currently taken by more than 40,000 students worldwide, and assessed in three languages – English, French and Spanish – any attempt to do justice to the sheer scale and complexity of such an international enterprise within the confines of this volume would be a futile exercise. Perhaps more significantly, the fact that more than three-quarters of the schools and colleges offering the Diploma Programme are *national* rather than international institutions (IBO 2004) not only says much about the perceived strengths of the IBDP in comparison to some of its home-based counterparts, but also provides a further rationale for the comparative focus on A-levels and the Diploma Programme which runs throughout the book.

In terms of its overall content and structure, the book is divided in two sections. Part One consists of two chapters, the first of which seeks to establish an historical context against which the evolution of the Diploma Programme can be more fully appreciated. In doing so, it chronicles the missed opportunities which characterise the English experience of curriculum and examination reform. Chapter 2 extends this contextual theme through a critical consideration of the international focus of the Diploma Programme, and argues the case for the importance of inculcating such a multicultural vision at a time when all students need to prepare themselves for life in a global community.

Part Two is devoted to a series of practitioners' perspectives on the IBDP. Chapter 3 includes three individual accounts – the first from an inner-city comprehensive, the second from an independent school, and the third from a tertiary college – of the challenges facing any institution intent on introducing the Diploma Programme. This is followed by a group of three chapters, each of which reflects critically on the teacher and student experiences of what could be considered to be the three main subject clusters of the IBDP curriculum – language, literature and the arts, individuals and societies, and mathematics and the sciences. These subject-specific perspectives are followed by Chapter 7, which opens with a critical overview of what many would argue is the philosophical linchpin of the Diploma Programme – the Theory of Knowledge (TOK) strand – and concludes with an assessment of the Extended Essay and the Creativity, Action, Service (CAS) requirement. Finally, Chapter 8 examines the issue of progression beyond the Diploma Programme – and given its focus, it is perhaps fitting that it emerges as the most student-centred contribution in a book which is, above all, designed to lead to a better understanding of the IBDP in practice.

References

DfES (Department for Education and Skills) (2004) *14–19 Curriculum and Qualifications Reform: Final Report of the Working Group on 14–19 Reform*, DfES, London.

DfES (2005) *14–19 Education and Skills: Summary*, DfES, London.

IBO (International Baccalaureate Organization) (2003) *Perceptions of the International Baccalaureate Diploma Programme: A Report of an Inquiry carried out at UK Universities and Institutions of Higher education*. Cardiff, International Baccalaureate Organization.

IBO (2004) www.ibo.org

Part I

In context

Chapter 1

The International Baccalaureate Diploma Programme (IBDP) and post-compulsory qualifications reform in England

Tim Pound

Contextualising the reform process

In the protracted, and occasionally acrimonious, debate about the reform of the post-compulsory qualifications framework in England, opinion remains divided on how best to match the needs of a heterogeneous mix of students with the demands of a modern skills-based economy. Within the contours of this debate, A levels have long been equated with the virtues of studying a limited number of subjects in depth. Originally conceived as free-standing and academically rigorous qualifications, A levels, according to their many admirers, have rightfully earned their reputation as the 'gold standard' of the post-compulsory curriculum. One obvious consequence of their formidable reputation for academic rigour, however, is that A levels have always been vulnerable to the charge that they are educationally exclusive and thus elitist. That the typical A-level experience has not included access to a broader range of knowledge and skills, increasingly demanded by both higher education and the contemporary workplace, has been a further cause for concern.

Such criticism has undoubtedly been thrown into sharper relief through comparisons between A levels and their international equivalents. What these have invariably concluded is that A levels are not simply out of step with other national systems, but, in terms of their narrow curricular focus, are little short of unique. For example, when set against the curricular breadth and balance of rival systems like the French *baccalauréat* and the German *Abitur*, the degree of subject specialisation inherent in A-level study becomes all too apparent. Yet since the former are effectively rooted in 'foreign' educational cultures, this has meant that their potential impact on the reform debate in England has hitherto been marginal.

The same cannot be said, however, about the IBDP. Perhaps the principal reason for this is that since the IBDP was originally devised as an international school-leaving qualification, its adoption by a small network of home-based international schools and colleges effectively placed it on the very threshold, as it were, of state provision. From these early beginnings, the IBDP has gradually made its presence felt across both the independent and maintained sectors, and the fact that it is now offered in more than 60 accredited institutions in England and Wales is a testament to its growing reputation for breadth and academic rigour. Moreover, in the continuing absence of a national qualifications framework combining guaranteed standards and broader patterns of study, this figure looks set to increase further – and, if some media reports are to be believed, the IBDP's growth may well be spectacular (*Independent*, 4 October 2004).

But while the IBDP has become synonymous with a degree of breadth and rigour that has arguably enabled it to eclipse the A-level system as the brightest star in the constellation of post-compulsory qualifications, few would dispute the fact that both qualification frameworks share a certain amount of common ground. Most obviously, each functions as a rite of passage between school and university or the world of work. Beyond this, however, the historical relationship between A levels and the IBDP becomes more complex. This is partly due to the fact that the conceptual origins of the latter are inextricably linked to the English experience of post-compulsory qualifications and curriculum development. Equally, as we shall see, the intrinsic merits of a baccalaureate model have long made their presence felt over the reform process in England. In this sense, it is not without significance that the various proposals to replace A levels with a broader qualifications framework, which have emerged over the last 40 years or so, have often shared a remarkably close affinity with both the content and structure of the IBDP.

One obvious starting point for a critical exploration of these issues is the controversy generated by the publication of the Crowther Report in 1959. While pronouncing in favour of retaining an examinations framework in which the study of three closely related A-level subjects had become the norm, the Crowther Committee clearly experienced some difficulty in defending its decision to ratify academic specialisation. In fact, it could only do so by asserting that specialisation satisfied a uniquely 'English' phase of post-adolescent intellectual development, which it subsequently defined as 'subject-mindedness'(CACE 1959: 262). From a historical perspective, what this endorsement meant in practice was that, unlike their counterparts across the rest of the developed world, schools in England could continue to prepare students for a narrow permutation of either arts or science courses, secure in the knowledge that such a programme had been officially sanctioned.

Not surprisingly, the Crowther Committee's justification of premature specialisation did not go unchallenged. One of the foremost critics of the report's defence of the English system was Alec Peterson, whose appointment as the first director general of what would become the International Baccalaureate Organisation (IBO) in 1967 meant that he would later become involved in both the planning and the piloting of the IBDP in 1968. As we shall see, Peterson's contribution to the debate about the upper-secondary curriculum in England in the late 1950s and early 1960s, following his appointment as director of what was then Oxford University's Department of Education, was fuelled by a deep sense of unease over the fact that, in preparing candidates for single-subject honours degrees, A-level examinations effectively discouraged the pursuit of broader patterns of academic study. Sceptical of attempts to introduce greater breadth into sixth-form studies through the use of what had become known as 'minority time' – in other words, the small portion of teaching time that remained after the timetabling of three A-level subjects – Peterson maintained that the introduction of complementary courses such as 'arts for science students' and 'science for arts specialists' lacked both credibility and status. If such courses were not formally examined, he argued, then they would never be taken seriously by their users and end-users – succinctly, the schools, the sixth-formers and, perhaps more importantly, the universities themselves.

Peterson, however, did more than voice his opposition to academic specialisation. Following a period of research funded by the Gulbenkian Foundation, which resulted in the publication of what proved to be a controversial report – *Arts and Science Sides in the Sixth Form* – he proposed an alternative four-subject examinations framework based upon existing A-level syllabuses and supplemented by what he designated as a 'unifying and complementary course' (Peterson 1960: 16), in fact a precursor of the IBDP's Theory of Knowledge (TOK) course. Formulated in the wake of the publication of the Crowther Report – which, as we have seen, gave subject specialisation its stamp of approval – Peterson's proposals ultimately failed to attract the kind of support needed to initiate change, and thus the equation between the A-level system and narrow academic specialisation was cemented further.

None the less, mindful of the growing number of less academically motivated students who elected to continue their education beyond the compulsory school-leaving age, successive governments throughout the remainder of the 1960s and 1970s grappled with the problem of how to broaden the post-16 qualifications framework as a whole in order to make it more responsive to a wider range of educational needs. Arguments in favour of greater breadth, however, would repeatedly collapse when confronted by a seemingly implacable conundrum – that a broader examinations framework could only be achieved at the expense of academic depth. The fear of a decline in standards would prove to be a potent factor in the rejection of all of the subsequent attempts to reform the post-compulsory qualifications framework – and, as we shall see, it undoubtedly played its part in undermining one particular set of proposals that were generally agreed to hold the greatest potential for a radical overhaul of the A-level system, those embodied in the Higginson Report of 1988.

While the IBDP continued to consolidate its growth not only in the context of international education, but also in a growing number of schools and colleges in England that had become increasingly dissatisfied with the lack of breadth and balance in the sixth-form curriculum, the narrow exclusivity of the English system continued to attract adverse criticism. Moreover, the expansion of vocational qualifications, which began in the 1970s and received additional impetus following the implementation of the Technical and Vocational Education Initiative (TVEI) in 1984, began to focus attention on the vexed issue of parity of esteem between the academic and vocational routes post-16. The crux of the problem lay with the A-level system and the value placed upon its reputation for academic excellence. This effectively meant that alternative qualifications that evolved under its shadow struggled to achieve status and recognition within an examinations framework in which A levels had come to function as some kind of benchmark, or 'gold standard', against which vocational qualifications in particular would be invariably judged and evaluated.

Official attempts to bridge the gulf between the academic and vocational routes began in earnest in the late 1980s, with the identification of a number of 'core skills' shared across each of the pathways, and the formal recognition of a number of 'principles' common to both. In practical terms, however, these initiatives failed to create a context in which students could confidently 'pick and mix' a combination of academic and vocational courses, let alone find themselves encouraged to transfer between one route and the other. Moreover, efforts to incorporate core skills into A-level syllabuses proved largely unsatisfactory both from the point of view of assessment and in the sense that concepts such as 'working as part of a team', to take but one example, sat uneasily alongside established academic assessment objectives such as those embedded in, say, English literature or history.

While the notion of parity of esteem continued to provide a focal point for those who criticised the divisiveness, lack of coherence and exclusivity of the English system, closely related issues – such as the country's comparatively low participation rate in post-compulsory education and training – served as an additional reminder of the need for more fundamental reform. The cumulative effect of these concerns was reflected in a series of independently funded reports during the early 1990s, each proposing the development of an 'overarching' qualifications framework to end the division between general and vocational education and training, to raise participation rates and to provide a broad and balanced curriculum responsive to the social and economic demands of a new millennium. These reports, such as the proposal to introduce a 'British *baccalauréat*', mark a pivotal point in the debate about post-compulsory curriculum reform, in that they collectively present the case for an inclusive and unifying system to promote greater breadth of study and to recognise achievement across both academic and vocational routes post-16.

This discernible shift in the curriculum debate in favour of a unifying framework none the less continued to run counter to government policy, which tended to fall back on the less radical option of treating both routes as separate entities. Such an approach, for example, had resulted in the unsuccessful attempt to broaden academic study through the introduction of the Advanced Supplementary (AS) qualification, followed by the development of the General National Vocational Qualification (GNVQ) in the early 1990s, an award specifically devised to raise the status of vocational qualifications, but one that failed to become established as a viable alternative to A levels (Hodgson and Spours 1999: 112). It also underpinned the text of the Dearing Review, which argued for the introduction of a 16–19 qualifications framework that would equate levels of achievement across general and vocational pathways, and encourage breadth of study through the proposed introduction of an overarching award or 'Advanced Diploma'. The fact that success in each route would still be rewarded by a fundamentally different set of qualifications, however, did not bode well for the development of a more unified system. In addition, given the text of Dearing's remit, which stressed the importance the government attached to 'maintaining the rigour' of A-level qualifications, the chances of this benchmark of academic excellence becoming subsumed under a more generic qualifications label were remote.

This fragmented and incremental approach towards the reform process can also be discerned in the most recently implemented attempts to establish greater breadth and inclusiveness in the post-compulsory curriculum – those associated with the

Curriculum 2000 proposals. At the core of these hastily implemented reforms lay a reformulated AS level, retitled the 'Advanced Subsidiary' and, in terms of standards, pitched midway between the General Certificate of Education (GCSE) and A level. This was accompanied by a revamped GNVQ, more tightly linked to the new A- and AS-level framework through three- and six-unit modular blocks and a shared grading scheme, which was given the title of the 'Advanced Vocational Certificate in Education' (AVCE). These revisions were introduced in the belief that the former would decisively counteract the problem of subject specialisation, while the latter would remove the stigma attached to vocational qualifications. Rather than achieving these long-coveted aims, however, the *Curriculum 2000* reforms have achieved only limited success (Hodgson and Spours 2003a). Moreover, what they will probably be remembered for above all is the sense of disbelief and outrage over the setting of grade boundaries – together with the rash of demands for the remarking of candidates' scripts – which greeted the first batch of results for the revised A levels in the late summer of 2002. An inadequate consultation process, coupled with a lack of detailed guidance from the Qualifications and Curriculum Authority (QCA) over the precise relationship between the newly segregated AS and A2 levels, had, it seemed, resulted in the unthinkable happening – the 'gold standard' of the post-compulsory curriculum was in danger of becoming irreversibly devalued.

Perhaps the greatest irony behind the recent crisis of confidence in the A-level system is that it might never have arisen in the first instance had Peterson's original proposals for overcoming subject specialisation not met with such implacable opposition. The point here, however, is not that students might have found themselves following some kind of Anglicised version of the IBDP, since the IBDP was specifically devised with international schools in mind. What they would have doubtless experienced would have been a further variant of Peterson's proposals, in which the drive to introduce breadth and balance into the sixth-form curriculum could well have resulted in a truly integrated qualifications framework. The implications of such a model for subsequent attempts to incorporate more vocational areas of study into the field of post-compulsory provision can now only be the subject of speculation, but it is unlikely that a curriculum originally predicated on breadth would have provided the kind of barriers to systemic reform that have thus far characterised the English experience.

What, then, lay at the core of the Peterson proposals? How can they be related to subsequent attempts at reform, and why did their rejection establish a precedent that would effectively enable the A-level system to dominate post-compulsory provision in England throughout the next four decades? The principal intention of the remainder of this chapter will be to examine these issues in more detail, and, in doing so, to provide a contextual background against which the practitioners' perspectives on teaching and managing the IBDP that follow can be more fully appreciated. A further purpose, however, is that in drawing attention to what a recent report rather euphemistically referred to as some 'longstanding English problems' (DfES 2003a: 8), a more informed sense of the relative merits of both the A-level system and the IBDP is likely to emerge.

'Arts and Science Sides in the Sixth Form'

Peterson's enquiry into subject specialisation actually began in 1958, the year before the findings of the Crowther Committee were published. His principal intention was to explore ways of overcoming the pattern of subject specialisation that resulted in only around 2 per cent of male and less than 10 per cent of female students combining both arts and science courses in their choice of A-level subjects in English schools (Peterson 1960: 6). In ways that would adumbrate his subsequent involvement in the development of the IBDP, Peterson's enquiry also incorporated an international perspective, in that comparisons were drawn between the evolution of sixth-form studies in England and those in France, Germany and the United States, which in common with most of the country's other leading economic competitors had adopted a broadly based post-compulsory curriculum. This brief comparative analysis led Peterson to conclude that the establishment of a broader, more 'integrated' curriculum beyond the compulsory phase of secondary education in other countries was directly attributable to strategic decisions of government policy. In England, on the other hand, the historical absence of state intervention had enabled the universities – in part through their monopoly of the examining boards – to exert a considerable degree of influence over the content of the 16+ curriculum. Thus students preparing for single-subject, three-year honours degrees were effectively discouraged from ranging beyond the strict permutation of subjects dictated by university-entrance requirements, and although many schools attempted to counterbalance premature specialisation through a programme of general studies, what Peterson discovered was that 'it is hard to get pupils to take seriously work which is neither examined nor considered worthy of a share in the homework programme' (1960: 7).

That Peterson was clearly frustrated by the constraints imposed by this unique historical alliance between the universities, the examining boards and the schools is apparent in the wording of his critique of the limitations of such a tradition, which is worth quoting in full:

> Nor is it easy to justify to critics not brought up in the system a curriculum which deprives one third of the nation's ablest pupils of any advanced Mathematics and the other two thirds of any serious contact with foreign languages or with the literature of their own country. To those bred in the tradition however it clearly has great attractions and any serious critique of the system or proposals for change must take account of the tradition and its origins.
>
> (Peterson 1960: 7)

Here we can perhaps discern – beyond the sense of frustration implicit in the opening negatives – the prospect of a broader baccalaureate-style framework already taking shape in Peterson's vision for future curriculum reform. What is of equal significance, however, is the way in which the strength of the English tradition was emphatically acknowledged – something that may, in turn, have prompted Peterson to adopt a more conservative approach to reform, in which preference was given to ways of increasing breadth *within* the framework of contemporary A-level provision, rather than to modifications that required a more radical intervention.

No doubt buoyed by the findings of his research – which indicated that when asked which three A-level subjects they would choose if free from all external influences and constraints, 40 per cent of all students canvassed (the largest group) opted for a combination of arts and science courses – Peterson proposed a four-subject curriculum. Underpinning this model was an ideological commitment to what had been defined as the four main categories or 'modes' of thinking and learning – the logical, the empirical, the moral and the aesthetic. In order to develop these modes, Peterson proceeded to identify what would become the four core subject blocks of his framework, and these were as follows:

- English language/literature
- mathematics
- one subject from the natural sciences
- either history or a second language.

The preferred combination was, of course, based upon a pattern of two arts and two science subjects. A three–one split would be permitted, Peterson conceded, but a limited degree of prescription would ensure that no student would be allowed to specialise exclusively in the arts or in the sciences. Further concessions were also proposed for those whom Peterson identified as being 'mathematically blind', and these involved mathematics being substituted by 'either a second language or a descriptive science such as Biology or Geology in which Mathematics is not essential in the early stages' (1960: 17).

In addition to this subject-specific core, a fifth block was proposed and devised primarily to enable students to develop a sense of the 'unity' of their studies through what Peterson defined as a 'training in clarity of thought' (1960: 17). Based on the French *baccalauréat*'s 'Classe de Philosophie', and with its emphasis on providing students with a broader understanding of subject 'methodologies' – or, in Peterson's words, an understanding of 'how scientists reach their conclusions, how a mathematical truth differs from a moral one and what is meant by poetic imagination' (1960: 18) – this essentially unifying course would later provide the inspiration for the IBDP's TOK component, which would first emerge under Peterson's direction some ten years later (Hill 2003: 50). Beyond this radical innovation, additional time was earmarked for religious knowledge, music, sport and physical education, together with arts and crafts such as painting or pottery. While the nature of these complementary subjects bears little resemblance to the Creativity, Action, Service programme that would eventually become a key element of the IBDP, the fact that Peterson singled them out as an integral part of his curriculum model provides clear evidence of his desire to give more formal recognition to non-academic and extra-curricular activities.

In a context in which A-level subject choice was primarily driven by the need to compete for a university place, the proposals embedded in Peterson's Gulbenkian

Report were always likely to be perceived as controversial. Well aware of the potential objections to his model for overcoming academic specialisation, Peterson devoted an entire section of his brief report to pre-empting potential objections to his new curriculum framework, many of which had arisen during 'subject panel discussions' involving practising teachers and university lecturers invited to Oxford to discuss his proposals. Having demonstrated that the Crowther Committee's belief in the phenomenon of 'subject-mindedness' lacked any empirical basis, Peterson was confident that the practical stumbling blocks to broadening the sixth-form curriculum, such as staffing and timetabling difficulties, could subsequently be overcome. However, when confronted by the lack of any centralised authority that could take the lead in matters of curriculum reform – a legacy, Peterson argued, that arose out of 'the idealistic liberal principle that no final authority equipped with powers is necessary' (1960: 36) – it was evident that the success or failure of his initiative would rest largely with the universities. Since individual departments and faculties continued to exert a controlling influence over subject choice at A level, if the universities could collectively agree upon a policy requiring a minimum level of general education from their candidates on entry, he argued, then the pattern of A-level specialisation could finally be broken. What he therefore proposed as a first step towards such reform was the introduction of a new set of matriculation requirements in which students would be expected to draw at least three of their four subjects from three out of the following five subject domains:

1   a general paper
2   mathematics
3   natural sciences
4   social sciences (history, geography and economics)
5   languages.

Yet again the very form of this proposal – in which academic breadth could only be achieved through some degree of prescription to regulate subject choice – reflects an educational philosophy that would ultimately find its full expression in the IBDP. However, the fact that such radical proposals clashed, in an ideological sense, with the 'liberal' principles that Peterson had already identified as the root cause of the state's failure to intervene in matters of curriculum reform did not bode well for their future reception.

Although they generated considerable interest, ultimately Peterson's proposals did not gain the level of support needed to initiate the kind of reform that he had envisaged (Pound 1998; 2004). A number of factors arguably contributed to this lack of success. First, Peterson may well have underestimated the strength of the relationship between, on the one hand, the schools and the universities, and, on the other, the examining boards that served the interests of both groups of stakeholders in the A-level system. Thus, while the idea of academic breadth may have been welcomed in principle, in practice it was difficult to argue the case for reforming a system that had clearly proved its worth in both preparing, and selecting, students for the rigours of a three-year honours degree – an issue about which the Working Group on 14–19 Reform under Tomlinson was equally sensitive (DfES 2003b: 27). Second, although Peterson's report undoubtedly attracted wider interest since its publication coincided with the 'Two Cultures' debate initiated by C P Snow, while it appeared to engage directly with Snow's analysis of the cultural divide by suggesting the means by which to bridge it, the cost of achieving this, in terms of the impact on students' workload and the examinations system as a whole, was perceived as too high. As a leading article in a contemporary edition of the *Times Educational Supplement* (*TES*) argued, even though Peterson had made a point of working within the existing framework, his proposals 'would clearly call for changes all round – in university entrance requirements, in the character of A level papers and so on' (*TES*, 7 October 1960). Third, in addition to increasing the examinations burden for the 'average' sixth-former, Peterson's four-subject framework appeared to ignore the needs of a new generation of sixth-form students. Thus, those who presumably remained bemused by the rhetorical excesses of the Crowther Report's description of the sixth-form years, as 'the seed-time for a life-long harvest' of intellectual discovery (CACE 1959: 270), would no doubt have felt equally alienated by Peterson's proposals for reform. As one of the subject panels invited to discuss Peterson's curriculum framework concluded, the non-academic 16-year-old 'has a right to a place in the sixth form, but he requires special treatment, he could not fit into Mr. Peterson's 4 "A" scheme' (OUDES, [1960–75]). Finally, although Peterson's enquiry may well have succeeded in casting considerable doubt over the conceptual validity of 'subject-mindedness', the Crowther Report's equally persuasive recommendations on the use of 'minority time' proved to have a more decisive impact on the debate about how to counteract excessive specialisation in the sixth form than Peterson's four-subject model.

In fact, in the very year that *Arts and Science Sides in the Sixth Form* was published, a group of leading grammar and public schools produced a manifesto entitled an 'Agreement to Broaden the Curriculum' (ABC). Outlined in the *TES* on 27 January 1961, this document proposed that a minimum of one-third of the weekly sixth-form timetable should be set aside for general studies, and the support that the more conservative ABC proposals received not only overshadowed the degree of interest shown in Peterson's reform initiative, but effectively paved the way for the eventual establishment of general studies as a discrete A-level subject.

The emergence of the IBDP

Although the publication of an 'Agreement to Broaden the Curriculum' effectively marked the end of his attempts to intervene directly in the debate over broadening the sixth-form curriculum in England, Peterson was none the less magnanimous in defeat, urging in a letter to *The Times* that 'the widest possible support' should be given to the ABC proposals 'for strengthening the "non-specialist" element in the sixth-former's work' (2 June 1961). Within six years of the publication of his letter, however, he had accepted the invitation to serve as the first director general of the IBO. Fortuitously, the timing of this invitation also coincided with a prearranged sabbatical from Oxford, and thus, in his own words, Peterson found himself with 'nearly a year to devote full-time to launching the IB' (1987: 23).

As his detailed account of this seminal period in the history of the IBDP makes clear, a considerable amount of developmental work had already been accomplished by the time of his arrival at the IBO in Geneva (Peterson 1972; 1987). The original idea for an 'international' qualification for school-leavers intent on a university education – which was first outlined by a group of teachers at the International School of Geneva in 1962 – had emerged in response to the experience of preparing an international student cohort for a number of different national leaving examinations. Apart from the obvious practical difficulties involved – notably the strain on resources – in an ideological sense the segregation of students into discrete national groups militated against the very ideals that underpinned the founding of the school.

Once the idea of such an international qualification had taken root, its appeal to the international schools community was self-evident, for rather than being removed from such schools and placed within their 'home setting' for the final two years of their secondary education, such students could, in theory, complete their education while residing abroad (Peterson 1972: 12).

Further developments, such as the establishment of the International Schools Examination Syndicate (ISES) in 1965 and the involvement of Atlantic College in Wales – the first in a proposed network of United World Colleges to be established – lent additional momentum to the task of devising an international qualification that would transcend national awards and become acceptable to universities worldwide. In his book *Schools across Frontiers*, Peterson pays particular tribute to the influence of the curriculum model developed at Atlantic College on the eventual framework of the IBDP, and also to the work of the educationist Kurt Hahn, who was instrumental in shaping the college's educational philosophy. Hahn's dedication to world peace and international cooperation, according to Peterson, had given rise to both an educational community and a curriculum dedicated to the promotion of 'mutual understanding between young people from different cultures' (1987: 4). Peterson himself contributed to the development of the college's first curriculum model, and although it was centred on a combination of three A-level subjects, it was supplemented by three college or 'subsidiary' courses, each studied over a two-year period. To complement the subject-specific courses, a programme of religious education, philosophy and current affairs was also included in the curriculum; and to ensure breadth and balance, at least one of the six main courses had to be selected from each of the following groups:

- a course in the mother tongue
- a course in a first foreign language (usually English for overseas students)
- a further course from the language and literature group of subjects
- a social studies course
- a mathematics or science course
- a course from the arts and crafts group of subjects.

(Peterson 1987: 12–13)

As Peterson himself remarks, the similarity between this framework – which he worked on during the summer of 1962 – and that subsequently adopted for the IBDP is certainly worthy of note (1987: 13). However, it was not until five years later, following the announcement of a grant from the Ford Foundation to the ISES for the purpose of conducting a feasibility study into the IBDP, that the prospect of a new international curriculum moved nearer. This proved to be a turning point, and, in Peterson's words, following the decision of the Ford Foundation to back the scheme, 'from this moment … the International Baccalaureate ceased to be a remote vision and began to look like a practical project (1972: 13).'

The extent of Peterson's own enthusiasm for such a project is perhaps summed up in his retrospective comment on the contributions made to the development of both individual syllabuses and the examinations framework by an international body of school and university teachers, who began devising syllabuses and working on an examinations framework some two years before he joined the IBO. What he noted was remarks that in most cases:

> they have been leaders of syllabus reform in their own country who have welcomed both the opportunity to meet with like-minded colleagues and the freedom to establish programmes unhampered by the necessity to compromise with the conservative traditions in national systems.
>
> (1972: 14)

That Peterson must have relished the opportunity to take a leading role in devising a new international school-leaving qualification is all too evident in this account of the evolution of the IBDP. His earlier experience as head teacher of Dover College, where, he sought to 'break the ethnocentric mould' of post-compulsory education by developing an international sixth form, coupled with his spell as editor of *Comparative Education*, had already established his 'international' credentials (1972: 9). Equally, his sense of relief at finding himself freed from the constraints associated with working towards reform within a system predicated on a deeply entrenched belief in academic specialisation is clearly registered through his reference to 'conservative traditions'.

It is thus hardly surprising that what took shape under Peterson's direction went considerably beyond his earlier proposals for curriculum reform in an Anglocentric context. What finally emerged, in fact, was a framework that remains substantially unchanged to this day. Six subjects were to be studied, three of them to a higher level to meet what he described as 'the specialized requirements of certain faculties in universities', while the remaining three were to be studied at subsidiary level. This provided the following familiar pattern of subject domains:

- Language A (including the study of literature, and of world literature in translation)
- Language B
- Mathematics

- Exact or experimental sciences (including physics, chemistry, biology and physical science)
- The study of man (including history, geography, economics, philosophy, psychology and social anthropology)
- A sixth subject to be chosen from the above (or from a course developed and taught within the school, and approved by the IBO).

(1972: 38)

Apart from the breadth of this framework and the element of prescription, which ensured that all students taking the IBDP would benefit from a general education beyond the age of 16, two additional components distinguished the IBDP from the narrow specialisation of the English system: first, a TOK course that would be internally assessed and, second, one afternoon of the school week set aside for creative/ aesthetic activities, or social and community service, which would be recorded on the diploma itself. The TOK course in particular arose from the desire to equip all students with a critical appreciation of the differing subject methodologies – in other words, with a developed sense of what it meant to think aesthetically, scientifically or historically. That it also reflected the underlying philosophy of the IBDP's encouragement of independent analysis is evident from Peterson's own description of the breadth of the programme as a whole:

> what matters is not the absorption and regurgitation either of facts or of predigested interpretations of facts, but the development of powers of the mind or ways of thinking which can be applied to new situations and new presentations of facts as they arise.

(1972: 40)

Given this combination of breadth and balance, along with an assessment pattern that ensured all students were obliged to follow a truly integrated curriculum, Peterson's remark (1972: 42) that such a programme would 'certainly shock some English readers' suggests something of the systemic divide between the IBDP and A levels, which the latter has consistently failed to close.

Promoting a broader qualifications framework in England: 1960–90

None the less, the quest to introduce academic breadth within the English system during the two decades that followed the publication of the Crowther Report continued unabated. For example, in the years between the publication of Peterson's enquiry into subject choice at A level in 1960 and the piloting of the first IBDP examinations at the end of the decade, no less than four sets of proposals appeared. The first, devised by the Committee of Vice-Chancellors and Principals and published in 1962, recommended that university entry should be determined by examination success in two specialist subjects supplemented by three 'general' courses, including the 'Use of

English' and a modern foreign language (SSEC 1962). Then, in 1966, the Schools Council proposed a new qualifications framework based on 'Major and Minor' examinations (SC 1966); and, in the following year, details of yet another Schools Council initiative emerged, on this occasion in the form of a more conservative model, which included two specialist subjects at A level supplemented by several 'elective' courses, the latter marked internally but subject to external moderation (SC 1967). Two years later, in a joint report with the Standing Conference on University Entry, the Schools Council proposed a more radical scheme for replacing A levels, this time involving a framework in which four or five subjects at 'Qualifying' level would be taken by students during the first year of their sixth-form studies, followed by three at 'Further' level in the following year (SCUE/SCJWP 1969). Once again, provision was made within this new framework for some element of internal assessment, yet none of these proposals secured enough support to pose a serious challenge to the A-level system. On the one hand, the universities voiced their concerns over any proposals that risked the erosion of academic standards, thus calling into question the continuing viability of the three-year honours degree. (For much the same reason, they were equally reluctant to endorse any system that involved a degree of internal assessment.) The schools, on the other hand, remained firm in their opposition to reforms that they believed would result, first, in an increase in the examinations burden placed upon their students and, second, in a revised qualifications framework that failed to address the needs of the less academically able sixth-former.

Given the nature of these objections, the prospect of any reform initiative emerging that satisfied both the schools and the universities seemed remote. That this certainly proved to be the case throughout the following decade is evinced by the fate of the 'Normal and Further' proposals (SCUE/SCJWP 1973), which were based upon a five-subject curriculum for students in the first year of their sixth-form studies. These were debated and subjected to minor revisions for a further six years before being finally rejected by the incoming Conservative government on the grounds that A levels continued to provide 'established, recognized and widely-respected standards' and served as the 'best guarantee for the continuation and success of three-year degree courses' (Hansard 1979–80: col. 1087).

Strengthening vocational provision

Once again, it seemed that the academic route post-16 had managed to withstand an attempt to reform it through the introduction of a broader qualifications framework – and, with the A-level system having emerged in a stronger position by the end of this particular phase of the reform process, attention now turned to the development of alternative pathways for widening access and participation in the post-compulsory sector. In fact, following the publication of an important policy document on vocational education and training by the Further Education Unit entitled *A Basis for Choice* (FEU 1979), together with a further report on *A New Training Initiative* by the Manpower Services Commission (MSC 1981), vocational provision was about to undergo a considerable transformation. New awards were subsequently introduced, such as the Certificate of Pre-Vocational Education and City and Guilds 365, and these were later followed by National Vocational Qualifications (NVQs) and regulated by a national qualifications body, the National Council for Vocational Qualifications, which was established in 1986.

Despite the introduction of an alternative range of qualifications designed for students for whom the traditional academic route had long been considered inappropriate, further developments – such as the schools-based TVEI – also reflected a desire for students following more traditional, and thus general, education courses within the post-compulsory sector to experience some form of vocational training or work-related learning. This belief in the need for *all* students to become equipped with the skills needed to contribute effectively to the workplace resulted in proposals both to incorporate, and ultimately to assess, a number of 'core skills' – such as communications, numeracy and information technology – across vocational and A-level qualifications (NCC 1990).

In one important sense, as far as A-level provision was concerned, what this amounted to was an attempt to encourage breadth through a policy initiative that did not threaten to subvert academic specialisation and thus academic standards. In fact, it was precisely this concern over the preservation of standards that had led to the introduction of the AS level in 1987, a prime example of a piecemeal reform that singularly failed to encourage greater breadth of study, largely because it was never fully supported by the universities, which continued to frame their offers around three full A-level grades (Macfarlane 1993). In much the same way, it also resulted in the decision to reject the reforms embodied in the Higginson Report of 1988. The dismissal of this radical policy document, which had set out a strong case for replacing the A-level system with a broader range of five 'leaner, tougher' examination syllabuses (DES 1988: 19), provides further evidence of the extent of the Conservative government's commitment to academic specialisation. Although the Higginson Committee had consulted widely before publishing its proposals, thus ensuring that they eventually attracted considerable support, its principal recommendation that A levels should be abandoned in favour of a broader modular framework appeared to touch a raw ideological nerve in the then prime minister, Margaret Thatcher, who reiterated her faith in the current system in the most unambiguous of terms. Ignoring what was arguably the committee's central preoccupation – that alone amongst its economic competitors, the UK did not appear 'to recognise the national benefits arising from a broadly educated and adaptable workforce' (DES 1988: 8) – Thatcher insisted that it remained 'absolutely vital that we continue to regard the deep study of some single subjects as important during the years from 16–18, particularly from 16–18, particularly for people going to university' (Hansard 1987–8: col. 434).

Despite the unmistakably personal nature of this forceful intervention, what the prime minister's statement also acknowledged was that, in a context in which vocational qualifications were increasingly regarded as a key mechanism in the drive to increase participation rates and to raise levels of achievement in the post-compulsory sector, A levels had to retain their elitist label as a rigorous test of academic ability. Moreover, given the anticipated impact of other recent democratising policy shifts –

such as the merging of the O-level examination with the Certificate of Secondary Education to form a common 16+ qualification, the General Certificate of Secondary Education (GCSE) – it became even more imperative that the 'gold standard' of the A-level system should be tenaciously defended. Thus, while the Higginson proposals could not be countenanced by the Thatcher government, the introduction of core skills could, since it would leave a more established 'core' – three specialised A-level courses – as firmly entrenched as ever. As the then minister of state for education commented (NCC 1990: 4), when requesting guidance on the development of core skills, 'Specialisation at A level, and the maintenance of standards, is vitally important. But it must not, and need not, be at the expense of developing broader skills, knowledge and understanding which will be needed in the twenty-first century.'

However, while the competence-based assessment framework of vocational education and training provided fertile ground for the incorporation of core skills, attempts to assimilate them within the framework of more traditional A-level syllabuses were largely unsuccessful. Yet despite this lack of success, the process of defining core skills at A level was by no means an entirely fruitless exercise, for in many respects it can be seen retrospectively as a tentative first step towards establishing shared systemic features across vocational and academic pathways.

Unifying frameworks and baccalaureate models: Proposals for qualifications reform since 1990

Official policy developments after 1990, following the publication of the government's White Paper on *Education and Training for the 21st Century* (DES 1991), arguably extended this particular initiative through the introduction of a new qualification, the GNVQ, devised for students staying on in full-time education in schools and colleges for whom the purely academic nature of A-level study would have proved inappropriate. However, the presence of a third distinct pathway in the post-compulsory sector proved to be at odds with those who favoured more radical reform. For example, a series of influential reports compiled during the early 1990s were united in their support for the development of a more inclusive and integrated qualifications framework. The first of these reports to emerge was published by the Institute for Public Policy Research (IPPR) and was aptly titled *A British 'Baccalauréat': Ending the Division between Education and Training* (Finegold *et al.* 1990). This report proposed the introduction of a modular qualifications framework over three levels, the first at foundation level at 16+ to replace, in the words of the report itself, 'the current jungle of one year full-time provision including GCSE' (Finegold *et al.* 1990: 25); the second an Advanced Diploma – in effect, a 'British *baccalauréat*' – which would take the place of A levels and their vocational counterparts; and the third a 'Higher' stage linked directly to undergraduate study and to more advanced vocational awards.

Given the title of the IPPR report, it was hardly surprising that the second stage of the proposed framework – the Advanced Diploma – received the most detailed attention. This involved three broad modular 'domains', which included both general and vocational courses. The framework as a whole was predicated on the need to provide students with breadth, balance and flexibility, while still providing scope for more specialised study, and it was conceptualised as follows:

> *Domain A: Social and human sciences.* This domain would include history and social science modules, as well as applied areas such as health, caring and business studies.
> *Domain B: Natural sciences and technology.* This domain would include maths, the natural sciences and engineering, as well as more skills-based modules.
> *Domain C: Arts, languages and literature.* This domain would include performing and visual arts and design, as well as languages, literature and media studies.
>
> (Finegold *et al.* 1990: 27)

Modules were to be offered at 'core' or 'specialist' levels, the latter ensuring that curricular breadth would not be achieved at the expense of depth, and these had to be selected from each of the three domains. Further modules providing accreditation for work or community-based experience were also included in the framework, and the award of the proposed diploma would depend on their successful completion.

Although the authors of the report make a point of acknowledging the influence of the IBDP on the framing of their proposals, the qualifications system outlined in the IPPR document bears all the hallmarks of having been shaped by what had become a distinctly English preoccupation – that of dealing effectively with the issue of parity of esteem. Thus, although the IBDP undoubtedly served as an exemplar for the development of a broad and balanced curriculum, its overtly academic function had to be modified if it were to be adapted for the context of post-compulsory curriculum reform in England.

This imperative to develop a more inclusive system to overcome the divisions between academic and vocational routes post-16 provided a central focus for a second report, *Beyond GCSE* (RS 1991), which also presented the case for the abolition of existing awards and the introduction of an integrated qualifications framework to bring an end to the division between the separate pathways. Within two years, a third report appeared, on this occasion published by the National Commission on Education. Entitled *Learning to Succeed: A Radical Look at Education Today and a Strategy for the Future* (NCE 1993), this report was equally persuasive in advocating the replacement of A levels and vocational qualifications, and the development of a broader and more inclusive framework leading to the award of a General Education Diploma.

This emphasis on the need to replace A levels and vocational awards with an integrated qualifications system was forcefully reiterated by yet another independent report – *Routes for Success* – compiled by the Confederation of British Industry (CBI) and also published in 1993. The CBI proposals, principally devised to address the issue of parity of esteem by raising the status of vocational awards, sought to do so by abandoning the differentiated titles of existing qualifications by assimilating them within an overarching framework. As the report itself argued:

As a priority, fresh thought needs to be given to the titles of A/AS levels, GNVQs and NVQs. Given the individual's need for maximum choice it may be better to focus on routes – the occupational, vocational and academic – and to highlight the scope for flexibility.

(CBI 1993: 18)

This collective plea for the relationship between education and training routes post-16 to be radically reformed appears at first sight to have gone largely unheeded by the Conservative government. None the less, with the publication of the Dearing Committee's *Review of Qualifications for 16–19 Year Olds* (Dearing 1996), it was clear that the issue of comparability between progression routes post-16 had been finally addressed. However, although Dearing's proposals for establishing broad levels of equivalence between general and vocational awards through the development of a national qualifications framework – together with his recommendations for the structure of GNVQs to become aligned with that of A levels – ostensibly held out the promise of greater parity of esteem, they fell considerably short of the kind of reforms demanded by the CBI. Yet, given the fact that a key element of Dearing's original remit had been to maintain the rigour of A levels, it was hardly surprising that the academic route post-16 emerged from his review in a strengthened position, as one of three discrete pathways open to learners beyond the compulsory school-leaving age.

In much the same way, because Dearing's proposals for the development of over-arching awards in the form of National Certificates and Diplomas depended on the attainment of a broader range of *existing* qualifications, while such awards remained optional the incentive for students to pursue greater breadth in their studies was at best severely limited. Thus, rather than giving serious consideration to the introduction of the kind of unified and integrated system favoured by those who advocated more radical change, Dearing's proposals for reform arguably amounted to a classic English compromise. As Hodgson and Spours (2003a: 18) have more recently argued, the Dearing Review was essentially a pragmatic response to the issue of curriculum reform, one that should be judged in the political context in which it was produced – in other words, that of an outgoing Conservative and incoming Labour administration.

In this particular respect, it is interesting to compare the Dearing recommendations with those produced by the Labour Party before it took office in 1997. Having criticised earlier attempts at reform for being 'piecemeal and uncoordinated' (LP 1996: 2), the Labour Party's report, entitled *Aiming Higher*, proposed a number of fundamental reforms to the system, including a reduced emphasis on the traditional barrier between school and post-compulsory education and training at 16+, in order to establish 'a coherent 14–19+ curriculum' (LP 1996: 17) in which students would have the option of following vocational courses from the age of 14+. Moreover, the report also underlined Labour's commitment to establishing greater breadth not only through the introduction of an overarching award but also through an 'integrated and unified approach' to curriculum reform, 'which breaks down the historic and artificial divide … between academic and vocational learning' (LP 1996: 2).

During a period in which, north of the border, Scotland was already proceeding with the introduction of an integrated 14–19 curriculum based on the *Higher Still* proposals of 1994, enabling students to combine both academic and vocational subjects from 14+ (SO 1994: 22), while in Wales the development of a 'Welsh Baccalaureate' was finally given official backing (Jenkins and David 1996), the new Labour government immediately adopted a less radical approach to reform (Hodgson and Spours 2003b: 167). In fact, under Labour the qualifications framework was soon subjected to yet another round of piecemeal reforms following the publication of the consultation document *Qualifying for Success* (DfEE 1997). The main policy changes that emerged from this document – which became known as the *Curriculum 2000* reforms – included, first, the establishment of greater equality between academic and vocational awards through the introduction of a new six-unit modular framework common to both, together with a rebranding of the GNVQ, which was to become the AVCE. This was further reinforced by the decision to merge the two separate regulatory bodies for academic and vocational qualifications into one single entity, the QCA.

Second, the principle of encouraging greater breadth of study, arguably one of the most radical proposals outlined in the original *Qualifying for Success* document, was also actively promoted. It was to be achieved through the subdivision of A-level syllabuses into two three-unit blocks, including a new Advanced Subsidiary (AS) qualification taken after one year, which in terms of standards was perceived as being roughly equivalent to a halfway stage between GCSEs and full A-level qualifications, now renamed 'A2s'. The intention behind this particular reform was to encourage A-level students to take a combination of four or even five AS subjects in their first year – with the additional subjects acting as 'complementary' courses to their main area of specialisation – before specialising in three during the second year of their A-level programme (Blackstone 1998).

Described in a recent QCA report as having encouraged only 'limited additional breadth in programmes' (2002: 3), the reformulated A level has done little thus far to counteract subject specialisation. According to Hodgson and Spours, in their detailed study of the impact of the *Curriculum 2000* reforms on A-level choice, 'the predominant pattern nationally has turned out to be four AS subjects in the first year and three A2s in the second year', with very few students choosing 'a contrasting fourth subject' at AS (2003b: 88). Indeed, in the absence of any kind of prescription governing subject choice, it is difficult to see how such an outcome could have been avoided. As a further report by the QCA makes abundantly clear, when compared with the IBDP, A levels are still remarkable for their singularity:

> Unlike the IB Diploma, A levels do not call for students to follow an overall programme. Each subject is offered as a discrete qualification, with little real guidance even for each subject as to the programme of study to be followed.
>
> (2003: 4)

To add to this systemic deficiency, the revised AS level also gave rise to a range of problems that subsequently bedevilled *Curriculum 2000* following its inception, including:

- difficulties over timetabling lessons, together with end-of-module examination clashes
- a concomitant marginalisation of extra-curricular activities, traditionally seen as an essential element of the sixth-form experience
- a significant increase in the examinations burden on students
- the adoption of more didactic styles of teaching, with less time for the nurturing of intellectual curiosity and independent thinking.

Perhaps more damagingly, the revised AS level and its ambiguous relationship to the A2 contributed directly to the first major crisis of confidence in the A-level system in its 50-year history when, following the publication of examination results in 2002, accusations of tampering with examination grades were levelled at the examining boards by the schools, only to be followed by a series of counter-accusations that called into question both the accuracy and integrity of the guidance provided by the QCA, and the extent of its ability to withstand political interference. At the heart of this crisis lay the issue of maintaining academic standards; the general perception that they had declined following the implementation of the *Curriculum 2000* reforms not only attracted widespread media attention, but also prompted an urgent review into the structural relationship between the AS and the A2, and the examining process as a whole (Tomlinson 2002a; 2002b).

The changes ushered in under *Curriculum 2000,* therefore, may well prove to represent a pivotal moment in the evolution of the 14–19 qualifications framework in England, a further example, perhaps, of an outmoded system being pushed to its very limits by a succession of piecemeal reforms – and in this instance, almost to the point of collapse. Identifying the AS award as one of the faultlines of the recent reforms, Hodgson and Spours draw attention to its divided function as both 'a stand-alone qualification at the end of the first year of study' and 'a stage towards the full A level'. They conclude,

> In this sense, it represents a halfway house to a new advanced level system by trying to combine, within the shell of an A level, features of the old and the new in an uncomfortable and unstable state.
>
> (2003b: 98)

Inevitably, it was the acknowledgement of this very instability which finally prompted the view that nothing short of a radical overhaul would restore confidence in the system. Although local initiatives to develop overarching awards to recognise wider achievement in both education and training (Butler, Lucas, Stewart 2003) continued to gain momentum – particularly in the wake of recently published Government papers such as *Schools: Achieving success* (DfES 2001) and *14–19: Extending opportunities, raising standards* (DfES 2002) which gave broad support for their introduction – the absence of any coherent national policy on the future shape of the 14–19 curriculum was clearly a matter for concern.

As a result, the Tomlinson 'Working Group on 14–19 Reform' was established in 2003 to advise the Government on a long-term replacement for the current 14–19 qualifications maze. Following an extensive consultation process and the publication of 'progress' and 'interim' reports which enabled key stakeholders and other interested groups to be kept fully informed of developments, the *Final Report* of the Working Group appeared towards the end of 2004 and was greeted with widespread approbation both in the 14–19 sector and in higher education circles. Tomlinson's recommendations for a more flexible and inclusive diploma framework over four levels, incorporating general academic and vocational awards, thus seemed poised, as the text of the 1990 IPPR report memorably put it, to end once and for all the division between education and training. Scheduled to be phased in over a ten-year period, the new framework was designed to assimilate existing general and vocational awards so that, for example, AS and A2 modules and their vocational equivalents would effectively become 'components' of the main learning programme of the Advanced Diploma. To supplement the study of specialist subjects, a compulsory 'core' was proposed to ensure that all students reached a minimum level of competence in three key areas – literacy and communication, mathematics, and ICT. Finally, an 'extended project' would become a further mandatory feature of the system as a whole, while work experience, involvement in community service, or achievement in sporting activities or the arts would be formally recorded across all four levels of the diploma framework.

Despite the marked absence of any element of prescription to broaden the spread of academic learning programmes, even this relatively cautious blueprint for reform was rejected by the Government. Within days of the publication of Tomlinson's recommendations, the Prime Minsister, Tony Blair, declared that he had no intention of allowing GCSEs and A-levels to become subsumed under an integrated diploma framework, prompting speculation in the media that he wished to avoid, at all costs, the stigma of being the Prime Minister responsible for the abolition of A-levels. In fact, when the Government's official response to the Tomlinson proposals – a White Paper entitled *14–19 Education and Skills* – appeared in February 2005, it pointedly referred, as we have already seen, to both sets of awards as the 'cornerstones' of the 14–19 curriculum and examinations framework.

Whether or not the fate of the Tomlinson proposals was determined by political expediency rather than prudent educational policy, the fact remains that at a time when schools and colleges are increasingly aware of the need to prepare their students for life in the context of a global community, the current qualifications framework is looking increasingly flawed and deficient. In contrast, one of the greatest strengths of the IB Diploma Programme lies not just in its insistence that all students study a second language and take mathematics and a science subject beyond the level of the GCSE, but in the *international* dimension of its curriculum. Above all, the IBDP appears to stimulate an appetite for learning and a breadth of vision which continues to inspire both teachers and students alike. As one of the contributors to this book so forcefully puts it, the Diploma programme 'has a habit of becoming a way of life for those who teach and study it, often appearing to be something of a mission for those involved, and frequently engendering evangelical zeal in its participants' – something which A-levels in their present form might find very difficult to emulate.

References

Blackstone, T (1998) *Qualifying for Success: The Response to the Qualifications and Curriculum Authority Advice*, DfES, London.

Butler, P (2003) 'The College Diploma: A Case Study' in G Phillips and T Pound (eds) *The Baccalaureate: A Model for Curriculum Reform*, Kogan Page, London.

CACE (Central Advisory Council for Education) (1959) *15 to 18: A Report of the Central Advisory Council for Education (England)*, HMSO, London.

CBI (Confederation of British Industry) (1993) *Routes for Success: Careership: A Strategy for All 16–19 Learning*, CBI, London.

Dearing, R (1996) *Review of Qualifications for 16–19 Year Olds: Full Report*, School Curriculum and Assessment Authority, London.

DES (Department of Education and Science) (1988) *Advancing A Levels: Report of a Committee Appointed by the Secretary of State for Education and Science and the Secretary of State for Wales*, HMSO, London.

DES (1991) *Education and Training for the 21st Century: Presented to Parliament by the Secretaries of State for Education and Science, Employment and Wales*, HMSO, London

DfEE (Department for Education and Employment) (1997) *Qualifying for Success: A Consultation Paper on the Future of Post-16 Qualifications*, DfEE, London.

DfES (Department for Education and Skills) (2001) *Schools: Achieving Success*, DfES, London

DfES (2002) *14–19: Extending Opportunities, Raising Standards*, DfES, London.

DfES (2003a) *14–19: Opportunity and Excellence: Government Response to the 14–19 Green Paper*, DfES, London.

DfES (2003b) *Principles for Reform of 14–19 Learning Programmes and Qualifications: Working Group on 14–19 Reform*, DfES, London.

DfES (2004) *14–19 Curriculum and Qualifications Reform: Final Report of the Working Group on 14–19 Reform*, DfES, London.

DfES (2005) *14–19 Education and Skills: Summary*, DfES, London.

FEU (Further Education Unit) (1979) *A Basis for Choice: Report of a Study Group on Post-16 Pre-Employment Courses*, FEU, London.

Finegold, D, Keep, E, Miliband, D, Raffe, D, Spours, K and Young, M (1990) *A British 'Baccalauréat': Ending the Division between Education and Training*, Institute for Public Policy Research, London.

Hansard (1979–80) *House of Commons Debates*, Fifth Series, Vol. 969, HMSO, London.

Hansard (1987–8) *House of Commons Debates*, Sixth Series, Vol. 134, HMSO, London.

Hill, I (2003) 'The International Baccalaureate' in G Phillips and T Pound (eds) *The Baccalaureate: A Model for Curriculum Reform*, Kogan Page, London.

Hodgson, A and Spours, K (1999) *New Labour's Educational Agenda: Issues and Policies for Education and Training from 14+*, Kogan Page, London.

Hodgson, A and Spours, K (2003a) *Beyond A Levels: Curriculum 2000 and the Reform of 14–19 Qualifications*, Kogan Page, London.

Hodgson, A and Spours, K (2003b) 'A Baccalaureate System for the English Context' in G Phillips and T Pound (eds) *The Baccalaureate: A Model for Curriculum Reform*, Kogan Page, London.

Independent (2004) 'Hundreds of schools set to allow pupils to take baccalaureate' by Richard Garner, 4 October.

Jenkins, C and David, J (1996) *The Welsh Baccalaureate*, Institute of Welsh Affairs, Cardiff.

LP (Labour Party) (1996) *Aiming Higher: Labour's Proposals for the Reform of the 14–19 Curriculum*, LP, London.

Lucas, G (2003) 'The Graduation Certificate' in G Phillips and T Pound (eds) *The Baccalaureate: A Model for Curriculum Reform*, Kogan Page, London.

Macfarlane, E (1993) *Education 16–19: In Transition*, Routledge, London.

MSC (Manpower Services Commission) (1981) *A New Training Initiative: A Consultative Document*, MSC, London.

NCC (National Curriculum Council) (1990) *Core Skills 16–19: A Response to the Secretary of State*, NCC, York.

NCE (National Commission on Education) (1993) *Learning to Succeed: A Radical Look at Education Today and a Strategy for the Future*, Heinemann, London.

OUDES (Oxford University Department of Educational Studies) [1960–75] Peterson Papers, Box 3.

Peterson, A (1960) *Arts and Science Sides in the Sixth Form: A Report to the Gulbenkian Foundation*, Abbey Press, Abingdon.

Peterson, A (1972) *The International Baccalaureate: An Experiment in International Education*, Harrap, London.

Peterson, A (1987) *Schools across Frontiers: The Story of the International Baccalaureate and the United World Colleges*, Open Court, Illinois.

Pound, T (1998) 'Forty Years On: The Issue of Breadth in the 16–19 Curriculum', *Oxford Review of Education*, Vol. 24, No. 2.

Pound, T (2004) 'After A-levels: Tomlinson and 14–19 Reform', *Prospero*, Vol. 10, No. 2.

QCA (Qualifications and Curriculum Authority) (2002) *The Second Year of Curriculum 2000: Experience Compared with Objectives*, QCA, London.

QCA (2003) *Report on the Comparability between GCE and International Baccalaureate Examinations*, QCA, London.

RS (Royal Society) (1991) *Beyond GCSE: A Report by a Working Group of the Royal Society's Education Committee*, RS, London.

SC (Schools Council) (1966) 'Sixth Form: Curriculum and Examinations', *Working Paper No 5*, HMSO, London.

SC (1967) 'Some Further Proposals for Sixth Form Work', *Working Paper No 7*, HMSO, London.

SCUE/SCJWP (Standing Conference on University Entrance and the Schools Council Joint Working Party) (1969) *Proposals for the Curriculum and Examinations in the Sixth Form*, HMSO, London.

SCUE/SCJWP (1973) 'Preparation for Degree Courses', *Working Paper 47*, Evans/Methuen, London.

SO (Scottish Office) (1994) *Higher Still: Opportunity for All*, HMSO, London.

SSEC (Secondary School Examinations Council) (1962) *Sixth Form Studies and University Entrance Requirements: Sixth Report of the Secondary Schools Examinations Council*, HMSO, London.

Stewart, J (2003) 'George Abbot School and the Surrey Graduation Certificate' in G Phillips and T Pound (eds) *The Baccalaureate: A Model for Curriculum Reform*, Kogan Page, London.

Tomlinson, M (2002a) *Report on Outcomes of Review of A Level Grading*, DfES, London.

Tomlinson, M (2002b) *Inquiry into A Level Standards: Final Report*, DfES, London.

Chapter 2

The International Baccalaureate (IB) and international education

Mary Hayden

The origins of the IB programmes and the context in which their development took place have been charted in a number of publications, including Peterson (1987 2003), Fox (1985 1998a; 1998b), Pound (2003), Sylvester (2003) and several writings by Hill (2002a, 2002b, 2002c, 2003a, 2003b, 2003c, 2003d). It is clear from reading such documentation, from conversations with those involved with the IB programmes over many years, from other forms of anecdotal evidence and from a simple observation of the numbers of schools now offering the programmes – currently over 1,400 (IBO 2004), some 35 years since the first trial examinations of the International Baccalaureate Diploma Programme (IBDP) were offered in 1969 – that the International Baccalaureate Organisation (IBO) has satisfied a need not being catered for by other education programmes, and has persuaded schools, parents and students of its attractiveness in many different parts of the world. It would be difficult in particular to argue against the success of the now well-established IBDP, which preceded the Middle Years Programme (MYP, first offered as an IB programme in 1994) and the Primary Years Programme (PYP, first offered as an IB programme in 1997).

Elsewhere in this volume, chapters by other contributors focus on a range of dimensions of the IBDP, providing a series of critical perspectives from the experiences of practitioners. In this chapter, the main focus will be on the 'I' in 'IB': on what might be inferred from the term 'International' in its title, and on how the IB and, in particular, the IBDP may be considered to contribute to what could be described as 'international education'. The chapter will also include a consideration of the original aims of the IBDP, focusing on what the international dimension of the programme might be in intention and in practice. The chapter will conclude with an evaluation of some of the challenges likely to face the IBDP, especially within the UK context.

What's in a name?

The origins of the title 'International Baccalaureate' given to the Diploma Programme are unclear. An initial 1925 suggestion by the International School of Geneva for the development of an internationally recognised entrance examination referred to a *maturité internationale* (the *maturité* being the Swiss university-entrance examination), but by 1962 the first small conference organised by that school to take the idea forward referred specifically to an 'international baccalaureate' (Peterson 1987), a title that has survived without record of any real challenge since. Precedents clearly existed at that time for the use of the term 'baccalaureate' to describe a university-entrance qualification in, for instance, the French *baccalauréat* and the *bachillerato* of a number of Spanish-speaking countries, including Colombia. More recently, research has suggested that a baccalaureate-style curriculum model would have the following characteristics:

- It is a curriculum or programme of study for upper secondary education which may be used as a school leaving examination
- It may be used as a qualification for admission to higher education, for entry into employment, and as a foundation for learning throughout life
- It is a programme of study which constitutes a broad and balanced curriculum
- It contains a compulsory core element offering learners a common experience, in addition to optional or elective elements.

(Thompson, Hayden and Cambridge 2003: 42)

The IBDP can be used as a school-leaving examination, as a university-entrance qualification and/or for entry into employment, and undoubtedly provides a foundation for learning throughout life. It also constitutes a broad and balanced curriculum, containing a compulsory core as well as optional elements, as represented diagrammatically by Thompson (1988). According to the characteristics described above, the IBDP therefore justifies its claim to be a baccalaureate.

The qualifier to the term 'Baccalaureate' in the IBDP's title might at first glance appear to be equally straightforward: the word 'International' is widely used in many contexts, educational and non-educational, and such wide usage might suggest that its meaning is obvious. Sadly, a closer examination – in the context of education at least – reveals such optimism to be ill-founded. Gellar, for instance, pointed out as long ago as 1981 that, as the number of 'overseas' schools worldwide grew, 'for want of a better one, the term "International Education" gained currency – a term that meant all things to some people and meant very little to many – a good example of Wittgenstein's "bewitchment of intelligence by means of language"' (Gellar 1981). Gellar's point is well made and is supported by Mattern, who argued that 'If I had a pound for every essay that has been made at defining international education, I would surely be a good deal richer than I am now', before going on to add that 'If I had read them all, however, I am not sure that I would be much further along towards a comprehensive definition: what constitutes or should constitute an international education remains a complex and controversial matter' (1971: 209). Similarly, Knight, in referring to consistent emphasis in the history of the International School of Geneva on terms such as 'internationally minded', 'progressive international education' and 'the idea of an international school', highlights what he perceives to be a problem in that 'so much have these phrases been commonly used, so much have they been assumed to have practical meaning, that they have become more akin to a series of mantra', before going on to suggest that 'it is important to take a colder look at the general concept "international education", and to ask whether this really is anything more than a mystical formula of incantation. What is the evidence?' (1999 p: 195).

Clearly, then, the very concept of international education is one which is neither well defined nor widely shared. Pasternak suggests that 'the question of whether international education exists, or not, is a conundrum to be considered by a party of pedagogical professors puffing their pipes in an opium parlour' (1998: 254) and, while resisting the urge to engage in too much pipe-puffing, it is worth referring here to one recent study that set out to clarify, from the perspectives of students and teachers in international schools around the world, the notion of what it means to experience an international education. Based on a survey of over 3,000 students in the 16–19 age group, who attended schools around the world that offered programmes including the IBDP, plus almost 300 teachers from a similar range of schools, the findings suggested the following five main clusters of factors contributing to the experience of international education. These are ranked in order of importance by 16-year-olds, 18-year-olds and teachers (though for teachers the rank order of the last two factors was reversed), as follows:

- exposure to students of different cultures within school
- teachers as exemplars of international-mindedness
- a balanced formal curriculum
- informal aspects of school
- exposure to others of different cultures outside school/links with the local community.

(Hayden and Thompson 1996)

This study, which reinforced many points previously identified in a smaller-scale study of first-year undergraduates reflecting on their own international-education experiences while at school (Hayden and Thompson 1995), was helpful in clarifying the perceived relative importance of various dimensions of international education from the point of view of participants. Both studies suggested, as observed by Thompson, that 'no single aspect of institutional arrangements is likely to act as a guarantee of delivery of an international education at the level of the individual student' (1998: 286). They also contributed to the subsequent development by Thompson (1998) of a model of a learning environment for international education, presented visually as a cube and based on the premise that international education is 'most likely to be caught, not taught' when an appropriate learning environment is provided. The Thompson model, founded on an

ABC of Administrative styles, Balanced curriculum and Cultural diversity, was subsequently extended by Schwindt (2003), who proposed three other faces of the cube: an interface between tertiary education and jobs; motives for enrolment on the part of the parents; and dividing the 'cultural diversity' face of Thompson's cube into two – focusing separately on the student population and others (teachers, parents, board members).

The formal curriculum then (in other words, the planned aspects of school experience), while clearly playing a crucial role in any education system, is but one dimension in the context of international education. As an example of the formal curriculum, the IBDP could therefore be argued to contribute to the promotion of international education when taken in conjunction with other factors. This should not lead us to underestimate the importance and influence of the IBDP. It does, however, make particularly interesting the exploration of the international nature of the programme in terms of its contribution to the 'bigger picture'. McKenzie, in discussing the use of the word 'international' in discourse relating to education and schools, makes a similar point to those of Gellar, Mattern and Knight, contending that 'through lack of rigorous definition, the precise meaning of the word has been and still is cloudy and confused in the phrases "international education" and "international school"', before going on to argue that in the context of the statement of aims of the IBO, the word 'international' is used with five different meanings: 'non-national, pan-national, ex-national (as in expatriate), multinational and transnational' (McKenzie 1998: 243). These aims, as stated by the IBO in 1994, are as follows:

- To improve and extend international education and so promote international understanding
- To facilitate student mobility and provide an educational service to the internationally mobile community
- To work in collaboration with national education systems in developing a rigorous, balanced and international curriculum.

As McKenzie points out, 'the means to reaching these aims [is] through the manufacture of two complementary products, described in the same document', namely an 'internationally recognised pre-university curriculum' and a 'university entrance examination, the IB Diploma, which gives access to higher education worldwide'.

In summary, McKenzie comments that the IBO:

> sets out to link its curriculum to the promotion of understanding between countries, and to use national systems of education where appropriate to develop a curriculum that is international in the sense that it is global in range. These two aims ride in tandem. Ancillary to these, it wishes to serve … the internationally mobile community by providing in countries across the globe an education that is consistent and that will give access to the best universities anywhere.
>
> (1998: 243)

In doing so the IBO, he claims, represents the five meanings of 'international' described above in the following ways. It is *non-national* in the sense that it is 'not subject to the requirements, standards, demands and orientation of a particular national system', and *pan-national* in its promotion of 'international understanding' or 'sympathetic mutuality' that 'seeks to build bridges between countries'. Catering for the 'internationally mobile community', it provides education for those who could be considered to be *ex-national*, while working 'in collaboration with national education systems' in developing an 'international curriculum' suggests a notion of 'international' that is *multinational*. Emphasis on international recognition of the IBDP by universities worldwide, meanwhile, implies a *transnational* dimension, whereby diploma holders may 'cross educational borders with the same ease that a valid passport permits movement from one country to another'. McKenzie is at pains to point out that, while he believes that 'much of the discourse of international education uses the qualifier "international" with these five meanings and seldom attempts to define them or to say which is being used when', he also believes that there is 'nothing inherently negative about this fluctuating quintuplet of meanings', given the range of different types of international schools offering different programmes to varying groups of students. He does, however, go on to declare a particular interest in the pan-national dimension, the 'most obviously ideological' of the five, which 'works consciously to reduce tensions and misunderstandings across nations by promoting global initiatives, knowledge and empathy through education', seeking to produce students who are 'not only citizens of the world but participants in trying to produce a future world fit for all its citizens'. Pan-national education, McKenzie argues, needs to be underpinned 'by a set of values congruent with the drive for international understanding'.

McKenzie's discussion is helpful in highlighting the complexity of the challenge facing those currently involved in the various IB programmes: administrators, curriculum developers, researchers, teachers and, indeed, students. Different dimensions of the concept of 'international' have also been noted by other researchers. Hayden (2001), for instance, highlights a dichotomy between what might be referred to as the 'ideological' and 'pragmatic' dimensions of international education, while Cambridge and Thompson (2001) make a similar distinction between what they describe as the 'internationalist' and 'globalizing' perspectives of international education, where the former may be 'identified with a positive orientation towards international relations, with aspirations for the promotion of peace and understanding between nations', which 'values the moral development of the individual and recognises the importance of service to the community and the development of a sense of responsible citizenship'. The latter, meanwhile, 'is influenced by and contributes to the global diffusion of the values of free market capitalism … in terms of … increasing competition with national systems of education, accompanied by quality assurance through international accreditation and the spread of global quality standards that facilitate educational continuity for the children of the globally mobile clientele'. Cambridge and

Thompson (2001) go on to point out that 'the internationalist and globalizing approaches to international education are rarely seen in their pure forms', with international schools generally managing to 'reconcile these contrasting approaches in their practice of international education' with 'each reconciliation ... unique to the historical, geographical and economic circumstances of that institution'. It could be argued that McKenzie's five interpretations of 'international' relate to the two dichotomies identified above, in the sense of 'pan-national' equating to 'ideological' and 'internationalist', and the other four interpretations to 'pragmatic' and 'globalizing'.

To conclude, the overall ill-defined construct of international education is argued here to consist of a number of dimensions, of which the formal curriculum is one, and to focus on two broad areas (ideological/internationalist and pragmatic/globalising). The IBDP is an example of a formal curriculum that relates to both main areas, where the latter can be subdivided into four of McKenzie's five meanings. Against this backdrop, the next section will consider the origins of the IBDP and, in particular, the international dimension of its aims.

Original aims

In reflecting on the earliest days of the development of the IBDP, Alec Peterson – a central figure in those developments – wrote:

> In terms of aims, we were seeking to design a genuinely international curriculum to meet all the various needs of those sixteen to eighteen year olds in international schools who were seeking entry to different forms of higher education all over the world. We believed that these needs and interests included the moral, aesthetic and practical education of the whole person and thus extended far beyond the purely intellectual and academic preparation normally sanctioned by university entrance examinations.
>
> (1987: 34)

He summarised the educational aims of the IBDP at that time thus: 'to develop to their fullest potential the powers of each individual to understand, to modify and to enjoy his or her environment, both inner and outer, in its physical, social, moral, aesthetic and spiritual aspects' (1987: 33).

His involvement with the earliest days of the IBDP, as is clear from his own account (Peterson 1987), grew very much out of a personal commitment to the desirability of broadening the sixth-form curriculum in England. Since the replacement of the broader School, and Higher School, Certificates by the highly specialised A level in 1951 (Kingdon 1991: 46), there had been criticism in various quarters of the excessive specialisation and its likely consequences for society. Growing levels of concern were highlighted by C P Snow's discussion (1959) of the 'Two Cultures' of scientific and literary intellectuals essentially ignorant of each other's fields, and by a report published by Peterson himself (then Director of the Department of Education at the University of Oxford), from a study funded by the Gulbenkian Foundation, entitled *Arts and Science Sides in the Sixth Form* (Peterson 1960), which suggested that students would not necessarily opt for the narrow range of subjects imposed upon them by the university-driven A-level system if given a free choice.

Previously head of a Shropshire grammar school, Peterson had subsequently been influenced by a period in the then Malaya as director of information services, which role included attempting to engender commitment in three culturally very different communities (Malay, Indian and Chinese) to the notion of one unified Malayan nation. Returning in 1954 as head of Dover College, he instigated an 'international sixth form', which led in 1957 to an invitation to participate in a NATO-organised conference on international education held in Bruges. It was here that he met for the first time Kurt Hahn, a German of Jewish origin, instrumental in founding Gordonstoun School, the Outward Bound movement and the Duke of Edinburgh's Award, and ex-head of Salem School in Germany, which had brought together children of former German and British enemies. An idealist with a commitment to the breaking-down of national and racial prejudices, Hahn was then involved in the translation into practice of a vision for the development of an international college, which would bring together young people from different backgrounds, former enemies as well as allies, to live and be educated alongside one another and, it was hoped, to form lifelong friendships across national boundaries, which would contribute in some way to increased international understanding and reduction in international conflict. In order that the students in question should be those most likely to be influential in their own countries in later years, it was agreed that the focus should be on those clearly destined for university, in terms of both academic potential and age – in other words, those in the last two years of secondary education, of approximately 16–19 years of age.

Opening in 1962 in South Wales, Atlantic College admitted 56 students from the UK, Scandinavia, Europe and North America, and clearly needed to offer a curriculum that was other than the specialised A level: unusually narrow when compared with equivalent programmes in other countries, and thus likely to lead to difficulties with university entrance for non-UK students, with results published late (mid-August) compared with university-entrance examination results in Europe, and with a heavy national emphasis in some subject areas, such as history. Indeed, the adoption of any national curriculum would have proved problematic in this respect, as well as causing additional concern about recognition of one national system's university-entrance examinations by universities of another national system.

It was clear, therefore, that an alternative to A level was needed in this context and, from its opening in 1962, Atlantic College offered its students a curriculum based on three A levels plus three complementary or 'subsidiary' Atlantic College courses, and recorded their achievement on an Atlantic College Leaving Certificate. Development of this curriculum was contributed to in large part by Peterson, who by this time had moved to Oxford, where research interests were then focusing not only on comparative education but also on moves to broaden the English sixth-form curriculum. Through the Atlantic College and Oxford connections, Peterson became involved in work being spearheaded by the International School of Geneva, where a small UNESCO-funded conference was organised in 1962 by the school's Social Studies Department for social studies teachers in international schools. This was where the first reference to the notion of an 'international baccalaureate' was made and, with additional work on the IBDP project during the 1960s and commitment to the new idea not only from Atlantic College, for whose purposes it was ideal, but also from other schools, including the United Nations International School in New York, from the Ford Foundation and from the Twentieth Century Fund, a range of trial examinations were offered in 1969 followed by the first full session in 1970.

This brief summary of the very beginnings of the IBDP, which does less than justice to the enormous amount of work and levels of commitment involved in developing the curriculum and negotiating its acceptability, is included here to demonstrate the earliest aims of the IBDP. Arising from different but related needs of Atlantic College, the International School of Geneva and a number of other international schools, the aims the IBDP was to satisfy could be summarised as follows, namely that the programme should be:

- sufficiently academically rigorous to allow university entrance
- internationally recognised for university-entrance purposes
- non-nationally based in terms of the curriculum
- sufficiently broad to avoid over-specialisation in arts or sciences.

Reading of more detailed accounts of developments from those very early days of the IBDP (Peterson 1987; Hill 2000) makes clear the various influences on the programme as it developed and suggests that, to use the terminology adopted earlier in this chapter, the 'ideological' aims began to achieve a higher profile. Writing in 1974, for instance, Gérard Renaud – previously a teacher at the International School of Geneva and by then IBO director general – made the point that 'the International Baccalaureate programme, conceived as a common school-leaving examination to satisfy the needs of university-bound students in multinational schools, has come to be thought of as an educational system whose principal characteristic ... is to be a vehicle for international understanding and the promotion of different cultures' (Renaud 1974: 11).

Influences leading to an increased emphasis on the ideological dimensions clearly included UNESCO, which in 1974 defined 'international education' as relating to education for peace, human rights and democracy, with aims identified as being the development of:

- a sense of universal values for a culture of peace
- the ability to value freedom and the civic responsibility that goes with it
- intercultural understanding which encourages the convergence of ideas and solutions to strengthen peace

- skills of non-violent conflict resolution
- skills for making informed choices
- respect for cultural heritage and the protection of the environment
- feelings of solidarity and equity at the national and international levels.

(UNESCO 1996)

Such influences can be seen in the aims of the IBDP today. The IBO's mission statement, for instance, is as follows:

The International Baccalaureate Organisation aims to develop inquiring, knowledgeable and caring young people who help to create a better and more peaceful world through intercultural understanding and respect. To this end the IBO works with schools, governments and international organisations to develop challenging programmes of international education and rigorous assessment. These programmes encourage students across the world to be active, compassionate and lifelong learners who understand that other people, with their differences, can also be right.

(IBO 2004)

Hill, meanwhile, has suggested that the intent of the IBDP is for students to:

1   Engage in a broad, academically rigorous education which still allows for specialization
2   Learn how to evaluate information and actions critically
3   Learn how to go on learning
4   Become intellectually flexible and creative to cope with uncertainty
5   Develop an appreciation of the human condition in all its local and global manifestations
6   Discuss and probe global issues and cultural differences to arrive at international understanding
7   Develop a sense of environmental responsibility
8   Become informed and responsible local and global citizens.

(2003a: 54)

These objectives, the first four of which are described as 'pedagogical' with the latter four being related to 'international understanding', are 'reflected in the syllabuses and examination papers of the IB Diploma Programme and the total curricular experience in schools', according to Hill, currently the IBO's Deputy Director General.

It would appear, then, that as they have developed, the aims and objectives of the IB programmes have kept faith with original intentions, but with emphasis being increasingly placed upon the ideological dimension of those intentions. An interesting question to ask, therefore, might be to what extent such intentions are actually translated into practice today.

Intentions and actualities

With Atlantic College in South Wales one of its earliest supporters, the IBDP in the UK has had steadily, if slowly, growing support to the point where more than 60 schools and colleges now offer the IBDP, two of them also offering the more recently introduced MYP, and another two also offering both the MYP and PYP (IBO 2004). To observers of developments in UK education over recent years, however, it will be clear that this presently still relatively small number of participating centres does not reflect the much greater increase in the IBDP's profile in the public eye. The many proposals for A-level reform raised – and usually quashed – since the 1970s (most recently in England by the Working Group on 14–19 Reform, or 'Tomlinson Task Force', and in Wales by the Welsh Assembly Government, who have sponsored the development and piloting of the Welsh Baccalaureate) have been accompanied by seemingly ever-louder calls from certain sectors for consideration of a model based on, or similar to, that of the IBDP. With every problem arising in the A-level system (most recently issues of assessment overload and the grading debacle of 2002, when some sections of the media appeared to suggest the IBDP almost as a panacea for all the ills of the national education system), more interest has been expressed by schools and colleges in the IBDP. What is not immediately obvious are the exact reasons behind the growing popularity of the IBDP as an alternative to A level, given the number of respects in which the two programmes differ. It has already been noted that there can be seen to be two complementary dimensions to the aims of the IBDP, which may be paraphrased as follows:

- *ideological*:
    - improving and extending international education, and thus promoting international understanding
- *pragmatic*:
    - facilitating student mobility, and providing an educational service to the internationally mobile community
    - providing an internationally recognised pre-university curriculum
    - providing a university-entrance examination that gives access to higher education worldwide
    - developing, in collaboration with national education systems, a rigorous, broad, balanced and international curriculum (where 'international curriculum' is interpreted here in the sense of being internationally recognised).

One of the difficulties associated with commenting on the current situation of the IBDP in the UK (or, indeed, elsewhere) – whether from an ideological or a pragmatic perspective – is the relative lack of systematically gathered data on which to base conclusions, although this is a position gradually being addressed by the University of Bath's IB Research Unit, as well as by growing numbers of IB

teachers and administrators worldwide engaging in research for postgraduate qualifications. What research has been done tends to focus on dimensions of the IBDP
described here as pragmatic, as in a piece of research commissioned by the IB
Research Unit in the form of a survey of perceptions of the IBDP in 71 higher-
education institutions in Scotland, England, Wales and Northern Ireland (IBO
2003a). In a clearly overall very positive set of responses, with respect to depth and
rigour it is reported that 96 per cent of respondents were satisfied with the level of
preparation of IBDP students for degree studies, and that while 'the A level system
was seen to have greater depth by some respondents, ... this was less the case with
Curriculum 2000'. A similar majority 'favoured a broad curriculum and were
particularly enthusiastic about this aspect' of the IBDP, and most 'appreciated the
confidence, wide knowledge and skills that the breadth of the Diploma Programme
seemed to endow'. Other aspects of the IBDP remarked upon favourably in the
study were the compulsory Theory of Knowledge course (with mention of the
'flexibility and adaptability of the thought processes it seemed to assist') and
extended essay ('seen to assist both research skills and the preparation of disserta-
tions'). The Creativity, Action, Service programme, while not apparently valued in
academic terms, was greeted positively in terms of its contribution to producing
'rounded personalities', and particularly positively by some from the medical
profession who 'see the service element as good preparation for medical studies'.
In terms of 'higher skills' (critical thinking, communication, self-management and
motivation), the majority of respondents perceived IBDP students 'as more
accomplished than those following the A level system'.

Thus, in the UK at least, even acknowledging that the study was commissioned
by the IBO and that it did not attempt to ascribe causality in terms of the attributes
of students and their capabilities, there is evidence to suggest that, from the higher-
education perspective, the pragmatic IBDP aims relating to the provision of a
recognised curriculum, access to higher education and the development of a
rigorous and balanced curriculum are being met. Indeed, this provision and access
clearly extends to the wider international context. Spahn (2001), for instance,
provides a helpful summary of those countries where the IBDP allows direct
access to higher education (subject to prerequisites of specific faculties), where
advanced placement (AP) is given and where specific restrictions are imposed on
which IBDP subjects must be studied. In the USA, a study conducted by Duevel
(1999) of 12 universities and 95 adults holding IBDP diplomas suggested that the
challenging nature of the IBDP, and a range of attributes including strong produc-
tivity/study skills, perseverance, analytical thinking skills, research skills and
development of a global perspective, provided good preparation for university-
level study.

One would assume that recognition by higher-education institutions is one
concern for schools/colleges contemplating offering the IBDP, but there will also
be a range of other considerations (some of which have been written about elsewhere in this volume). Again, systematically conducted research is relatively thin
on the ground, although there is undoubtedly plenty of anecdotal evidence on

which to draw. Clearly, the reasons why schools opt for the IBDP will be linked, at least in part, to available alternatives and to their own school philosophy. The United World Colleges (UWCs), for instance, are committed to the IBDP for reasons discussed earlier in relation to the founding UWC, Atlantic College. International schools with a highly mobile and culturally mixed student population, meanwhile, may well favour the IBDP for reasons such as those motivating the International School of Geneva's 1960s initiative. In other contexts, there may well be different reasons for favouring the IBDP, and it is interesting to note Hill's observation that of the 1,080 IBO schools in May 2000, 'approximately 43% are state schools. Of the remaining 57%, approximately one third are private, national schools. This means that only about one third of all schools offering an IBO programme are private independent international schools' (2000: 24). Indeed, by 2003 international schools accounted for only 18 per cent of the total number of schools offering IB programmes (IBO 2004).

In the USA, a study by Spahn (2001) investigated why US schools adopt the IBDP, how they go about implementing it and what effects the programme has on the institution after its implementation. Based on a questionnaire sent to all US schools offering the IBDP, and case studies of four of them, Spahn's findings suggest that 'while a rise in academic standards was the major reason for adopting the IB, the majority of schools that did so also found that their culture changed due to higher expectations from the IB' (2001: 6). Of 155 responding schools, 70 per cent referred to introducing the IBDP as a way of raising academic standards – whether as a response to perceived falling standards (bearing in mind concerns raised in the 1983 report *A Nation at Risk* by the National Commission on Excellence in Education, and subsequent relatively poor US performance in international league tables) or, from those with an already respected academic curriculum, the need for a programme suitable for their 'gifted and talented' students or, for 'magnet' schools, the possibility of offering something different from the widely offered AP programme (Spahn 2001). While reference was made in some of the schools studied to the international dimensions of the IBDP, these were all very much from a pragmatic perspective, such as attracting 'foreign' students, offering a curriculum with external international standards and creating racial balance within a school by 'stemming white flight' of students away from the area. As Spahn says, 'the large majority of the schools were attracted to the IB because of its high academic standards', while 'its international aspects were of secondary importance'. Indeed, the growth of the IBDP in the USA, he says, 'seems to be due more to its content rather than its philosophical underpinnings' (2001: 102).

Reasons specific to the UK might be expected to differ not only from other contexts worldwide, but also within the UK itself. The narrowness of the A-level system already referred to, for instance, has never applied to the context of Scotland, with its own broader curriculum post-16; it is interesting to note that only 1 of the 49 UK schools offering the IBDP is located in Scotland, and that this school – the International School of Aberdeen – is clearly one for which the pragmatic international dimensions, such as those concerning the international mobility of students from different nationalities, are important (ISA 2004). Other than in

Scotland, a preference for the breadth of the IBDP over A level might be assumed to be a selling point and, indeed, anecdotal evidence suggests a groundswell of support within other parts of the UK for an increase in breadth in the post-16 curriculum (as evidenced in the pilot Welsh Baccalaureate already noted, and in the Tomlinson proposals in England).

One of the few systematic studies of UK schools offering the IBDP has been conducted by McGhee, who undertook a case study of four schools (one international school offering only the IBDP; one independent school offering the IBDP alongside A level; a comprehensive school offering the IBDP alongside A level; and a City Technology College offering the IBDP plus various vocational qualifications, but not A level), focusing on why they chose to adopt the IBDP and what challenges they faced in its implementation. The 'driving factor' in all four schools' decision to adopt the IBDP had been 'shaping a unique place in the local context' (McGhee 2003); in one case, creating an international sixth-form centre, with the IBDP helping to save the dwindling sixth form; in another, raising standards of achievement by providing a challenging programme. Challenges faced in offering the IBDP included costs (especially initially, in terms of the need for staff training and additional resources); 'training, gaining and maintaining staff' were all mentioned as crucial (though having been met in different ways by different schools). When asked about the international dimension of the IBDP, each school viewed this positively, with the IBDP being 'an integral part, and, indeed, a symbol of, the international-mindedness the school was also trying to foster in other ways'.

Again in the UK context, in a small-scale study conducted at the University of Bath, some of the 'less tangible' aspects of the IBDP, culled from various IBO documents, were explored with 19 IBDP graduates registered as university undergraduates and 3 IBDP teachers – as well as 3 members of university staff – including the aims of the IBDP that it:

- facilitates mobility (geographical and cultural)
- promotes international understanding
- promotes the preservation and appreciation of own language and cultures.

(Hayden and Wong 1997)

In general, all respondents in this study were very positive in respect of the IBDP's contribution to meeting the first of these aims; curriculum breadth, language learning and extending of the possibility of higher education were all mentioned as factors facilitating mobility. In relation to the second aim, students, teachers and others 'generally agreed that … IB students tend to be international in their outlook, although it was unclear whether it is the international school environment or curriculum which makes them so or indeed the students' internationally mobile background, often experienced long before the IB programme'. Living and mixing with students of other nationalities was felt by students and others to be 'most influential' in promoting international understanding 'rather than the IB curriculum', although it was acknowledged that multiple factors acting in combination were most likely as the overall influence in this connection. Students 'reinforced the view that the IB school environment is more important than the IB subjects in encouraging them to be "international"', the variety of nationalities at the school being particularly emphasised. One student pointed out that 'living with people of other countries was most important: I don't think studying the IB in a normal English school would have that kind of international influence'. Another believed it was 'not so much the IB as an educational programme which promotes international understanding, but rather the school environment you study it in', while another argued that international under-standing 'had not been promoted at all through the IB curriculum, but through living with students of other nationalities'. In relation to the third aim addressed, 'preserving one's own culture was perceived by students to be highly supported by Language A in particular: numerous references were also made ... to the IB's broad curriculum and its emphasis on learning two languages', while teachers felt that the IBDP 'makes positive attempts at preserving students' culture and languages through mother tongue learning in Language A'. Informal learning through mixing with other students in the school environment was, again, valued more highly, with one student commenting that 'the IB course *itself* did not give me a greater appreciation of my own culture', while another apparently was unaware of the IBDP's aim in this respect, saying, 'I don't know if the IB's aim was to expose the students to their own cultures', making the point that while some cultures were promoted within the IBDP, this was not true for all – although one teacher's comment here was interesting in highlighting that not all interna-tional school students of this age are enthusiastic about their own culture, and that some 'actually oppose anything to do with their religion or culture and want to be as American as possible'.

Other student perspectives on the IBDP experience have been gathered in inter-views with ex-IBDP students recorded in publications such as *IB World*, where positive references by different students have been made to the rigour of the programme; critical-thinking skills; extra-curricular activities; the international perspective; the service element of Creativity, Action, Service; Theory of Knowl-edge; 'learning how to learn'; the extended essay; getting to know students of other cultural and linguistic backgrounds; and discovering new areas of interest through the prescribed breadth, which a narrower choice would not have uncovered (IBO 1995; 1996a; 1996b). As one student put it, 'The IB ... made me aware of new ways of looking at the world' (IBO 1996a). Other positive student reflections and profiles included in Hill's discussion of the IBDP focus on the academic rigour and breadth of the programme, as well as primarily on the 'pragmatic' aspects of its international dimension (2003a).

Challenges for the future

It is clear that the IBDP has made an impact on the UK education scene in terms of the numbers of schools and colleges offering the programme, and through influence on new developments already noted in England and Wales. It is well regarded by universities, and its profile continues to grow in education circles generally. Given that 'the IBO has no ambition to see its diploma become the national qualification of the UK or indeed of any other country', but rather wishes 'to see it welcomed as an attractive and distinctive alternative, competing on equal terms' (IBO 2003a), it would appear that the IBDP story in the UK is, indeed, a successful one.

The original aims discussed by Peterson, arising from the needs of Atlantic College and schools such as the International School of Geneva, appear to be being met, summarised as the provision of a rigorous, internationally recognised and thus internationally portable university-entrance qualification, with an 'international' rather than a 'national' focus that can be followed by, and be appropriate for, students from different national and linguistic backgrounds, encouraging them to develop critical-thinking skills and an open-minded approach to learning and to others. There is no reason to imagine that the success of the IBDP in the UK will not continue, notwithstanding challenges such as cost (particularly relevant perhaps in the context of state-funded schools and colleges) and steps to broaden post-16 provision nationally. It is interesting, however, to reflect on what might be some of the consequences for the IBDP in the UK if, in due course, the Welsh Baccalaureate becomes well established, and a broader 16–19 curriculum is introduced in England. Would the IBDP, if the alternative national programme were to be equally broad and rigorous, continue to be as attractive as it currently appears? Setting aside the issue of cost, if the major difference between the two programmes were to lie in the international dimension alone, would that of itself continue to attract national state, as well as international, schools and colleges to the IBDP? Currently there seems little likelihood of the international dimension of the IBDP being challenged within the national system. Notwithstanding moves to introduce international dimensions to education – such as the first International Education Week, initiated by the DfES in November 2003 (Hastings 2003), and the Teachers' International Professional Development programme (DfES 2004) – and strides being made by individual state schools in internationalising the student experience across the age range within the constraints of the national system – the John Bentley School in Wiltshire being just one example (Hamilton 2003) – there is little evidence of international influence upon the existing *Curriculum 2000* programmes. If the international dimension of the national system were to strengthen markedly, this might perhaps lead to a sharpening focus on the meaning of 'international' in the national context and, indeed, in the context of the IBDP. It has already been noted that the international dimension of the IBDP could be considered to fall under two main headings: 'pragmatic' and 'ideological'. According to the definitions considered earlier, there would seem to be no doubt that the 'pragmatic' aims are currently being achieved. The 'ideological' dimension is, however, more challenging, and it could be argued that the IBO has, over the years since its inception, become more ambitious in its stated aims for this dimension. From what appear to have been original aims that the IBDP could be used as a means of facilitating the teaching of students from different backgrounds and of encouraging critical-thinking skills and an open-minded approach to learning and to others, with – as has been argued – the formal curriculum being but one dimension of the provision of the experience of an international education, more recently articulated aims place a heavier emphasis on the ability of the IBDP (or, indeed, of the IB programmes more broadly) to promote international understanding *per se*.

Anecdotal evidence from some students and teachers may well suggest that such aims are being met. Hill (2003a), for instance, refers to a survey of approximately 1,700 students and teachers relating to the period 1998–2000, in which the promotion of intercultural awareness was said to be affected by a number of dimensions of the IBDP. There are, however, perhaps two (linked) issues to raise here. One is the extent to which the effects of the formal curriculum can be distinguished from those of the school environment; as Hayden and Wong's study (1997) suggested, the school environment and the personal contact with a mix of nationalities that it provided, together with international travel, were perceived to contribute more to international understanding than was the IBDP itself. Indeed, Hill points out that in the survey referred to above:

> Respondents often related the IB programme to the school context, so that in the international schools a frequent response was that intercultural awareness occurred principally 'via the cultural mix of students and teachers'. In national state and private schools the corresponding response (from about half the schools) was that intercultural understanding was enhanced through interaction with 'foreign teachers and students, foreign visitors, and intercultural comparisons'.
>
> (2003a)

In an international context, where 43 per cent of schools offering IB programmes in 2000 were 'state schools' (Hill 2000: 24) and where claims have been made that the IBDP has evolved 'from a program for international schools to an international program for schools' (Hagoort 1994: 11), such an issue is clearly of relevance to IBDP aims with respect to promoting international understanding. In the UK context, where some, if not many, IBDP schools are 'national' rather than 'international' in character, it could be equally important. The IBDP has many strings to its bow, and it is clear that different strings will be more highly favoured in some contexts than in others. Against the backdrop of the still relative narrowness of A level, the breadth of the IBDP is one of its strong selling points in the UK, as are its international credibility, its contribution to a school carving out a distinct identity for itself locally and its contribution to attracting non-UK students as part of its recruitment strategy. It would appear that the contribution the IBDP can make to developing an 'international outlook' is also an important factor for at least some schools.

What is more debatable is whether it can be argued that the formal assessment of the IBDP can judge the extent to which a student is internationally minded. Indeed, it would be difficult to incorporate the assessment of such attributes systematically to ensure that, across all dimensions, such judgements could be made about all students, regardless of the combination of subjects studied. Another interesting point relates to the extent to which the IBDP can be said to engender or increase a student's international-mindedness, given issues related to the impact of the school environment and, indeed, the growing numbers of students now following the PYP and MYP of the IBO, whose international-mindedness will already, it is claimed, have been nurtured by participating in those two programmes prior to embarking upon the IBDP. 'What is the evidence', as Knight (1999) asked in another context, that engaging in the IBDP does actually lead to international-mindedness? And, if it cannot be shown to do so, is this in any sense a problem, provided that claims for the programme are cautiously made? Would it be a problem if UK-based and/or, indeed, other schools were to offer the IBDP for its rather more pragmatic characteristics (academic and international) alone?

Recently, the IBO, through its research unit, has embarked upon a 'School/ University Transition Study' with two main foci: a progress and performance study, considering academic performance in the IBDP and subsequently in higher education (and the relationship between them), and an international values study, exploring how the claimed values of international-mindedness are exemplified in the IBDP and subsequent higher-education experiences (IBO 2003b). The results of this study should make a helpful contribution to understanding in this area. It would, however, be rash to expect, however informative the outcomes of this study, that this complex area will be simplified. The question of values, attitudes and associated behaviour is notoriously complicated in its definitions and implementation in any educational context: the international dimension does nothing to aid simplification. A programme such as the IBDP, if its aims include promotion of the 'ideological' dimensions of international education, will continue to need to be clear in its definitions and cautious in its claims, if such aims are to be capable of being systematically and demonstrably achieved.

References

Cambridge J C and Thompson J J (2001) 'A Big Mac and a Coke?' Internationalism and Globalisation as Contexts for International Education, unpublished paper, University of Bath.

DfES (Department for Education and Skills) (2004) *Teachers' International Professional Development*, www.teachernet.gov.uk

Duevel L M (1999) *The International Experience: University Perseverance, Attainment and Perspectives on the Process*, unpublished PhD thesis, Purdue University, Indiana.

Fox E (1985) 'International Schools and the International Baccalaureate', *Harvard Educational Review*, 55(1): 53–68.

Fox E (1998a) 'The Emergence of the International Baccalaureate as an Impetus for Curriculum Reform', in M C Hayden and J J Thompson (eds) *International Education: Principles and Practice*, Kogan Page, London pp. 65–76.

Fox E (1998b) 'The Role of the International Baccalaureate in Educational Transformation: Chile as a Case Study', in M C Hayden and J J Thompson (eds) *International Education: Principles and Practice*, Kogan Page, London pp. 235–41.

Gellar C (1981) 'International Education: Some Thoughts on What It Is and What It Might Be', *International Schools Journal*, 1: 21–6.

Hagoort T (1994) 'A Message from the President', *IB World*, 6: 11.

Hamilton P (2003) 'Response to Ruth McGhee's article: 1', *IB Research Notes*, 3(2): 9.

Hastings S (2003) 'Fun and Games', *TES Go Global Supplement*, 7 November 2003.

Hayden M C (2001) 'International Education and the International Baccalaureate Programmes', unpublished paper presented to the International Baccalaureate Organisation Academic Advisory Committee, 5 April 2001.

Hayden M C and Thompson J J (1995) 'Perceptions of International Education: A Preliminary Study', *International Review of Education*, 41(5): 389–404.

Hayden M C and Thompson J J (1996) 'Potential Difference: The Driving Force for International Education', *International Schools Journal*, 16(1): 46–57.

Hayden M C and Wong C S D (1997) 'The International Baccalaureate: International Education and Cultural Preservation', *Educational Studies*, 23(3): 349–61.

Hill I (2000) 'Internationally-Minded Schools', *International Schools Journal*, 20(1): 24–37.

Hill I (2002a) 'The History of International Education: An International Baccalaureate Perspective', in M C Hayden, J J Thompson and G R Walker (eds) *International Education in Practice: Dimensions for National and International Schools*, Kogan Page, London pp. 18–29.

Hill I (2002b) 'Early Stirrings in International Education Part III: The Dawning of the IB Diploma', *International Schools Journal*, 21(2): 10–24.

Hill I (2002c) 'The Beginnings of the International Education Movement Part IV: The Birth of the IB Diploma', *International Schools Journal*, 22(1): 17–30.

Hill I (2003a) 'The International Baccalaureate', in G Phillips and T Pound (eds) *The Baccalaureate: A Model for Curriculum Reform*, Kogan Page, London pp. 47–75.

Hill I (2003b) 'Early Stirrings in International Education Part V: The ISA Primary Curriculum and Early Donors to the IB Project', *International Schools Journal*, 22(2): 12–24.

Hill I (2003c) 'Early Stirrings in International Education Part VI: Alec Peterson and the Establishment of the IB Office', *International Schools Journal*, 23(1): 64–78.

Hill I (2003d) 'Phenomenal Growth of the IB', in A D C Peterson *Schools across Frontiers: The Story of the International Baccalaureate and the United World Colleges*, Open Court, La Salle, Illinois.

IBO (International Baccalaureate Organisation) (1995) 'Class Notes', *IB World*, 8: 1–5.

IBO (1996a) Class Notes, *IB World*, 11: 1–4.

IBO (1996b) Class Notes, *IB World*, 12: 1–5.

IBO (2003a) *Perceptions of the International Baccalaureate Diploma Programme: A Report of an Inquiry Carried Out at UK Universities and Institutions of Higher Education*, IBO, Cardiff.

IBO (2003b) 'School/University Transition Study: Draft Specification', unpublished internal paper.

IBO (2004) www.ibo.org

ISA (International School of Aberdeen) (2004) www.isa.aberdeen.sch.uk

Kingdon M (1991) *The Reform of Advanced Level*, Hodder and Stoughton, London.

Knight M (1999) *Ecolint: A Portrait of the International School of Geneva 1924–1999*, International School of Geneva.

McGhee R (2003) 'Implementing the International Baccalaureate Diploma Programme in UK Schools: Rationales and Challenges', *IB Research Notes*, 3(2): 3–8.

McKenzie M (1998) 'Going, Going, Gone ... Global!' in M C Hayden and J J Thompson (eds) *International Education: Principles and Practice*, Kogan Page, London pp. 242–52.

Mattern W G (1991) 'Random Ruminations on the Curriculum of the International School', in P L Jonietz and D Harris (eds) *World Yearbook of Education 1991: International Schools and International Education*, Kogan Page, London pp. 209–16.

Pasternak M (1998) 'Is International Education a Pipedream? A Question of Values', in M C Hayden and J J Thompson (eds) *International Education: Principles and Practice*, Kogan Page, London pp. 253–75.

Peterson A D C (1960) *Arts and Science Sides in the Sixth Form: A Report to the Gulbenkian Foundation*, Abbey Press, Abingdon.

Peterson A D C (1987) *Schools across Frontiers: The Story of the International Baccalaureate and the United World Colleges*, Open Court, La Salle, Illinois.

Peterson A D C (2003) (2 edn) *Schools across Frontiers: The Story of the International Baccalaureate and the United World Colleges*, Open Court, La Salle, Illinois.

Pound T (2003) 'The Resistance to Reform: From Crowther to Curriculum 2000', in G Phillips and T Pound (eds) *The Baccalaureate: A Model for Curriculum Reform*, Kogan Page, London pp. 7–28.

Renaud G (1974) *Experimental Period of the International Baccalaureate: Objectives and Results*, UNESCO Press, Paris.

Schwindt E (2003) 'The Development of a Model for International Education with Special Reference to the Role of Host Country Nationals', *Journal of Research in International Education*, 2(1): 67–81.

Snow C P (1959) *The Two Cultures*, Cambridge University Press.

Spahn B A (2001) *America and the International Baccalaureate: Implementing the International Baccalaureate in the United States*, John Catt Educational, Great Glemham, Suffolk.

Sylvester R (2003) 'Further Mapping of the Territory of International Education in the 20th Century', *Journal of Research in International Education*, 2(2): 185–204.

Thompson J J (1988) In Fox E (1998a).

Thompson J J (1998) 'Towards a Model for International Education', in M C Hayden and J J Thompson (eds) *International Education: Principles and Practice*, Kogan Page, London pp. 276–90.

Thompson J J, Hayden M C and Cambridge J C (2003) 'Towards a Structural Typology for Baccalaureate-Style Curricula', in G Phillips and T Pound (eds) *The Baccalaureate: A Model for Curriculum Reform*, Kogan Page, London pp. 29–46.

UNESCO (United Nations Educational, Scientific and Cultural Organisation) (1996) *Declaration and Integrated Framework of Action on Education for Peace, Human Rights and Democracy*, UNESCO, Paris.

Part II

In practice

Chapter 3

Implementing the IBDP:
Three retrospective accounts

A comprehensive-school perspective
An independent-school perspective
A tertiary-college perspective

Ian Andain, Jill Rutherford and Peter Allen

A COMPREHENSIVE-SCHOOL PERSPECTIVE

In *Change Forces with a Vengeance*, Fullan (2003) warns that 'premature clarity is a dangerous theory.' I would hazard a guess that many of the staff at Broadgreen High School had similar emotions, although certainly not articulated in the same way, when in 1991 I suggested introducing the International Baccalaureate Diploma Programme (IBDP), because the A-level system was failing to equip our students with the sorts of skills and knowledge that the late twentieth century demanded: the need for more breadth and a high profile for science and technology, to name but two. Not that I lacked support for the initiative. Some three years earlier the Higginson Report had been published (DES 1988), and its proposals had been vetoed by the then prime minister, Margaret Thatcher, while the Oxford University report to the Advisory Council on Science and Technology (Pring *et al.* 1989) had been all but ignored. It was just that Broadgreen did not quite fit the profile of an International Baccalaureate (IB) school. Ours was, and is, an inner-city co-educational community comprehensive in Liverpool, with 5 per cent of students statemented and 54 per cent entitled to a free school meal. We also have two specialist units on site – a Deaf Resource Base (for both profoundly deaf and hearing-impaired students) and an Access Resource Base (for disabled students). Notwithstanding this, there were a number of factors that moved the debate forward. First, there was a *Guardian* leader, 'The Vacuum after 16', published on 15 August 1990, which was blunt in its judgement of A levels: 'no other developed state in the world has such a narrow end to its school exam (system).' Second, the process of introducing the National Curriculum stimulated massive interest in the whole school curriculum and, of course, the relationship (in so far as there was one in 1991) between the 11–16 and 16–19 phases. One thing at least was clear – that relationship was better served by the IBDP than by A levels. Third, the staff at Broadgreen had generally recognised that the speed of change was unlikely to slow down, and were therefore open to new ideas. It must be emphasised that at this stage, however, there was no suggestion of dropping A levels: rather, the two systems would operate in tandem, despite the cost.

In our application for International Baccalaureate Organisation (IBO) accreditation, we identified the following reasons for wishing to offer the IBDP:

- to increase opportunities for academic study and employment in a wider international context, in order to meet the challenge of the single European market
- to escape the narrow specialist boundaries inherent in the A-level system
- to create a more international ethos in the school
- to create more effective partnerships with industry.

Before the days of delegated funding and chequebook management, we needed to find some sponsorship to develop the IBDP. We decided to approach businesses on Merseyside, and were eventually rewarded with grants from Glaxo (as it was then), British Nuclear Fuels and Pilkington Glass. This financial support was crucial, not only because it signified that businesses saw value in the IBDP, but also because most IBDP staff-development workshops were held outside the UK. The three grants were supplemented by generous financial support from the Merseyside Training and Enterprise Council, which allowed the school to run an advertising campaign for the IBDP in an area that is very traditional in its attitude to post-16 qualifications. We targeted potential students, parents and employers through a variety of marketing techniques: a video explaining the IBDP; information sessions at venues likely to attract large numbers (for example, Liverpool Football Club); and information packs. It would be a gross exaggeration to say that we were overwhelmed by student applications for the IBDP in that year (we actually had one student!), but slowly the currency of the programme has gained acceptance, and much of the reason for this was the quality of the marketing campaign in those first three years.

Looking back on that period, I am struck by how the IBDP seemed to be in tune with so many of the themes that dominate our thinking today:

- Coleman's idea (1990) of 'social capital', now citizenship but embodied in the IBDP's Creativity, Action, Service (CAS) element
- a broad and balanced programme (DES 1988)
- academic achievement
- teamwork skills
- school collaboration.

The IBO has always been enthusiastic about the IB 'family of schools', and the concept of teachers working together and sharing good practice. It is instructive, therefore, to note what Fullan and Hargreaves (1998) had to say about the early 1990s in England and Wales: 'Market competition and school self-management may make teachers more diligent in courting parental support and involvement. But this kind of institutional competitiveness also divides schools and their teachers from each other.' To date, all our IBDP students have had the chance to participate in revision summer schools and to go abroad to support their CAS activities, and at least three-quarters of the teaching staff of 86 have experienced a range of IBDP workshops, both in this country and abroad. Having said that, however popular travelling abroad was with staff, not all colleagues were as enthusiastic about the IBDP's syllabuses as some. Many in the Modern Foreign Languages Department, for example, felt that the then new modular A-level courses were far superior to the French course in the IBDP, mainly because they believed it built up student confidence as each module was successfully completed, whereas the IBDP still relied on an end-of-course examination, which the department felt was a retrograde step. Other colleagues in the Mathematics Department considered the higher-level mathematics course in the IBDP to be far too difficult (a view, it must be said, that still has resonance). And, of course, as the 1990s drew to a close, and the difficulties of maintaining two very different systems grew, so did the debate about which the school should adopt.

It was certainly clear that we did not attract enough students into the sixth form to sustain the luxury of choice at that level. The debate was made more complicated because of the views of some of our committed and able sixth-formers. Many chose the A-level route because it was the easier of the two – three subjects (four if you include general studies), not six; no Theory of Knowledge (TOK); no CAS requirements; and no extended essay. We had to acknowledge the painful fact that at that time A level seemed the easier option. Ingrained in the UK student psyche in the late 1990s was the notion that 'difficult' or 'disliked' subjects could be permanently dispensed with at 16. I was certainly aware that if we abandoned A levels, then a number of our Year 11 cohort would decamp to other sixth-form providers (we did in the end lose about 24 students). However, while cost was a deciding factor in moving to one system, the benefits of the IBDP were too strong for the governors to ignore, and in 1997 the decision was taken to admit our last A-level candidates. It also has to be acknowledged that it was an attractive proposition to be unique in a city of 11–18 schools, where everyone else was offering the same diet, and we believed it would help our students when they were applying for university. Few admissions tutors would fail to look twice at a candidate doing the IBDP from an inner-city comprehensive school. It is true that I cannot quantify this observation, but it remains a fact that the school has almost a 100-per-cent record of entry to university for those students who wish to apply. It is also true that many of those students did not complete the full IBDP. Some dropped subjects because they found them too difficult or because the amount of work they needed to put in was too taxing. Not every student has the capacity to fulfil the demands of the IBDP, but every student can benefit from it. We have many students, currently studying at university, who achieved certificate qualification rather than the full diploma. They still gained a university place, based on an offer that did not require the mandatory 24 points, but which satisfied admissions criteria in the relevant subject areas and, importantly, recognised the immensely enriching experience of the TOK and CAS elements of the IBDP. Many university admissions officers have also commented favourably on the extended essay, which gives many students their first taste of original research.

The certificate option in the IBDP also gives students who are not of the first rank academically the opportunity to participate in the IBDP, and thus benefit from the programme without prejudicing their chances of a place at university. It certainly enabled the school to extend recruitment to a wider range of students than we had initially calculated. Increasingly, we are attracting students who do not aspire to university, but who see the IBDP as an appealing qualification for employers because of the breadth it offers. Having said that, it was clearly a blow to lose able and talented students in the first instance. It did not, however, prevent us from increasing the number of our IBDP students, in part by offering opportunities to mature students (through a partnership with a local tertiary college), but increasingly through a growing number of overseas students, particularly from Africa and Asia. In fact, our post-16 students are turning Broadgreen into an international school rather than an inner-city comprehensive.

Over the past few years, events seemed to have conspired to make the IBDP a much more attractive option to students. *Curriculum 2000*, of course, was an attempt to produce a more balanced A-level curriculum, which at the same time significantly increased the amount of work students were expected to complete, thus making the IBDP appear less onerous. Then, the pressure created by the first set of AS examinations became the first factor in undermining the whole philosophy of *Curriculum 2000*. The next factor was almost certainly the government's Green Paper *14–19: Extending Opportunities, Raising Standards* (DfES 2002a), which even made reference to the IBDP (favourably, it must be added). It was, however, the grade-boundary fiasco that undoubtedly produced the most vociferous reaction from our Year 11 students, and prompted a much stronger interest in the IBDP. In October 2001, the school received its second Ofsted inspection and was one of the first cohort of schools to have a separate inspection of our sixth-form provision. This was clearly a major challenge, because it was certainly the first state comprehensive to have the IBDP inspected and incorporated into an Ofsted report. Notwithstanding the inevitable Ofsted-'speak', it was very positive:

> The Sixth Form is successful. Its students achieve well in the IBDP, having entered with mainly modest GCSE qualifications. They are successful at entering higher education. The IB Diploma Programme is broad and offers very good opportunities for students to develop initiative, study skills and personal qualities. The enrichment programme is extensive.
>
> (Ofsted 2001)

This view has been further endorsed by a visit from Her Majesty's Inspector of schools (HMI), specifically to look at the IBDP. These fact-finding visits are not formally reported on to the school, but it was gratifying indeed to hear the word 'inspirational' used in the context of our IBDP provision. Comments like that do not drop lightly from the lips of HMI.

A further problem – and one I would imagine is common to many state schools – is that Local Education Authorities (LEAs) have tended to shy away from formally endorsing the IBDP, which in turn has dissuaded parents and students from embracing it. There must be many reasons for this – a lack of knowledge of the IBDP probably being the principal one – but others suggest themselves:

- not enough serious curriculum thought given to the post-16 sector (now, of course, the 14–19 sector)
- an unwillingness to confer 'approved' status on an IBO-accredited school where there is significant competition for post-16 students
- satisfaction with the status quo as an acceptable national examination system;
- too great an expense
- an inability to influence post-16 provision because previous reorganisations have focused such provision in the sixth-form college/further-education/ tertiary sectors.

However, there are now tentative signs that some LEAs are experiencing a road-to-Damascus conversion, and are beginning to see the IBDP as an integral part of all students' post-16 entitlement. For example, Liverpool's '14–19 Curriculum Entitlement Statement' now includes a formal reference to the IBDP. All young people, it states, will have access to:

- courses at the appropriate level (including Entry Level and Levels 1, 2 and 3)
- appropriate types of courses leading to the award of qualifications and combinations of qualifications including academic and vocational, and access to the work-based learning route in line with government policy
- nationally and internationally recognised qualifications including GCSE, GNVQ, AS/A2, NVQ, AVCE and the International Baccalaureate
- key skills in line with government recommendations
- language and basic skills support as required
- community citizenship programmes such as YAR, Duke of Edinburgh and Award Scheme Development Accreditation Network (ASDAN) awards.

In February 2003, Kent County Council held a conference in Dartford billed as 'Raising Standards of Education through the Global Dimension', which took as its focus the IBDP's emphasis on 'diversity' and 'choice', now apparently the new watchwords for a number of LEAs. This has certainly been reinforced by the failure of *Curriculum 2000* to promote breadth, and the concomitant lack of emphasis on the quality of learning and on learning skills, both of which the IBDP fosters. In particular, TOK and the extended essay highlight issues around 'types' of knowledge, around research, around the concept of the 'essay' and around how we learn generally. By its very nature, the IBDP encourages visual, audio and kinaesthetic learning, and students are invited to reflect on methods of learning.

Of late, much has been made of the concept of learning communities. David Miliband's speech of 17 October 2002, to the annual meeting of the Association for Foundation and Voluntary Aided Schools, makes this point strongly:

But networks of collaboration – local, regional or national learning communities – are also about culture and not just incentives. They are vital to a new culture of learning in the schooling system. That is why I celebrate the growth of networks of schools ... We want to see a schooling system growing from the bottom up rather than the top down, partnerships fuelled by vocation and interest and commitment, as well as contracts and funds, not central diktat.

(DfES 2002b)

At the time of writing, Liverpool is on the verge of inaugurating a network of 14–19 schools to ensure that its entitlement statement can be realised. Not only is Broadgreen in a network of three schools where the IBDP will be on offer to all post-16 students, but in addition the IBDP will be franchised to another two schools in similar networks. In what is certainly a groundbreaking initiative, involving Broadgreen, the IBO and Liverpool LEA, a franchise agreement framework has been agreed that will permit the IBDP to be taught in schools not formally accredited by the IBO. The hope and expectation is that the IBDP will gradually be available to all students in the LEA. With new technologies, it is perfectly feasible to offer programmes of study without a teacher's immediate monitoring, support and intervention. Videoconferencing and the growth of schools' intranet facilities mean that learning can take place remotely. In essence, Liverpool LEA has decided to provide a solution to a problem that the Tomlinson Working Group has been addressing, namely 'inclusion'. The 2000 figures showing students in full-time education from 16 to 18 make depressing reading (Table 3.1).

Increasing choice and providing more coherence is what is likely to increase student numbers, and Broadgreen sees the IBDP as being an integral part of Liverpool's 14–19 philosophy, whatever the Tomlinson proposals may lead to in the future. Indeed, while the much-needed reform of the English educational system post-16 may still be a long way off, it looks very much as if the IBDP will continue to provide the only viable alternative to a post-16 examination system that is continuing to fail its students. As David Miliband pointed out in a speech, 'Moving Forward at 14–19', to a joint conference of the Secondary Heads Association, the Association of Colleges and the National Association of Head Teachers on 2 March 2004, 'We have the 4th highest drop-out rate in the industrialised world; the cultural and educational signals associated with a "school leaving" exam at 16 need to be overcome' (DfES 2004).

Table 3.1 Number of students aged 16–18 in full-time education in 2000

Age	Percentage in full-time education
16	71.6
17	58.7
18	36.9

By way of conclusion, I was struck by a section in the Vision 2020 conference paper 'One World One School', which suggested in its section on 'Innovation in Pedagogy' that schools should trial a higher-education teaching style at post-16 (SST 2000). This is exactly what the IBDP strives for in its insistence that all students follow a TOK course and complete a supervised extended essay. A number of university lecturers have remarked on the maturity of our IBDP students, and the ease with which they adapt to university life, a salutary acknowledgement of the quality of thought behind the IBDP. As a nation, we cannot afford to ignore the example set by the IBDP – if it can work in an inner-city comprehensive, it can work anywhere.

AN INDEPENDENT-SCHOOL PERSPECTIVE

In Years 9–11 at Oakham School, Rutland, most students take ten GCSE courses, and there is minimal choice. All students take coordinated science, mathematics, history, geography, English literature and language, French, a second modern foreign language or Latin, and a creative arts subject. This deliberate decision to maintain breadth in the academic curriculum is reflected in other activities. (For example, all students are encouraged to participate in music, drama, sport and service activities.)

The reduction in breadth post-16, even with the new AS/A2 system, was always seen as a loss for the school and the students. Most students take four AS subjects and three at A2, thus dropping at least six of their GCSE subjects. It was therefore natural for the school to look at ways of keeping a broader curriculum, and for a while an 'Oakham Baccalaureate' was considered. However, it quickly became obvious that the International Baccalaureate Diploma Programme (IBDP) fulfilled every requirement that the school was looking for, with the addition of an international dimension that would encourage students to look outwards into Europe and beyond.

Before 2000, the trustees decided to introduce the IBDP and to run it in parallel with the A-level system in Years 12 and 13. Students were to be given free choice between the two programmes, and those new to the school (between 20 and 50 per year) were also to be given free choice between the IBDP or A levels. Since the school was fully subscribed, the decision to adopt the IBDP had nothing to do with issues of recruitment. What has certainly changed, however, is that the proportion of international boarders has increased, and this has inevitably had an impact on the composition of the student body.

Three years after the IBDP was first introduced, there is a shared perception amongst both teaching staff and students that it offers a comprehensive package of skills and knowledge, underpinned by a coherent philosophy. The emphasis is on the acquisition of skills in communication (in your own language and that of another), in numeracy (everyone takes one of the four mathematics courses), in oral presentations (part of the assessment in English, other languages and Theory of Knowledge, or TOK) and in giving something back to the community (the service element of Creativity, Action, Service, or CAS). There is also increasing evidence that IBDP candidates are receiving fair and sometimes generous offers from universities, while A-level candidates with comparable GCSE grades are being rejected. The IBDP grading system goes beyond that of an existing A grade at A level. Offers from the top universities range from 36 to 40 points, five below the maximum points score. About 36–38 IBDP points would be equivalent to three As at A level, so the IBDP grading system permits differentiation at higher levels of academic ability, and therefore allows university admissions tutors to refine their offers.

Managing the introduction of the IBDP

Before starting to teach the IBDP, a school has a choice of appointing an internal IBDP coordinator with knowledge of the institution or appointing an external candidate with IBDP knowledge. There are advantages in both. An internal candidate knows the school and its staff, and can attend IBDP workshops to learn about the administration of the programme. However, this does take some time as the International Baccalaureate Organisation (IBO) passes much of its administrative role over to the IBDP coordinators in schools. It is also a steep learning curve for those with no previous IBDP experience. The advantage of appointing a newcomer with IBDP experience is that he or she can take a missionary role in both informing stakeholders and raising levels of staff awareness of the IBDP relatively quickly.

Oakham decided to appoint an external candidate with IBDP experience. Perhaps more crucially, the appointment was made one academic year before teaching began. This gave the IBDP coordinator time to inform, persuade and recruit students, and to set up appropriate systems within the school. The IBDP timetable is different from that of A levels. There are no modular examinations in January and June, but terminal examinations in May of the second year. Effectively, this is a five-term programme, with the coursework component being submitted by mid-March of the second year. The examination regulations are also slightly different from those of the UK awarding bodies, and at Oakham it was decided to place the administration of IBDP examinations within the IBDP coordinator's remit, but in liaison with the schools examinations officer.

It goes without saying that the IBDP coordinator has to be biased in favour of the IBDP. It is not enough to say that this is a good programme, and so are A levels. The introduction of a new and very different academic package to the school therefore necessarily involved presentations on the IBDP to students, staff and parents. These were well publicised and well attended by the latter, who think they know about A levels because they did them, but are uncertain at any mention of the IBDP. Questions at these sessions tended to focus on two main issues – is the IBDP more difficult than A levels, and how do universities and prospective employers feel about it? As far as the first part of the question is concerned, most Oakham students have the perception that the IBDP is harder than A levels, but it really depends on the subjects chosen and the organisational abilities of each individual student. In responding to the second part, the following points are worth bearing in mind.

- The IBDP is the oldest public examination offered in England and Wales. It is 35 years old, and so tried and tested. GCSEs are less than 20 years old, while the revised AS/A2 system is 3 years old and still has teething troubles. Some 50,000 students per year take IBDP examinations around the world.
- The IBDP is a package that holds together well. It was conceived and designed by educators and not politicians, and has had – and still has – no national political input into the philosophy or syllabuses.
- The emphasis is on developing skills and maintaining breadth. To compete in the new Europe, young English people will find themselves in competition with those who are trilingual and have continued up to 12 subjects (for example, in Poland) to the end of schooling.
- There is more flexibility within the IBDP than at first appears. Students may specialise in sciences (taking two higher-level (HL) sciences and HL mathematics) or in languages (English, German and Latin) or, with the advent of the trans-disciplinary courses, in two arts subjects (music and visual arts).
- Assessment is terminal and does not test the same skill more than once, so examination durations are reasonable. All subjects have coursework varying from 20 to 100 per cent (visual arts, theatre arts and TOK) of the final marks.
- Criterion-based assessment is used in grading the papers, not norm-referencing, so all students who deserve a top grade based on written grade descriptors will gain one.
- Universities, both in the UK and around the world, recognise the IBDP as an entry requirement, and most list specific IBDP requirements on their websites. Some US colleges give sophomore status for IBDP candidates, or extra credits.
- Taking an HL subject prepares a student just as well (some say better) for degree courses as taking an A level in that subject.

Implementing the IBDP

In managing the IBDP, a decision has to be made between offering a small range of subjects – so giving students less choice, but making for ease of timetabling, and entailing lower start-up costs – and a large range of subjects – so giving students more choice, but having timetabling ramifications and involving higher costs. Oakham started the IBDP with a sizeable financial and staffing commitment. Some 35 courses were offered in the first year, and this involved the recruitment of up to 14 new teaching staff over two years. Despite the scale of this investment, some combinations of subjects were still not possible, as there are both IBDP group requirements and school blocking restrictions.

It is perfectly possible to start the IBDP with a smaller range of subjects. For example, only one standard-level (SL) science may be offered at first, and fewer languages and levels of language courses. Short cuts, but acceptable ones, include teaching HL and SL together for some subjects. While not popular with students or teachers, the science courses are written with a common core for HL and SL, and options can be selected that are common for both levels. Similarly, both levels of geography, music, visual arts, Latin, design technology, mathematics and mathematics methods were first taught together. Some of the Latin lessons were also co-taught with A level.

Within a 40-minute-period timetable, IBDP lessons were taught on a weekly basis as follows: 6 × 40 minutes of HL, 4 × 40 minutes of SL and 2 × 40 minutes of TOK. This gave a total of 32 lessons, equivalent to taking four AS levels in blocks of eight lessons. Over the length of the IBDP, this works out to be slightly less than the 240 hours recommended for HL and slightly more than the 150 hours for SL.

Some of the main challenges that have to be faced in the years following the implementation of the IBDP are:

- informing various stakeholders (teaching staff, trustees, students and parents)
- planning the timetable and deciding upon which subjects to offer
- counselling students on their subject and course choices
- ensuring sufficient training of IBDP teachers
- managing the complex administration procedures of the IBO
- spreading IBDP deadlines over a sufficiently long time, so that students are not too pressurised at the end of the programme
- publicising university recognition of the IBDP.

Teacher and student perceptions of the IBDP

There can be no doubt that A levels and the IBDP offer quite distinct teaching and learning experiences. The package of the IBDP may be more quickly recognised by the student – each subject gains an equal grade (up to 7 points), so it is fool-hardy to focus on one to the exclusion of another. There are many more elements and deadlines to be met within the IBDP – extended essays, TOK essays, orals – so good organisational skills are essential. However, since IBDP students cannot compare their own learning experience with that associated with A-level courses, those who teach across both programmes are better placed to make critical comparisons. At Oakham, for example, there is a majority view that teaching the IBDP is a different experience to teaching A levels. This is partly due to the non-modular nature of the IBDP, and the fact that all subjects are taught for two years (in reality, 19 months). This holistic and concurrent structure, together with the fact that examinations come at the end of the programme, means that teaching is 'of the subject' and not, until the last few weeks of the course, 'to the examination'. This provides more freedom to explore and consolidate. Moreover, the differences in both content and assessment patterns have an impact on teaching and learning styles. In history, for instance, the thematic nature of many topics within the two-year programme provides time to develop real depth and quality of learning, which can be very rewarding from the perspective of the teacher. However, preparing for IBDP lessons can be demanding, as there are few textbooks (especially in history) that are geared towards its specification. This means that, in practice, there is a greater onus on the IBDP teacher to synthesise materials from university-level books to present to the classes. While more and more publishers are producing IBDP-specific textbooks – such as Cambridge University Press, Biozone and IBID Press – such textbooks are not that common for some subjects.

In English, a big selling point for the IBDP is the ability and requirement to study other literatures. This makes students realise that English literature operates, like every other literature, in a pan-cultural context. Without this understanding, their knowledge of their own literature must be imperfect. World literature, Part 1, provides a wonderful opportunity for cultural breadth, and becomes a natural development from the other cultures' texts of GCSE. The oral commentary and presentation do a great deal to sharpen thinking, organisation and presentation skills at this higher level – again, a natural follow-up to GCSE oral work in English and modern languages. The additional study of TOK, for example, encourages a broader, more deeply considered response to the role of literature in society. As one teacher commented:

> The choice of texts for AS/A2 is dictated by the exam board, and this choice is dull and limited. With the IBDP, the teacher is very much in control of what is selected, and the texts may be very exciting and unusual because of this.

IBDP courses are structured differently to those at A level. This is in part due to the modular nature of the current A-level system, and in part to the internationalism of the IBDP subjects, which need to be taught in 117 different countries. As one physicist at the school commented, 'The [International Baccalaureate (IB)] is more traditional and, I believe, prepares students better for a physics course at university.' Similarly, a historian takes the view that:

> The structures of the history IB courses and examinations are, I think, more straightforward than those for the AS and A2 units, and relate more closely to the demands of university-level history. The AS and A2 system is complicated because each unit assess[es] skills in [a] particular way, whereas the IB units are more consistent in their objectives. In terms of content, IB demands greater skills of synthesis and, if level 7 answers are to be produced, an awareness of historiographical difference throughout.

Whether students respond differently to IBDP and A-level teaching is important. From the perspective of the school's teachers of economics, and of business and management, the view is that:

Four assessments for AS/A2 mean students have a much better idea of where they are, what they need to do – e.g. A2 business will have completed five out of six units by the fifth term, so there will be few surprises in August. This feedback has a significant impact on their attitude and motivation. With the Diploma Programme, it is very much more speculative – IB students have to revise and be far more familiar with a much greater range of material. There is an issue here with organisation skills and so on.

One central question is whether taking the IBDP instead of A levels makes a young person a different student, or whether IBDP students happen to be different from their A-level counterparts right from the outset of the two courses. Based on anecdotal evidence at Oakham, we think that the students are different at the beginning, and that the IBDP enhances these differences. As one member of staff commented, 'By the end of the seventh-form course, I felt that many of my IB students were confident at handling major themes through conceptual and historiographical frameworks. This will equip them well for the demanding universities.' While another remarked:

> Are the students different? Domestically, I'd say not a huge amount, but inter-nationally, yes. But I think the bigger difference is not between AS and IB, but between new sixth form and ex-Oakham fifth form – but that's a question you didn't ask! But, because IB has a disproportionate number of newcomers compared with A levels in this school, there are differences in the ethos/industry/attitude, which I attribute to where they have come from rather than the course itself.

The IBDP and A levels

Although the perception of some students is that the IBDP is harder, it is once again a perception and not necessarily based on hard evidence. The IBDP time-table at Oakham is the same as that of AS levels. Students are taught for 32 periods of 40 minutes per week. AS students usually take four AS levels with teaching over eight periods each. On a weekly basis, IBDP students take three HLs for six periods, three SLs for four periods and TOK for two periods. In Year 13, A2 teaching is reduced to 24 periods per week for those taking three A2 levels, but remains at 32 for IBDP students. Suggested private study time per week – of about 16 hours – is comparable for each programme.

The IBDP, however, is more condensed. Examinations come in early May (November for southern hemisphere schools), and this can mean just one week of the summer term before they start. Effectively, this gives a five-term IBDP, but it is not split up by modular examinations, and the summer term of the first year of the IBDP is a full teaching term. IBDP students require self-motivation, good organi-sational skills and a curiosity to find out more. One Oakham teacher has likened the difference between A levels and the IBDP to that of horses and pigs. In A levels, the horses jump the jumps, get around the course and win a rosette. In the IBDP, the pigs are looking for truffles in a field. The route that they take may be direct, or it may be circuitous, leading to the discovery of more truffles. It is this sense of academic adventure, particularly in TOK and the extended essay, but also in other areas of the programme, that the IBDP inculcates.

In schools and colleges where there is a choice of courses, it is not easy for students to make reasoned decisions. At Oakham, since A levels and the IBDP are both offered, choosing one or the other is the first big academic decision that students and their parents have had to make. They need detailed information, counselling and guidance, and will still change their minds, perhaps several times. For the student who wants to keep options more open, the IBDP may be the right programme. Universities do notice SL, as well as HL, subjects. For example, one recent offer was based on 36 points with 7, 7 or 6 in any of HL history, HL English and SL biology (to read anthropology at LSE). Some students may opt to take four HL, and two SL, subjects to keep more options open. So those students unsure about whether to read engineering or French and Spanish can keep the languages, mathematics and physics at HL. We give students a free choice of either A levels or the IBDP, but we recommend that IBDP students are self-motivated and have developed (or are prepared to develop) good organisational and study skills. GCSE requirements are at least a B at GCSE for HL subjects, and a C for SL subjects.

Words from students are better than any words from teachers, so here are two examples:

> I chose to do the IB as it was different. I wanted a range of subjects and did not want to do exams every term like the A-level students. The IB has been good for me and, although I moan about it, I have enjoyed it: I'm more in touch with the foreign students, I have six subjects (one of which was mathematics) and when the results come in I hope I get a feeling of achievement that everyone deserves. It has been hard work, a lot more than A level, which is a downside. It was not what I expected. Sixth form was brilliant with the IB, and I enjoyed it; seventh form has involved a lot more work than I anticipated.

> The IB really appealed to me because of the smaller class sizes. As an art student, it gave me a different dimension as a university candidate. However, maintaining a relatively full timetable made portfolio completion challenging, but when you're passionate you make time, and organisation was the key to keeping on top of things. The amount of work is more than A level, but there are many personal benefits to taking the IB, such as the CAS log and TOK that encouraged my extra-curricular activities and broadened my horizons.

The IBDP in a post-Tomlinson era

The IBDP philosophy and that of the 14–19 Working Group are remarkably similar in a number of ways. We all want to educate young people to be good citizens of the world and lifelong learners, and to be equipped with the skills they will need in the future. But the IBO strategic plan foresees an enhanced global role for the organisation, with the IB network becoming far larger than its current position in the UK. To quote the Director General of the IBO, in his foreword to a report on perceptions of the IBDP by UK universities, 'the IBO has no ambition to see its diploma become a national qualification of the United Kingdom or indeed of any other country. It does, however, want to see it welcomed as an attractive and distinctive alternative' (IBO 2003).

The Tomlinson *Final Report* gives a template for 14–19 learning, but says that this will take some ten years to implement. For those who are familiar with the IBDP, there are some obvious resonances between the two. For example, the proposed 14–19 core is designed to ensure that all young people:

> acquire the functional mathemathics, functional literacy and communication, functional ICT and common knowledge ... they require to succeed and progress in learning, HE, employment and adult life ... [and] ensure that all learners develop and demonstrate a range of generic skills, including research and analysis, problem solving ... [and] independent study.
>
> (DfES 2004)

The IBO mission statement, on the other hand, reads as follows:

> The International Baccalaureate Organization aims to develop inquiring, knowledgeable and caring young people who help to create a better and more peaceful world through intercultural understanding and respect. To this end the IBO works with schools, governments and international organizations to develop challenging programmes of international education and rigorous assessment. These programmes encourage students across the world to become active, compassionate and lifelong learners who understand that other people, with their differences, can also be right.
>
> (IBO 2005)

The requirement of IBDP students is that they study mathematics, a science, a subject from the humanities, their own language and literature, together with those of at least one other country, and usually an arts subject. In addition, the core is a course in TOK (which encourages critical thinking and reflection), writing a 4,000-word extended essay in a subject of their choice and fulfilling CAS requirements in which they must contribute something towards the community. The IBDP assessment policy is based on both knowledge and skills acquisition. It also requires a skill to be assessed only once in the total package, not in every subject. Communication – in writing and speech – is seen as essential, so students are asked to write in various genres; present commentaries on texts as part of the examination in language A1; and take part in group work for their second language, science and the TOK presentation.

For the 65 schools and colleges in England and Wales currently offering the IBDP, the challenge of adopting the IBDP can be great. Approximately half of these institutions are state-funded institutions (at present the IBDP gains funding equivalent to 4.5 A levels), but the IBDP is an expensive programme and will remain so because of small candidatures across a large range of subjects. None the less, the impact of the IBDP within a school is immense. It is, however, not a programme of study for all our students. Those who are determined to specialise at age 16, whether in sciences, languages or the arts, may still do so within the IBDP, but they must continue with a breadth of disciplines at SL.

This focus on academic breadth is also complemented by the skills-based components of the IBDP, in which students' communication, ICT and numeracy skills are developed alongside an understanding of the cultures of others. Many IBDP students may not see the value of the programme until some time after they have finished it, but they often report back that they find themselves equipped with the range of skills that both universities and employers require.

Each year, more independent schools in the UK are gaining accreditation to offer the IBDP. Certainly, IBDP students are gaining good offers from universities where the value of the IBDP is fully recognised. Parents are also more aware of the IBDP from the many articles in the press that have appeared in recent years. Although achieving IBO accreditation may be seen as a way of avoiding the *Curriculum 2000* reforms, most independent schools continue to offer AS/A2 as well as the IBDP. Taking the decision to become IBO-accredited is a major decision for any educational institution. It involves changing the culture of the institution, as well as increasing staffing and budgeting for IBDP training. To offer the IBDP does not necessarily mean that a school has automatically become an IB 'World School'. This takes time and, more importantly, a willingness to adopt the IB philosophy in its fullest sense.

A TERTIARY-COLLEGE PERSPECTIVE

The right step for a tertiary curriculum

In 1990 it seemed a natural development to offer the International Baccalaureate Diploma Programme (IBDP) at Henley. South Oxfordshire, under the educational guidance of its then director of education, Tim Brighouse, had decided to go tertiary in the 1980s, and in 1987 the sixth-form college and the nearby technical college joined together to form The Henley College. Its first principal, Graham Phillips, had visionary ideas for its curriculum. The two former colleges had offered a wide range of A levels, mainly at the academic King James College, and a more limited range of vocational courses, chiefly in secretarial studies and engineering at the technical college. Graham Phillips wanted to put Henley on the educational map, and was fully aware of the attractions of the IBDP for the new college, seeing it as one way to establish its new identity.

Senior staff visited Atlantic College, the obvious and nearest major IBDP centre, for fact-gathering and research, and then initial curriculum planning began in earnest. A formal application to the International Baccalaureate Organisation (IBO) was made, and in the late 1980s there was still an IBO office in Bloomsbury, from where the late Robert Blackburn made the journey to grant approval. The staff had the right educational experience, and the library met the IBDP's academic demands. The first cohort of students began the course in 1990, and the local education authority (LEA) blessed the launch with a grant of £15,000, which went a long way towards producing some marketing materials, sending staff on training events abroad and sustaining some minority languages. In its first years, Henley was able to offer Japanese, Afrikaans, Italian and Polish, in addition to its two mainstream languages, French and German, by using local part-time teachers to give one-to-one support to students who had a background in the language concerned.

It was not an easy birth, and the introduction of the IBDP met some opposition from within the institution's own ranks. At one heated Academic Board meeting, at which the formal introduction of the course was up for approval, a few members objected to the additional costs of the IBDP, and could not see that it offered anything different from A levels. To some extent, a short-sightedness blighted the early years of the course at Henley, as a number of staff thought that the IBDP was an expensive luxury.

To launch the new course, it was decided to offer as full a programme as possible, so apart from English, two modern languages and mathematics at higher and standard level, the sciences were provided at both levels, along with history, economics and geography. It was a bold decision, but inevitably costly when the course failed to recruit its target numbers. This led to a situation where some very small groups were taught – higher-level mathematics and physics, for example, had about half a dozen students. In fact, recruitment in the first year barely hit 30 in total, and then fell back as some students switched to A levels. The main problem was the course's newness and unfamiliarity. In a tertiary environment, the college's courses rely heavily on the teachers in the 11–16 schools promoting them, and in the early 1990s the IBDP was relatively unknown. The media hardly mentioned the IBDP, and it was generally thought to be a course that only international schools offered. When potentially good scientists asked their teachers at school whether they should do the IBDP or A levels, the answer was invariably in favour of the latter.

An IBDP coordinator was subsequently appointed, and Henley was fortunate to have recruited to a lectureship in history a former member of staff of Atlantic College, who was very familiar with the programme. In the first year of its launch, there were alarmingly low applications. The coordinator decided to review all the applications for A levels, and found a number of students who, it was felt, might make good IBDP candidates. They were written to, and it was later discovered that they knew little of the IBDP, but after some persuasion, many of them were converted. It was a modest start, with around 30 recruited, but the calibre of the students was high and, at the end of the first two years, the pass rate was 100 per cent. The students who completed the IBDP had high praise for the experience and secured their places at university, although in the early years many admissions tutors claimed to have no knowledge of the IBDP. Times have certainly changed since then.

The lean and hard years

The years following the implementation of the IBDP were marked by cynicism and idealism in fairly equal measure from the staff. The cynics thought the IBDP elitist, expensive and not as progressive as A levels. The idealists, who were closer to the course, usually by teaching on it, could see that it offered its students something unique. Every cohort of students in the early years, although comparatively small, did well, achieved remarkable results and loved the course. In one year there were only 16 students who completed the programme, and, incredibly, 14 of them gained grade 7 in English, with the other two gaining grade 6. This feat has not been repeated since.

Throughout the first few years of the IBDP at Henley, there was a constant battle against financial constraints, and the incorporation of colleges in 1993 did not bring in any additional funding. The bright future, which was to be free of the restrictions of the LEA, never came; there was another quango, the Further Education Funding Council, and many colleges were facing deficits. Each year the IBDP came under scrutiny, and with its steady but uneconomic recruitment in the low to mid thirties, it was just not financially viable. In terms of funding, the IBDP was equivalent to three A levels, but, of course, with its six subjects and Theory of Knowledge (TOK), it cost much more. At senior level, there was strong pressure to abandon the programme. A-level courses had grown in number, with the introduction of new and popular subjects like psychology and media studies. There was also a feeling that a true tertiary college ought to be offering more General National Vocational Qualifications, and the IBDP was undoubtedly expensive. The college was in financial crisis, and other cuts in courses were being made, so there were those who asked why the IBDP should be protected. The battle lines were drawn to save or abandon it. On one side, there were its critics, many of whom had never supported the concept of the IBDP in the first place: these included most of the senior management and a number of departmental heads. On the other side, there were a few lone voices in support; critically, they were in important positions. One was the principal, who had always been an enthusiastic advocate of the IBDP; another was one of the heads of school in which the course was based; and a further supporter was the head of humanities, who had been the first coordinator. The battle was fierce, but the IBDP won the day, with the principal placing the educational arguments above the financial ones.

The decision to continue with the IBDP was certainly vindicated. Student numbers began to increase, and there was wide coverage in the media, which undoubtedly helped to raise the profile of the IBDP in the national consciousness. It was an important milestone for the college to have become one of the first state tertiary institutions to offer the programme and, subsequently, to have been perceived as a leader in the field. One consequence of this was that Henley was visited in these early years by representatives of many other colleges, from Derby to Exeter, all of whom were keen to see the programme in action in a state institution.

The IBDP at Henley was destined to survive, but, none the less, cuts had to be made in order for the course to have some semblance of viability. Consideration was given as to whether students should be asked to pay for their relatively expensive examinations, whether to recruit more full-cost students from over-seas or whether other strategies – like combining IBDP and A-level groups in the classroom – could save money. In most cases, the latter strategy was rejected by the subject specialists, but it is worth noting that the subject leaders of art, economics, Spanish and German had always welcomed IBDP and A-level students in the same classes, and had taught them together with considerable success for both programmes. Ultimately, the decision was made to prune the IBDP, which in practical terms meant the loss of higher-level sciences, and a reduction in teaching hours from four and a half to four hours a week, while A levels were still allocated four and a half hours. With hindsight, it is ironic to think that it was considered possible to deliver a superior IBDP course in fewer hours than an A-level course. Were IBDP students perceived to be more capable than A-level students? No doubt some of them were, but that is a question consid-ered below.

The IBDP had thus survived tough times of financial stringency and underfunding. At the same time, some other courses were not so fortunate at Henley: hairdressing and motor-vehicle engineering had been suffering low recruitment for some time, and were not thought to be an essential part of the tertiary future, so while the IBDP continued, other courses were discontinued, with the concomitant staff redundancies.

The uniqueness of the IBDP curriculum

It is very difficult to gauge the differences between the IBDP and A levels in terms of the experience of the student. A handful of students have done both, but usually for negative reasons. In a tertiary college, there is ample opportunity for students to change their programme, and there are always a few students who try the IBDP and find it is not for them. What are their reasons? For some it is too demanding and, although they begin with enthusiasm, they find the workload daunting and get behind with deadlines. They are often marginally qualified and, after a year struggling to keep up with their more successful peers, they are persuaded to switch to A levels. Of course, they usually fare no better on an A-level programme, as the academic problems persist. Equally, some students do not like the prospect of continuing with a language or mathematics, and so find the narrower curriculum of A levels more appealing. On the other hand, a small number of students switch from A levels to the IBDP, but those who have done so tend to have more positive reasons: usually, they want the kind of intellectual challenge offered by the IBDP, and have not been enthused by the traditional sixth-form diet of A-level work. They also want the company of like-minded people, and, of course, they regret having to drop subjects on an A-level programme.

It is interesting that *Curriculum 2000* has not brought about the predicted broadening of the academic experience, since relatively few A-level students mix languages with sciences, or mathematics with an arts or humanities programme. It is always intriguing and puzzling why England is the only European country to offer its 16- to 18-year-old students such a narrow curriculum. The newly proposed diploma may contain a number of elements, but breadth does not seem to be at its heart, nor will it be assured.

So what does the IBDP have to offer to students in a tertiary college? In a sizeable college, it gives the student a sense of identity. The IBDP group is fairly close and homogeneous, not only because the students all study broadly the same programme, but also because they share similar aspirations: of going to university, of travelling or working abroad and, in some cases, of wanting to do something different. IBDP students mix freely with students across a range of courses, but they still have the support of the rest of the group. When times get hard, and they do in the second year of the programme, the students can draw on a high level of emotional support from their peers. They all know each other well, and their social lives are quite active. IBDP students are often exhausted yet exhilarated, not just from the academic rigours of the course, but from everything else they do.

They participate in a number of visits overseas to places like Seville, Berlin and, uniquely since 1993, on a skiing exchange to Zell am See in Austria. Their geography field trip takes them to the south of France, and their service activities have included creating a garden in a day for other students to enjoy, a kind of '*Ground Force* comes to Henley'. Moreover, the IBDP has attracted some unique individuals, who have achieved success not only on the course, but also in other arenas. Among the IBDP diplomates, the college has had the national ice-dance champion, and an Olympic swimmer who was also a Commonwealth silver medallist. In addition, Henley has had a member of the winning Cambridge rowing eight, a professional actor and its fare share of Oxbridge successes. IBDP students often make up the core of the college ski team, and one year formed virtually the whole of the volleyball team.

The international mix of students is an attractive aspect of the course. Henley has engaged in limited overseas marketing, mainly in the Middle East and Hong Kong, but has always been able to attract a growing number of students from Europe to the IBDP. Mainly from personal recommendation, students have come from a range of countries and, with their broader experience, they always enrich the course. How much better it is to read Flaubert with a native French speaker in the class! With Americans in the group – and the college has had three successive sisters – the study of the American dream in *The Great Gatsby* is made more comprehensible, and to have an Italian student in the class, who understands Italian politics, makes the reading of Dario Fo come more intellectually alive.

The last few years and the future

The last few years have been more comfortable financially, and have certainly been more fulfilling and even energising, given the increasing spotlight on the merits of the programme, both locally and nationally. Numbers on the course have grown steadily, reaching a peak of 60 enrolments in 1999. Larger overall numbers mean that most teaching groups are viable. With 50–60 students on the programme, the college can provide three good-sized English classes and three standard-level mathematics classes. Recently, mathematics methods has been offered for the able mathematician as an alternative to mathematics studies. French classes are quite large, while higher-level Spanish and German continue to be taught together with A-level modules. There has been a rise in demand for Spanish ab initio, and now there are two groups. Geography, economics and history are all popular, but the real star in terms of popularity is psychology, which now runs to two classes with 40 students. With a rise in numbers, the sciences have been reinstated at higher level, and, most recently, physics has been reborn. The college has still not been brave enough to offer higher-level mathematics, as demand for it has been low. A workable compromise is to offer the keen mathematician the opportunity to take A-level mathematics in addition to the IBDP. This may sound heavy, but students do not need to attend standard-level classes; they just need to take the examination. Art continues to be taught alongside A level, and proves to be a popular group 6 option.

Funding has been better since the IBDP became a load-banded course and its high hours attracted a more sufficient level of financial support. More recently, it acquired its own recognition as a course for funding purposes, but still the extra elements are not adequately recognised, namely TOK and support for the extended essay. The latter relies on goodwill from academic staff, in order for it to be properly supervised.

Looking ahead to the rest of the decade, the IBDP has a definite future in the post-16 sector. The Tomlinson proposals, appear to have borrowed many of the best aspects of the IBDP: the extended essay or project, and the Creativity, Action, Service activities or enrichment, but where the IBDP will still score over an English diploma is that the extended essay is a serious piece of academic research, and very good preparation for the higher-order skills needed in higher education. The enrichment activities are designed to develop the different sides of the young person, from the creative to the active, as well as to create the opportunity to serve others, so important in today's world. One of the most memorable service activities organised by the college was the renovation of the overgrown gardens of a number of elderly residents in Henley. This brought the whole student group together in planning the work, begging plants and shrubs from local nurseries and actually seeing a demanding project through, even if it did lead to a few rose bushes being pulled up inadvertently, having been mistaken for weeds. The residents were enormously grateful, and the college's community relations were considerably enhanced.

In a post-Tomlinson era, there is also the issue to grapple with of grade inflation at A level. If there is to be an A*, then it will almost certainly have been influenced by the IBDP's grade 7. Thankfully, most universities do not ask for a 7 in any subject, but it is still there to reward exceptional achievement, and consequently the students value it if they achieve it. On the question of key skills, most colleges struggle to deliver this kind of programme to students – or, more accurately, to get them to engage enthusiastically with the concept. The IBDP delivers these skills more effectively by its obligatory mathematics and English. In fact, in order to qualify for enrichment funding, it was decided at Henley to ask the IBDP students to take key skills in communications rather than information technology, which is what most A-level students generally take. This was delivered in English lessons, and although the examination is quite demanding at level 3, because of the time pressure to complete the tasks set, the students did well and virtually all of them passed.

To their credit, most universities now recognise the value of the whole IBDP, and make offers accordingly. It is invidious to unpick the IBDP, and just take from it whatever constituents the university wants. The IBDP student has worked hard across six subjects and more, and is well equipped for the demands of higher education. We have found in early July, when the results are available on the Internet – who said that the IBDP is not progressive? – that most of our students secure their first choice of institution, and are welcomed at universities who value the experience the IBDP diplomates bring with them.

At Henley, we have been privileged to offer the IBDP for many years now, and countless students have benefited from the opportunity to study for it. They have matured as thinking and critical human beings, and will contribute enormously to the global world they will inherit.

References

A comprehensive-school perspective

Coleman, J (1990) *Foundations of Social Theory*, Harvard University Press, Cambridge, Massachusetts.

DES (Department of Education and Science) (1988) *Advancing A-levels: Report of a Committee Appointed by the Secretary of State for Education and Science and the Secretary of State for Wales*, HMSO, London.

DfES (Department for Education and Skills) (2002a) *14–19: Extending Opportunities, Raising Standards*, DfES, London.

DfES (2002) www.dfes.gov.uk/speeches

DfES (2004b) www.dfes.gov.uk/speeches

Fullan, M (2003) *Change Forces with a Vengeance*, Routledge, London.

Fullan, M and Hargreaves, A (1998) *What's Worth Fighting For in Education?* Open University Press, Buckingham.
Ofsted (Office for Standards in Education) (2001) www.ofsted.gov.uk/reports/104/104696
Pring, R *et al.* (1989) *Enquiry into the Attitudes of Sixth-Formers towards Choice of Science and Technology in HE: A report to ACOST*, Oxford University Department of Educational Studies.
SST (Specialist Schools Trust) (2000) www.schoolsnetwork.org.uk

An independent-school perspective

DfES (Department for Education and Skills) (2004) *14–19 Curriculum and Qualifications Reform: Final Report of the Working Group on 14–19 Reform*, DfES, London
IBO (International Baccalaureate Organisation) (2003) *Perceptions of the International Baccalaureate Diploma Programme: A Report of an Inquiry Carried Out at UK Universities and Institutions of Higher Education*, IBO, Cardiff
IBO (2005) www.ibo.org

Chapter 4

Individuals and societies

David Lepine

Introduction

The great strength of the International Baccalaureate Diploma Programme (IBDP) lies in its coherence, and this is evident in the group 3 subjects.* In the IBDP, group 3 is concerned with individuals and societies. It has very broad aims, including the 'systematic and critical study' of 'human experience and behaviour' in a wide range of areas:

- physical
- economic
- social
- historical
- cultural (including the history and development of social and cultural institutions).

Such study is intended to develop awareness of the diversity of human attitudes and opinions, and an appreciation of this diversity. The methodological aims of group 3 subjects are to 'analyse critically and evaluate theories, concepts and arguments', as well as collect and analyse data so as to test hypotheses, and interpret data and source material. Group 3 also aims to ensure that students recognise that these methodologies are 'contestable' and require the tolerance of uncertainty. These general aims form the basis of the individual subject aims and detailed programmes of study.

There are a number of common elements in all group 3 subjects, which are worth identifying before discussing individual subjects. Some practical and technical matters apply to all IBDP subjects; others are specific to group 3. Unlike AS/A2, the IBDP is a two-year course, although in practice it is a four-and-a-half-term course, as examinations start at the beginning of May and time is needed for

---

*I am most grateful to my colleagues at Dartford Grammar School, Kent, for their help in writing this chapter. They have been very generous with their time, ideas and materials.

revision. For many group 3 subjects, a terminal examination is a considerable advantage. The essential analytical and literary skills of these disciplines need a two-year course to be developed and matured. The recommended time allocation for all subjects is 240 teaching hours at higher level and 150 hours at standard level. The assessment format is a combination of external assessment in examinations and internal assessment in coursework. The coursework element is worth up to 25 per cent of the total mark, and is marked internally and moderated externally. The International Baccalaureate Organisation (IBO) offers the full range of teacher support expected of any examination board: syllabuses, which are generally clear and detailed; examination papers; mark schemes; subject reports; and other subject-specific support material as appropriate. In addition, the IBO operates a teacher forum as part of its online curriculum, where teachers discuss practical issues. Subject by subject, there is an ongoing debate in which questions are raised, and advice is given, about courses, assessment and resources. There is also a list of resources, books, journals and websites, suggested and recommended by teachers. School-based syllabuses can be devised too, an example of which will be discussed below. In general, group 3 syllabuses are less content- and examination-driven than their A-level counterparts. They have coherent aims and flexible programmes of study, in which flexibility is not at the expense of coherence. They are supported and developed in the Theory of Knowledge (TOK) and extended essay components of the programme. The international ethos of the IBDP is strongly represented in the aims and syllabuses of group 3 subjects, particularly in its emphasis on world history and a global perspective in geography, information technology in a global society (ITGS) and business studies. The discussion of individual subjects that follows is not intended to be comprehensive, and some popular subjects, notably psychology, have not been included.

History

Aims

The history programme of study has succinct, coherent and closely thought-through aims. It seeks to promote the acquisition and understanding of historical knowledge from different cultures, thereby increasing international awareness and understanding. This awareness of the past is intended to lead to a better understanding of the present. It also promotes the subject as an intellectual discipline by developing historical skills, an appreciation of 'the nature and diversity of sources, methods, interpretations' and the ability to communicate this knowledge and understanding. Overall, the aim is to develop a lasting interest in the subject.

Syllabus content

The syllabus content closely reflects these aims. The standard-level course, twentieth-century world history topics, consists of seven topics:

- the causes, practices and effects of war
- nationalism and decolonisation
- single-party states
- peace and cooperation
- international organisations and multiparty states
- the cold war
- the state's relationship with religion and minorities.

In practice, it is recommended that only two or three topics are studied; the examination requires only two questions to be answered, each from a different topic. The most popular topics are the causes, practices and effects of war; single-party states; and the cold war. These topics also form a coherent course, the third being a continuation of the two other topics for the period after 1945. Within each topic, it is necessary to be selective in the content studied. There is clear guidance in the programme of study listing key themes and case studies, but there is not time to cover them all. Choices should be informed by a study of past examination papers; those issues that only appear rarely are readily identified.

To prevent a purely Eurocentric approach, the syllabus ensures that there is a world history component. This divides the world into five regions: Africa; the Americas; East and South-East Asia, and Oceania; Europe (which includes Russia); and South Asia and the Middle East (which includes North Africa). Each of the seven topics requires knowledge from more than one region. This is an essential component in the choice of content taught within a topic. From a non-European perspective, a single-party regime or civil war from the 'home region' and a European dictatorship or civil war could be combined. From a European perspective, Chinese history in the twentieth century is an attractive option, introducing an unfamiliar but stimulating culture and history. China's civil war, the communist regime under Mao and its role in the cold war complement the three most commonly taught topics. The cold war in Asia provides a non-European dimension for the topic on the causes, practices and effects of war, while the regimes of Castro, Nasser and Péron provide comparative material for the more familiar figures of Hitler, Mussolini and Stalin.

The most interesting and stimulating aspect of the twentieth-century world history topics is the thematic and comparative analysis that they encourage, an approach more often found in university courses than at 16–19 level. This approach should be an integral part of teaching and learning methods, and be explicitly built into them. None-the-less, the often open-ended nature of such analysis can disconcert some students. To overcome this, grids and tables can provide the structures to support the development of their analytical skills. By its nature, this approach is cumulative and becomes more important as the course progresses. The emphasis of the standard-level course on twentieth-century history can be seen as a weakness, as a narrow chronological range is studied. There is no opportunity to combine topics from contrasting chronological periods, although this is partly offset in the higher-level course, which begins in the mid eighteenth century.

However, this is a weakness of much history at 16–19 level; in practice, many A-level courses have a similar chronological span. From a British perspective, there is little British history, but some can be found in the European regional option. What is distinctive and attractive about the IBDP course is its international approach and commitment to world history.

The standard-level course includes a prescribed subject intended to develop candidates' use of source material, and is examined in the document paper. There are three options, all related to the seven world history topics, although they relate most closely to the topics on the causes, practices and effects of war; single-party states; and the cold war. The options are changed every five years. From 2003 to 2007 they are:

- the USSR under Stalin (1924–41)
- the emergence and development of the People's Republic of China (1946–64)
- the cold war (1960–79).

These should be taught in the context of the topic, rather than separately, since knowledge of the wider context is essential in developing the necessary historical skills. The skills required are the standard historical skills that are widely taught in secondary-school history – succinctly, the ability to 'comprehend, analyse, evaluate and use' source material critically. The IBO marking schemes give valuable guidance on the level of sophistication required in the evaluation of historical sources. In particular, candidates are expected to have a secure grasp of historiography when evaluating secondary sources. To ensure this, the specific teaching of different interpretations is advisable. These historical skills are also assessed in the historical investigation – the coursework element. In addition, they complement the TOK component, which considers the nature of historiography, problems of evidence and history as a scientific discipline.

The higher-level course consists of the standard-level course with the addition of one regional option from the five regions: Africa; the Americas; East and South-East Asia, and Oceania; Europe; and South Asia and the Middle East. This offers an extraordinarily wide range for study and, although many schools choose to study their own region or Europe, there are other possibilities. Imperial and post-colonial history could be studied in either the Africa or the East and South-East Asia regions, and the history of the USA in the Americas region. In contrast to the world history topics, the regional options take a more traditional chronological approach. All cover a 250-year period from the mid eighteenth century to the end of the twentieth century. Within this, there is a careful balance of subtopics. Each option is divided into 22 sections, and at least one question on each section is guaranteed in the examination. Most schools should find a section on their country in this period. The European option has sections on Spanish and Scandinavian history, as well as the more usual focus on Russia and Germany. The IBO recommends that a 100-year period is taught, and this is sufficient to cover a wide range of questions in the examination. Studying the nineteenth century in the regional option complements the twentieth-century emphasis of the standard-level course, and provides valuable context for twentieth-century developments as well as the practical benefits of a wider range of questions on the higher-level examination paper.

An alternative but more specialised related course, the history of the Islamic world, is offered at both higher and standard level. It has many similarities with the history syllabus, and comprises core topics on Islamic history from the time of Muhammad to the crusades and the Mongol empire, and optional topics on other historical periods and Islamic culture. It shares the same form of assessment and marking criteria as the history syllabus.

Assessment

Assessment is carried out in two forms: external, in the form of examinations, and internal, through coursework. At standard level, there are two examination papers: Paper 1 is a document paper examining historical skills, and Paper 2 tests the twentieth-century world history topics. Higher level has an additional paper, Paper 3, on the regional option. Paper 1 has four questions, each with a standard format, testing the comprehension, comparison, evaluation and synthesis of a range of primary and secondary sources, one of which will be non-written. Paper 2 has five essay questions on each topic, which are a mixture of the specific, on individuals or events, and the general, open-ended, thematic and comparative. Candidates have to answer questions on two different twentieth-century topics in this paper. Paper 3 is chronologically organised and has 25 questions, of which candidates have to answer any three. The questions focus on individual states, rather than on the thematic and comparative approach of Paper 2. Some questions on Papers 2 and 3 are broadly phrased, instructing candidates to compare, evaluate or analyse a topic, instead of the more usual narrowly focused questions, asking something specific. Candidates need to be taught the appropriate examination techniques to provide analytical and perceptive, rather than narrative and unfocused, answers.

The internal-assessment component forms 25 per cent of the marks at standard level and 20 per cent at higher level, a significant proportion of the total. It consists of an historical investigation, and is intended to be a problem-solving exercise. It is flexible and broadly defined, yet highly structured and relatively short at 2,000 words. Investigations can range from traditional research essays to fieldwork, oral history, local history and historical interpretations in the arts. The structure requires a plan, summary of evidence, evaluation of two sources, analysis, a conclusion and a bibliography, and marks are awarded for each component. In view of the structure and word length, investigations need precise and sharply focused questions to be successful. The weighting given to the examination papers and the coursework differs for higher and standard level, reflecting the extra paper that higher-level candidates sit. The degree of understanding required for higher and standard levels is the same, and common marking schemes are used.

Practicalities

The implementation of the IBDP history course presents few practical problems, although at the planning stage it is important to bear in mind that it is a course lasting four and a half terms. The twentieth-century world history topics can be taught in 22-week courses, allowing for two and a half hours' teaching per week. On this basis, two and a half topics can be covered comfortably. The higher-level regional option requires less time, and the 100-year period can be taught over four terms with one and a half hours' teaching per week. In addition, it is recommended that 20 hours are allocated to the historical investigation, although not all of this requires class time. Where there are time constraints, it is possible to combine the higher- and standard-level courses in one twentieth-century course. However, this can dilute the focus on the thematic and comparative approach necessary for the standard-level course. Resourcing the course does present some difficulties. There is no twentieth-century world history post-GCSE textbook for the standard-level course, but, as the IBDP becomes more popular, one will no doubt be written. The new generation of A-level textbooks cover the European aspects of the course very well, particularly up to 1945, but increasingly up to the 1990s, too. Many of them raise historiographical issues in helpful ways. There have also been a number of good new books on the cold war written for sixth-form students. Finding materials on non-European topics remains a problem. Twentieth-century Chinese history is probably the best covered, with recent additions to Pearson's Seminar Studies series and Hodder's Access to History series. Collections of source material for the prescribed subjects for the document paper are widely available for Russia, but less so for the cold war and especially China. Because the question format used in the examination is relatively new, few books have IBDP-style questions, but their standardised format makes them easy for teachers to generate. At higher level, there is plenty of material on nineteenth- and twentieth-century European and American history. With a carefully chosen range of books, both standard and higher level can be properly resourced, and the availability of resources will determine the choice of topic content studied. Support provided by the IBO is generally good. The subject guide is clear and detailed, as is the support material for the internal assessment. Marking schemes for essay questions, Papers 2 and 3, can be rather generalised, but those for the document paper, Paper 1, are detailed and give important guidance on the level of evaluation expected.

Student experience

The IBDP course, at both standard and higher level, provides the essentials of any post-16 history course for students. It fosters interest in history, develops powers of analysis and emphasises the importance of understanding the past and how it is different from the present, that it is indeed a foreign country where they do things differently. This includes an awareness of how the present has developed out of the past. It also develops a full range of historical skills, the transferable skills that make history such a useful and highly valued academic discipline: historical analysis, the evaluation of historical evidence, communication and research skills, and making judgements. However, one of the most attractive features of the course is the intellectual stimulus of its thematic and comparative approach, where there is scope for original thought. Students are encouraged to make links and connections, to identify similarities and differences in widely varying contexts. This, in turn, develops their ability to appreciate cultural differences and achieve greater clarity of analysis. It also enables them to develop a broader historical perspective and to identify historical trends. In the process, students can take an original approach, appreciate that there are not always definitive answers and gain a sense of exploration as they follow ideas through and test their observations and hypotheses, explaining contradictions and noting paradoxes. The balance of breadth and depth in the course makes this approach practical, and it is reinforced in the examination, where there are some broad open-ended questions, which invite wide-ranging comparisons.

Comparison with A level

A level, like the IBDP course, contains the essential features required of a post-16 history course. Both include the evaluation of historical evidence and a coursework component (or the option to include one). However, there are significant differences. The most obvious difference is in the content of the courses. All A-level courses must contain a substantial element of British history – most are 50-per-cent British history, and world history courses are rare. The IBDP course is a two-year course, rather than two one-year courses. As well as avoiding the continuous pressure of meeting examination requirements, it allows more time and space for students to develop their analytical and essay-writing skills. AS level requires shorter, more structured answers, and there is little time to develop the essay skills that are expected at A2. A-level courses in general take a more traditional approach, focusing either on individual states or European history, with fewer opportunities for thematic and comparative work, despite the synoptic element required in all syllabuses. Above all, A level lacks the intellectual coherence of the IBDP course. The IBDP's compulsory twentieth-century world history core at standard level has been carefully thought through and realised in the course structure. A level has no equivalent of this core course. Consequently, there can be great variety in what students study, since there is no common element. The A-level experience is too often fragmentary. The two component courses that make up the syllabus are unrelated and studied in isolation. Potentially interesting contrasts and comparisons are left unexplored. In these respects, the IBDP course has much to offer that A level cannot provide.

Geography

Aims

The geography programme of study aims to give students a global perspective and a sense of world interdependence, by developing understanding of the interrelationship between people, place and the environment. This includes a recognition of the need for social justice, an appreciation of diversity and a concern for the quality of the environment and its future management. It seeks to develop a range of geographical methodologies, and awareness of their relevance in analysing contemporary world issues.

Syllabus content

The geography syllabus consists of three parts, which are common to both higher and standard level:

- geographical skills
- core theme
- optional themes.

Part 1, geographical skills, is made up of eight skills, which are not taught separately but integrated into the core and optional themes. They range from mapping skills and quantitative techniques, such as the use and interpretation of statistical data, to geographical investigation, fieldwork and report-writing. Part 2, the core theme on population, resources and development, is compulsory. Its focus is on human interaction with the physical environment, and it examines the nature of human populations and their ability both to exploit and develop resources, and the need for sustainable development. The emphasis is on the interrelationship between population, resources and development, and the complexity of the geographical issues involved. Quantitative geographical skills, especially the synthesis of the large amount of data available for some topics, are needed to establish broad trends and identify anomalies. Part 3, the optional themes, is divided into three sections. At higher level, four themes are studied from particular sections; at standard level, any two themes can be studied. Section A has six physical geography themes, which are as follows:

- drainage basins
- coasts
- arid environments (all three of which include their management)
- lithospheric processes and hazards
- ecosystems and human activity
- climatic hazards and change.

Section B has four human geography themes, and these are:

- contemporary issues in geographical regions
- settlements
- productive activities
- globalisation.

The contemporary-issues theme uses the concept of a geographical region to explore current geographical issues and develop a 'sense of place'. The definition and choice of a region are left to the teacher, although broad guidelines are given. Two regions have to be studied, one of which should be familiar to the student, preferably the home region. Small manageable contrasting regions work best. The globalisation theme includes a major focus on tourism, which enables comparison between the home country and overseas. There is scope for an integrated physical and human approach, and a wide range of the geographical skills set out in Part 1, which underpin the course. Section C has one skills-based theme, topographic mapping. This forms a very effective synoptic topic, with opportunities to teach the geographical skills required in Part 1, and can be integrated into the fieldwork assignments.

From this brief outline of the course, several key features stand out. As would be expected in an IBDP course, there is a very strong commitment to internationalism, to the global perspective. This is at the heart of the compulsory core theme on population, resources and development, as well as some of the optional themes, such as globalisation. These are intended to lead to an understanding of less economically developed countries. Closely related to, and arising out of, this global outlook is the importance the course gives to understanding interrelationships, particularly between the developed and the less developed world, and the interdependence of the two; and, more broadly, the interaction between different parts of the world. Themes should not be studied discretely in isolation; candidates are rewarded for making links and having an awareness of the complexity of many geographical issues. A further great strength of the course is its flexibility, both in the choice of optional themes and in the use of case studies. This enables the course to reflect teacher strengths, the availability of resources and the location of the school. A school in a desert region would be able to study the optional theme on arid environments. Studies of river or coastal management allow a UK student to make a detailed study of current issues relating to flooding and land use. The balance between human and physical geography is also flexible; it can be almost entirely human, or more evenly weighted between the two. The standard-level course can be solely human, by selecting optional themes from Section B, but the higher-level course has to have a physical component, with two optional themes from Section A. However, the physical geography themes have a strong human geography dimension, with an emphasis on how people affect them and are affected by them. This reflects international teaching traditions, particularly US practice where syllabuses put less emphasis on physical geography.

Case studies are an integral part of the teaching methods needed for the core and optional themes, and there is considerable flexibility in their use. Although the content and learning outcomes of these themes are closely defined, and the required economic and population theories are specified in the syllabus, they are set out generically without precise case studies or examples. There is, however, strong and helpful guidance on the appropriateness of case studies, which should include examples from both more economically developed countries and less economically developed countries, as well as the home country. Teachers and students are expected to keep up to date with new geographical developments and events, and to use current examples. Appropriate examples or events, such as natural disasters, from the two-year cycle of the course should be incorporated. This is reflected both in the stimulus material in examination questions and in the marking scheme.

Assessment

Assessment is both external and internal. At both higher and standard level, there are two examination papers. Paper 1 tests the core theme and has two structured questions intended to elicit extended responses; candidates have to answer two out of three questions. Paper 2 tests the optional themes with a choice of essay questions or a structured stimulus response for each theme. At higher level, four questions have to be answered; at standard level, two questions. The difference between higher and standard level is reflected in extra questions required at higher level in Paper 2, and in the weighting between the papers. There is a common marking scheme for both levels, although grade boundaries differ slightly. The degree of understanding required for the higher- and standard-level courses is the same. The internal assessment, worth 25 per cent of the total mark at higher level and 20 per cent at standard level, consists of two investigations on different themes, resulting in written reports of 1,500–2,000 words at higher level and 1,000 words at standard level. At higher level, these have to be hypothesis-based and include fieldwork to produce primary data, but, at standard level, studies based on secondary research are acceptable. Group work is acceptable for data collection, but not for its analysis or in report-writing. The IBO subject guide provides clear and detailed guidance on the format of the written report. The subject matter is very flexible and can reflect a school's local conditions and opportunities. Travel and expense are not necessary – for example, local microclimate or land-use studies make highly suitable fieldwork topics.

Practicalities

Planning and implementing the course is relatively straightforward. The IBO syllabus is very clear and detailed. Terminology is specified and a glossary is easily produced. The structure of the course allows a considerable amount of integration in the teaching of topics, which can be maximised with a clear overview of the course at the outset of planning. For example, the core theme on population, resources and development can be combined with the optional theme on drainage basins in a module on water-resource management and food supply in the Nile valley. More generally, one country can be used to provide case studies across several themes. The two fieldwork assignments can also be integrated by devising investigations that include a broad range of skills on two contrasting topics, one for each of the assignments; two days for data collection is usually sufficient. Resourcing the syllabus presents few problems. Standard A-level textbooks cover it effectively, and some, such as *Advanced Geography* (Nagle 2000), are intended for the IBDP course as well as A level. There are important resource implications in the requirement to use current material. Old textbooks should be avoided, and regular use should be made of the news media and Internet, in order to provide appropriate material that ensures existing departmental resource bases are current.

Student experience

The clear geographical philosophy evident in the syllabus gives students a distinctive global outlook. It develops their awareness of global problems, environmental issues and the role of politics in geographical issues. It encourages an empathetic approach, giving them an understanding of different viewpoints and cultures in less economically developed countries. At a more basic level, students gain a good knowledge of global location, and the emphasis on using current case studies ensures that their knowledge is up to date. Their analytical geographical skills are strongly developed throughout the course, particularly independent research and presentation skills. The fieldwork assignments provide important opportunities to carry out individual research in depth, and reward initiative. Overall, the course gives a rounded appreciation of the subject as a whole, and forms an excellent basis for studying geography further at university.

Comparison with A level

There are many common elements in both IBDP and A-level geography. The principal difference between them is the considerably greater course content in A level. This emphasis on content creates pressure on teachers to get through the syllabus to meet examination requirements, with the consequent loss of opportunities to develop skills and explore issues in more depth. There are also some differences of emphasis in syllabus content. The IBDP course has more human than physical geography, a greater emphasis on population, less emphasis on the geography of productive activity and no direct opportunity to study glaciation and mountain environments. However, this is counterbalanced by a more coherent geographical philosophy that underpins the IBDP course, which tends to be implicit in A level. This is unashamedly political, particularly the aim to recognise the need for social justice and to 'combat bias, prejudice and stereotyping'. The geography course strongly reflects the international ethos of the IBDP, and the importance it gives to a global perspective and understanding of world interdependence. The IBDP is a more flexible course, with a greater choice of modules, which also allows a balanced human and physical course to be selected, and gives teachers the opportunity to teach to their strengths and areas of expertise. In general, the IBDP course is less well resourced and, therefore, more reliant on teachers' efforts to produce teaching materials, but most teachers are already doing this. The combination of its philosophy, flexibility and the opportunity to teach in greater depth makes the IBDP a very attractive course.

Business and management

Aims

The aims of the course are very broadly defined. It seeks to provide a holistic view of business; explore the subject from different cultural perspectives; and enable students to think critically, make decisions and appreciate the nature, pace and significance of change. Its objectives state more precisely the content and skills it promotes. These are the understanding of business concepts and principles; the role of social and cultural factors, and ethical considerations, in the actions of organisations; and the impact of organisations on the environment. The skills it aims to develop are problem-solving; data assessment and collection; research and presentation skills and methodologies; and the ability to distinguish between fact and opinion, and to apply theory to real-life situations.

Syllabus content

The higher-level course consists of six compulsory modules, and the standard-level course of four compulsory modules. Modules are broken down into topics and subtopics. However, although the four standard-level modules are also studied at higher level, their topics and subtopics differ. The four standard-level modules are:

- introduction to organisations
- marketing
- human resource management
- accounting and finance.

Module 1, introduction to organisations, is concerned with the structure and objectives of organisations, and the environments in which they operate. Their growth and evolution in an international setting, including the external environment, is of particular importance. Integration with other modules is encouraged, such as Module 4, accounting and finance. Module 2, marketing, focuses on marketing strategies to achieve organisational objectives, and in response to the changing environment, and requires an understanding of the impact of new technologies. It also covers sampling techniques and the validity of data collected. Module 3, human resource management, studies the way people influence, and are influenced by, organisations so as to achieve organisational objectives. Module 4, accounting and finance, examines how organisations manage their financial resources, and how accounting and financial information is used in decision-making and financial control. It is divided into two parts: management accounting, which covers internal analysis and reporting, and financial accounting, which covers external influences on decision-making. Financial calculations and analysis feature highly in the examination papers.

At higher level, Module 1, introduction to organisations, is broadly similar to the standard-level Module 1, with additional topics on decision-making and change; internal growth; mergers, demergers and takeovers; and economies and diseconomies of scale. Module 2, the external environment, is an expanded version of one of the topics within Module 1 at standard level. It uses a political, economic, social and technological analysis to study the environments in which organisations operate. The IBO recommends an integrated case-study approach be used to teach this module. Module 3, marketing, is based on the marketing module at standard level, with the addition of sales forecasting; sales budgets and variances; marketing objectives; and market share. More depth is required in the study of market research and marketing plans. Module 4, human resource management, is an extended version of the equivalent standard-level module, with an additional topic on corporate culture, and more depth in the topics on human resource planning and organisational structure and communication. Module 5, operations management, which is not studied at standard level, consists of topics on operational decision-making, quality assurance and customer care, and covers both manufacturing and service industries. It is important that this module is integrated with the study of labour markets, financial control and marketing. Module 6, accounting and finance, has the same focus and two-part structure as the standard-level module, but requires a greater depth of knowledge and more advanced accounting skills.

The approach of the course is international, and this is fully reflected in the examination. It should therefore be taught throughout using global case studies. The relevant theories, theorists, models, concepts and techniques specified in the learning outcomes for each topic or subtopic tend to be more wide-ranging than those found in A-level syllabuses. As in the geography syllabus, students are expected to be aware of current issues and case studies, and need to keep up to date with examples from the two-year cycle of the course. There is considerable flexibility in the order in which the course can be taught, although Module 1, introduction to organisations, is the obvious starting point. Thereafter, modules can be taught in parallel or be integrated for teaching purposes.

Assessment

Unlike many group 3 subjects, there is a substantial difference between the degree of understanding required at higher and standard level in business and management. At standard level, the emphasis is on describing features; learning outcomes refer to describing rather than explaining. Students are expected to understand the content and applications of modules, and to carry out some limited analysis. At higher level, they are required to analyse and evaluate. This is an important differentiation between higher and standard level. The much greater demands of higher level are set out in the content and learning outcomes of the modules and the internal assessment. Both levels have external and internal assessment, and both have a common pre-seen case study (of about 2,000 words) as the basis of Paper 1. All case studies are global, not UK-based. At standard level, Paper 1 consists of four compulsory questions on the case study. Paper 2 contains five data-response questions on the four modules, three of which have to be answered. The internal assessment at standard level, which forms 20 per cent of the total mark, is based on a written assignment of 1,000–1,500 words, which applies 'tools, techniques and theory' to a real business situation, and offers recommendations for future actions. Although primary data is not explicitly required, the exemplar material provided by the IBO does contain primary data. The subject of the assignment must be taken from one of the topics or subtopics of the four modules.

At higher level, Section A of Paper 1 consists of four compulsory questions on the same case study used at standard level. Candidates then choose one of two further questions in Section B. Additional information is presented in Section B, which involves quantitative data analysis and specific decision-making techniques, such as decision trees, investment appraisal, cash-flow forecasts and critical path analysis. Paper 2 has six data-response questions on the six modules, four of which have to be answered. The internal assessment at this level is significantly more demanding than at standard level, and forms 25 per cent of the total mark. It is based on a research project and written report of 2,000–2,300 words, which either addresses an issue facing an organisation or analyses a decision to be made by an organisation, and must contain primary data, as well as be forward-looking and present recommendations for future action. Students can choose the subject of their project, but it must relate to a real organisation and be of practical value. It is intended to be a working document. The format of examination questions at both levels puts particular emphasis on careful reading and timing by students to ensure that all aspects of the task are completed. Efficient time allocation is essential; few students answer all five questions on the higher-level Paper 1. Familiarity with marking schemes is important in judging the depth, detail and level of development expected in answers. Examination questions and marking schemes are best introduced early in the course. All calculations are expressed in dollars.

Practicalities

The syllabus guide is very detailed and helpful, giving full details of modules, and the topics and subtopics into which they are broken down. The content and learning outcomes of each topic and subtopic are specified, and their depth and breadth are defined, as well as the recommended teaching time for each module. In addition, there is a thorough five-page glossary with clear definitions of key terms and concepts, in order to ensure consistency and prevent misunderstanding. The syllabus guide contains detailed marking schemes for the internal assessments, but does not have general marking criteria for modules. Examination marking schemes and examiners' reports are even more essential than usual to teach the course successfully.

Resourcing the IBDP syllabus does present problems, since there is no recommended textbook. Although the content is readily covered by the standard A-level textbooks, they take a largely UK perspective, and present UK case studies and examples that are not appropriate for the IBDP course. An exception is *Business Studies: AS and A Level* (Stimpson 2002), which contains global case studies. Further global material can be found in the media and on the Internet. The latter is a vital resource for the course; good material can be found there, but it is a time-consuming process.

Student experience

As with other group 3 subjects, the distinctive feature of the IBDP business and management course is the extra dimension its international approach gives. Students gain a stimulating, wider perspective of the subject: they encounter different theories on leadership and motivation, and develop an appreciation of key issues for the future, such as globalisation and global branding, and, above all, the impact of different cultures on business. The approach enables them to apply their knowledge and to test business theories in the real world, particularly through the use of case studies and in the internal assessment. This is made more relevant through the focus on current issues. The emphasis on the ethical dimension of business and on issues of social responsibility also promotes a questioning and balanced approach to controversial topics, such as multinational companies, trade unions and advertising. In addition, the course develops an important range of skills: independent study; literary, analytical and research skills; the ability to work in groups and present information in a variety of ways; and the more specialised information and communication technology (ICT) skills used in business.

Comparison with A level

The IBDP and A-level courses share a considerable amount of content, but, in the IBDP course, topics are generally covered in more depth. A much wider and more diverse set of teaching materials and textbooks are used, particularly ones written by US authors who are not well known in the UK. It is also possible to follow a topic through more fully and logically. In the marketing module at higher level, some of the content is more usually found in first-year degree courses, but does not require that level of understanding. The major difference between the two courses lies, once again, in the international approach of the IBDP, which is reflected in the global case studies and such key issues as globalisation and global branding. The A-level course is mainly focused on UK businesses. IBDP standard level is roughly equivalent to AS level, and higher level to A2. Some aspects of the standard-level course are studied in the A2 course, especially in the marketing module and the accounting and finance module. The IBDP, with its global dimension, gives a broader, more rounded and more relevant understanding of the subject than A level.

Information Technology in a Global Society (ITGS)

Aims

ITGS is the systematic study through critical investigation and analysis of the impact of information technology (IT) on society. It aims to develop understanding of the advantages and disadvantages of IT, both at the local and global level; its social significance at the individual, community and organisational level; and its ethical implications, while recognising that there are diverse opinions about its impact on individuals and societies.

Syllabus content

At present, this subject is only offered at standard level, although a higher-level syllabus is currently being prepared. The standard syllabus is divided into three sections:

- social and ethical issues
- IT systems in a social context
- areas of impact.

Section 1, social and ethical issues, is broken down into 11 units, ranging from security, privacy and intellectual property to equality of access, control and cultural diversity, which explore the social and ethical issues raised by IT. Section 2, IT systems in a social context, is concerned with technological understanding, and is divided into four subsections: hardware and networks; applications; communication systems; and integrated systems. Section 3, areas of impact, focuses on the effect of IT on society. It has two parts: Part A covers business and employment, and Part B five other areas, namely education; health; art, entertainment and leisure; science and the environment; and government and politics. Part A is compulsory, and the IBO recommends that two or three areas from Part B are studied. An integrated approach is essential when teaching the course, and is reflected in the examination questions. The three sections are not intended to be studied in isolation, and they can be taught in any order. The syllabus guide gives clear guidance on alternative integrated approaches. Awareness of the interrelationships between the three sections is a very important aim of the course. However, many students coming to the course will be unfamiliar with the social and ethical issues raised in Section 1. To be able to apply and discuss them effectively when studying Sections 2 and 3, IT systems in a social context and areas of impact (which can be used to teach Section 1), the students need a grounding in the issues, so as to provide definitions and analytical frameworks. There are considerable advantages in teaching these first before using a fully integrated approach. This can be done in about 15 hours' teaching, and then returned to throughout the course. The TOK course helps develop the required analytical concepts and skills. In such a rapidly changing field, it is important to be aware of new developments and their implications. Students and teachers need to update their material continually.

Assessment

At standard level, external assessment makes up 60 per cent of the total mark, and internal assessment 40 per cent. The external assessment consists of two examination papers. Paper 1 has four compulsory short-answer questions, testing in an integrated way Sections 1 and 2 of the syllabus, social and ethical issues and IT systems in a social context. Paper 2 has six structured questions, assessing all three sections of the course, also in an integrated way. Question 1 is a compulsory question on business and employment, and there are five other questions, one on each of the five other areas of impact, two of which have to be answered. The internal assessment has two parts, a portfolio and a project, each worth 20 per cent of the total mark. Students must compile a portfolio of three pieces of written work on social and ethical issues concerning three different areas of impact, each 800–1,000 words in length. These are based on recent media reports within the last six months, not textbooks. The project is an IT solution to a problem set in a social context. It has three components: a product developed through the integration of IT skills; a written report of 2,000–2,500 words; and a logbook. Examples of successful projects include a website on how to improve IT privacy; desktop publications; and a website for a school exchange.

Practicalities

Providing resources for the course causes some problems; there is no recommended textbook, and much of the relevant material has a US bias. Widely used and easily available A-level textbooks can be adapted, such as *Computer Confluence* (Beekman 2003) and *Computers in Your Future* (Pfaffenberger 2003). The media and Internet are vital sources of material, and their use can be integrated into the teaching of many aspects of the course. The IBO website is an especially useful guide to, and source of, teaching material.

Student experience

As well as acquiring a broad understanding of the impact of IT on society, students learn valuable analytical skills and practical IT skills from the course.

Their understanding has the characteristic international perspective of the IBDP, in particular an awareness of the 'digital divide' between more and less economically developed countries, and the impact of their different problems, experiences and perspectives on the social and ethical issues raised in Section 1 of the syllabus. Analytical and reasoning skills are strongly developed in this part of the course. Students gain an awareness of different, often conflicting, viewpoints and the difficulty of resolving them, and an appreciation of a balanced approach that accepts/includes uncertainty. This understanding is developed through discussion and debate. Throughout the course, research and independent study skills are acquired, and there are interdisciplinary links with geography, business and management, and sociology, as well as some understanding of philosophical thinking.

Comparison with A level

The IBDP course has a much wider scope than A-level courses, which tend to be practically based. The IBDP course is not primarily intended to develop practical IT skills, but to examine the wider impact of the subject. The emphasis is academic, rather than practical. It does not require advanced computer literacy, although there is scope for students with these skills to use and develop them in the internally assessed project and class-based tasks. Its appeal is therefore wider, attracting not only computer enthusiasts with advanced skills, but also those with average skills who are interested in the subject, for whom a practical course is not appropriate. The strength of the IBDP course, apart from its global perspective, is this balanced approach, combining a broadly theoretical outlook with scope for practical development, both of which give it a wide appeal and relevance.

A school-based syllabus: Classical Greek and Roman studies

Introduction

School-based syllabuses are a good example of the flexibility within the IBDP curriculum. They allow a school, or group of schools, to devise their own syllabus for subjects not offered by the IBO. They are thus a very attractive feature of the curriculum, offering considerable potential, but require a great deal of work and a high degree of responsibility, particularly in assessment. School-based syllabuses can only be studied at standard level, and have to be approved by the IBO. When drawing up a school-based syllabus, it is best to share the work with other schools, or to use or adapt an existing syllabus with the school's permission. The advantages of school-based syllabuses make the effort worthwhile. They are highly flexible and can be tailor-made to a school's circumstances, the strengths of departments and teachers, the availability of resources and the interests and needs of students. Once set up, they work very well.

Successful group 3 school-based syllabuses have been drawn up for classical civilisation and international politics, among other subjects. The classical Greek and Roman studies syllabus discussed here was drawn up by the Kirstin School, Auckland, New Zealand.

Aims

The primary aim of this course is to give students a knowledge and understanding of aspects of Greek and Roman civilisation, and to help them understand their own cultural background. It also aims to develop historical skills, logical thinking and the ability to communicate fluently and coherently, both in writing and speech.

Syllabus content

Ten topics are studied from a total of 12 – six Greek and six Roman. They are a mixture of literature, history, philosophy and art history. The six Greek topics comprise:

- the *Odyssey* as an introduction to Greek myth
- Athenian democracy from Solon to Pericles
- Greek theatre, both tragic and comic, through the plays of Sophocles and Aristophanes
- the career of Alexander the Great
- the philosophy of Socrates and Plato
- Greek vase painting or sculpture.

The Roman topics are:

- Virgil's *Aeneid*
- art and architecture as seen in the ruins of Pompeii and Herculaneum
- social life in the Rome of Caesar and Cicero
- Roman religious practice
- the age of Augustus – his reforms, conquests and systems of government
- Juvenal's *Satires*.

Each topic is broken down into component units, and key books and relevant editions, as well as chapters and lines for literary texts, need to be specified. In art history topics, the examples to be studied are clearly identified. The syllabus content has strong links with other IBDP subjects, such as art, theatre studies, philosophy and TOK.

Assessment

Assessment is a key issue in school-based syllabuses. The forms of assessment and marking scheme are drawn up by the schools involved, and submitted to the

IBO for approval. In this syllabus, there are three assessment components: class work, seminars and an examination. Class work forms 30 per cent of the total mark, and consists of ten end-of-unit tests, made up of essays written under examination conditions. The marking scheme used is an adaptation of the IBO's history marking scheme. Seminars form 20 per cent of the total mark. Students are required to present two seminars, one each year. These take the shape of a 2,000-word research paper, which is presented in written and oral form, with the oral presentation being recorded on audio cassette. The marking criteria for seminars have four strands:

- knowledge and understanding of the topic
- interpretation and analysis of the topic
- presentation
- use of language.

An examination makes up the remaining 50 per cent of the total mark. It consists of two papers: Paper 1, which has three document questions, two of which have to be answered, and Paper 2, which has seven essay questions, three of which have to be answered. The examinations are set and marked by the schools involved, and are moderated externally.

Practicalities

There are few problems to be encountered when resourcing this course, and a full list is provided in the syllabus. Generally, books on Greek topics are more widely available than those on Roman ones. As well as being scarcer, books on the Roman topics tend to be more specialised, and are often not directed towards sixth-form study. They also tend to be more expensive, such as those on Roman religion and Pompeian wall paintings. The flexibility of the course enables the full potential of local resources, museums and ancient monuments to be used in teaching it. Some of the course can be taught through fieldwork visits, such as Roman art and architecture at Pompeii. Other parts of the course, such as Greek theatre, can be taught by non-specialists.

Student experience

As well as the intrinsic interest of the subject, the most valuable experience this course offers students is its truly multidisciplinary approach. It uses skills from history, literature, art, religion and drama. These enable students to make connections between different intellectual disciplines. The nature of the syllabus and its method of assessment lend themselves to seminar-based teaching and learning. Thus, students develop the advanced research and presentation skills that they will need for university study.

Comparison with A level

Traditional A-level classical civilisation courses have tended to concentrate on Greek topics. This IBDP syllabus offers more breadth by including more Roman topics. Because it is a school-based syllabus, and is tailor-made to meet the requirements and use the strengths of a school, it has more to offer than A-level courses. However, there is not the support and guidance provided by an examination board. School-based syllabuses are very time-consuming to establish, and there is an ongoing commitment to setting examinations, a considerable undertaking.

Conclusion: What do students gain from group 3 subjects?

Each subject has its own intrinsic value, stimulating interest and offering a body of knowledge that is, above all, grounded in an understanding of individuals and societies. All syllabuses have a coherent philosophy and the characteristic IBDP international outlook. Together they develop a range of valuable, indeed essential, skills in any post-16 programme of study. The most important of these is the power of analytical and critical thinking, and the associated research skills and capacity to work independently, which require students to collect, evaluate and use a wide range of sometimes contradictory material. In addition, they learn to present a logical coherent argument fluently, both in writing and speech. They confront different perspectives, which often challenge their own preconceptions, and are encouraged to respect and appreciate diversity. In doing so, they become more aware of the provisional nature of conclusions, and learn to tolerate complexity and uncertainty.

References

Beekman, G (2003) (5 edn) *Computer Confluence*, Pearson Education International, Upper Saddle River, New Jersey.

Nagle, G (2000) *Advanced Geography*, Oxford University Press.

Pfaffenberger, B (2003) (5 edn) *Computers in Your Future*, Prentice Hall, Upper Saddle River, New Jersey.

Stimpson, P (2002) *Business Studies: AS and A Level*, Cambridge University Press.

Chapter 5

Language, literature and the arts

Michael Coffey

Introduction

This chapter will consider the main implications of teaching language, literature and the arts in the International Baccalaureate Diploma Programme (IBDP) from a further-education perspective in the UK, where A levels are usually offered to academically able 16- to 18-year-olds.* Because of its evaluative and analytical nature, the chapter should also be helpful to managers and teachers in schools and colleges who are considering adopting the IBDP. Three of the six groups of the IBDP hexagon (see Preface, Figure 1) will be considered, and the implications of different teaching permutations of these three subject domains will also be discussed.

As the subject areas in this chapter are wide-ranging, each will be dealt with separately, and under the following headings: syllabus content; aims, objectives and outcomes; teaching and learning styles; assessment; and administration and resource implications. By the end of the chapter, readers should have some idea of the nature of these parts of the diploma, and of the constraints and achievements that students, lecturers and managers experience in implementing the IBDP at a further-education college.

A major difference in philosophy between the IBDP and A levels is that the former is designed as a course: it is in a full sense of the word a curriculum, whereas A levels are designed to be primarily an assessment tool. Details fleshing out these approaches will be provided further on in the chapter. In terms of grading strategies, both differ substantially too. The IBDP is criterion-referenced. Because it is taught around the world, teacher-awarded coursework marks and examination scripts have to be graded according to written criteria. The moderation and final-marks award meetings also follow the assessment criteria. Notable features of the IBDP are the consistency of its standards and the stability of its syllabuses over time. While A-level marking does include the awarding of marks according to assessment objectives in the initial stages of assessment, final grades are not

---

*I would like to thank Claudine White, Chris Thomas, Anthony Arratoon and Mary Fair, without whose help this chapter would not have been possible.

criterion-referenced. Despite the fact that the examination boards would no doubt claim that they seek to maintain the same standard year on year, the national debate during the past few years over A-level grade inflation would tend to question this claim. As a case in point, my experience as both a student and teacher of A levels would suggest that A levels are now easier to achieve than they were 20, or even 10, years ago.

Glossary of IBDP terms

Before we examine the differences between A levels and the IBDP, a brief consideration of some of the essential terminology that characterises the two programmes (Table 5.1) will help to clarify many of the issues that are addressed in the chapter as a whole.

Overview of IBDP language courses

IBDP languages are taught at four levels of language competence, each with different focuses on the target language and with different pedagogic approaches. These four courses are: A1, A2, B and ab initio. At the basic levels, ab initio and B, the target language is studied, while at the highest levels, A2 and A1, what is studied are examples of the language's culture and the best expressions of that culture's thoughts. The distinctions between the courses are quite clear, and, not unexpectedly, they exert a considerable impact on the type of student that will be attracted to each course.

A1 is a group 1 subject in the IBDP hexagon, and the three others belong to group 2. Any one of these four courses can be offered in a further language as a group 6 option. Thus, students must study two, and may study three, languages in the IBDP. A1, A2 and B are offered at two levels: higher and standard level. As ab initio is a beginner's level, it is just offered at standard level. The difference between these levels is not just one of time allocation – 240 hours compared to 150 hours over the duration of the course – but also of the level of student ability: thus, the assessment criteria are different. Let us compare, for example, in A1 Paper 2

Table 5.1 Comparison of A-level and IBDP terminology

General term	A-level term	IBDP term
syllabus booklet	specification	subject guide
section of syllabus	unit	part
attainment targets	assessment objectives	general criteria
work file	coursework folder	dossier/portfolio (of work)
(arts) work file	work journal	research workbook
(literary) book	text	work
—	qualification	course

Table 5.2 'Criterion C: Message' at higher and standard level

Achievement level	Higher level	Standard level
9–10	The message has been communicated very well.	The message has been communicated well.
	The ideas are relevant and stimulating.	The ideas are relevant.
	The development of ideas is thorough and imaginative; supporting details are appropriate and convincing.	The development of ideas is methodical and thorough; supporting details are appropriate.
	The organisation of ideas is clear and flows well.	The organisation of ideas is clear.

the external assessment entitled 'Criterion C: Message' for both higher and standard level (Table 5.2).

As with the assessment criteria for A-level English literature, those for A1 higher-level English attempt to measure not just the literary features of a student's work, but the language-related and intellectual abilities, in this case the ability to persuade, entertain and inspire.

My experience suggests that A1 higher-level English is roughly comparable to a combined old A- and S-level English literature course, in terms of course continuity and the requirement to combine ideas from a broad field of possible responses. A1 standard-level English might be comparable to a slightly harder International General Certificate of Education (IGCE) English literature course; B higher-level French to A-level foreign-language French; and ab initio Spanish to GCSE foreign-language Spanish. The range of linguistic and extra-linguistic competencies in the IBDP is therefore very much wider and subtler than those tested at A level. However, it is crucial to mark out the differences between these courses, and these will be examined in the following sections of this chapter.

Much work has been done within the International Baccalaureate Organisation (IBO) in the last few years to define the appropriate levels of students for each course. As a result of the many comments made by IBDP heads, coordinators and teachers, and the findings of subject reviews, the opening pages of each language guide now set out in considerable detail the types of students who are suitable for each course. I have taken these into account in Table 5.3, which compares the four IBDP language courses. Although my own experience of teaching these courses would suggest that the student profiles for the higher-level courses might look something like those in Table 5.3, it should be emphasised that other permutations exist.

Languages A1 and A2 could be described as 'language use' courses, while languages B and ab initio could be termed 'language acquisition' courses. These guidelines, however, assume that each course is appropriate for a certain group of students, with each group being typified by its language competence. However, because the IBO gives schools and colleges freedom in course selection – and

Table 5.3 Comparison of IBDP language courses

	A1	A2	B	ab initio
Type of work	15 interesting works	6 works and 2 topics	A few works and 3 broad topics	Snippets of literature and around 7 topic areas
Language ability of student	Bilingual or expert reader	Fluent language user	Second-language student	Complete beginner, or negligible knowledge
Typical student profile	Loves reading, has good organisational ability and has proven ability to work hard	Capable, motivated student, who enjoys literature and can sustain worthwhile research	Still mastering one or more aspects of the language, or the routine of working; does not want to analyse too many books	Learning a new language; at beginner's level, but not for long!
Aims of course	To assess literary response; written expression must be up to explaining subtle ideas; emphasis on essay-writing	To assess reading skills and imaginative work in equal measure	To assess language skills, mainly written and spoken	To test 7,000 items of vocabulary and correct use of basic tenses; student must be understood in, and understand, target culture

because of the differing levels of motivation amongst individual learners – there is, in practice, some flexibility in the kind of course that is suitable for any given student. For example, an expert user of English may want to study English culture and media as well as read its literature, or write creatively as well as study a range of literature critically. If students are able to study literature in another language, then they can opt to study English at A2 rather than A1 level, providing the timetable allows for this. Clearly, it will be much harder to get top marks in A1 than in ab initio, so the IBO urges centres to help students make the right selections bearing in mind what the students are going to learn throughout the two years of the course.

Group 1 subjects

Syllabus content

A1 is a wholly literary course, which may be offered in one of more than 80 languages. Further-education colleges, accustomed to accepting students on to courses with little prior background information about them, need to plan IBDP induction really thoroughly. European students (and those from other continents) will need greater induction support for their UK studies. For some of our students English is their strongest language, but for others English can be their fifth language (in order of languages learnt). Our IBDP students often need support in the following ways:

- acquiring the metalanguage and techniques of studying literature
- subject-specific help with their English.

Extra English support is therefore vital for their effective progress in the IBDP. Some 70 per cent of our students come from outside the UK, and so English culture must be taught alongside the study of literary texts, if these students are to gain the full benefit of studying A1 English. Understanding the references, the humour and the symbols of the literature they read will help them ask transactional questions of the books – for example, 'What does this book mean to *me*?' – since IBDP literature questions customarily have the reader at the centre of their rubric.

Funding is available for additional learning support in literacy and numeracy, and a 'Searchlight' test taken at the start of the course flags up those students who are not working at level 3 in these areas. A further Searchlight test at the end of their first year measures their progress in these key skills.

The main features of the A1 English course content that differentiate it from A-level English literature could be summed up as follows.

- At least 35–45 per cent of all the works studied should be written in a language other than English, and be studied in translation. The international element is a significant feature of this course. As is now the case with AS/A2, texts written in English from other nations are allowed, but not texts in translation.
- Around 50 per cent of the teaching and assessment focuses on comparative literary analysis, for example, comparing themes or techniques across set works; the other 50 per cent comprises critical analysis of individual works.
- Some 30 per cent of the entire course is orally assessed, and 50 per cent of the final mark is based on the coursework students have completed over the two years. This includes the oral work.
- Prose is divided into 'the novel and the short story' and 'other', that is, essays, travel narrative, autobiography and satire. Students study both fiction and non-fiction.
- As well as essay-writing, a creative response to literature is also encouraged, so students can analyse and explore works in non-essay forms. A rationale is required whereby students explain the purpose of their writing.
- A1 is a linear course, not modular, so formal testing occurs at the end of the two years. However, much of the coursework is handed in well before the examinations at the end of the course.

As the A1 course is divided into four parts, lecturers at college teach two parts per year, although the pace of progress on the course is determined by the individual tutor. The lecturer also decides on the overall theme and works to be studied in each part of the programme. (A-level syllabuses, on the other hand, prescribe the topic. For instance, AQA's 'The literature of WWI' is the Unit 6 theme for 2001–2 and 2002–3.) In addition, students are encouraged to nominate themes and individual works for study. Three elements of A1 English cohere well with Key Stage 4 practice in the English National Curriculum, and these are:

- a creative response to literature
- the testing of oracy
- a world literature element.

Aims, objectives and outcomes

The aims of both the IBDP and A-level courses are generally similar. However, some important differences exist. For example, the heritage (or historical) element to A-level English literature is a mandatory attribute not found on the A1 English course. The synoptic element, which tests students' ability to work across the genres, is a further strength to the A-level course that is not found formalised in the A1 programme. The IBDP world literature list, however, is extensive; navigating through the literatures of different languages and cultures is one of the pleasures of A1 English teaching. Choice of works is reached through a balance of authors, genres and links (decided by the teacher) and prescribed works (set by the IBO). Further differences centre on:

- the use of language
- the separation of an understanding of the work from an understanding of the examination question
- the nature of the criticism being encouraged
- the international perspective.

The A1 course is written in a more direct and accessible way than the A-level course. As an example, let us take one aim from both programmes:

IBDP: 'to encourage a personal appreciation of literature and develop an understanding of the techniques involved in literary criticism.'

A level: 'to encourage candidates to appreciate the significance of cultural and historical influences upon readers and writers.'

The former starts with the learner's appreciation; the latter does also, but then limits the possible influences on a writer's work, and refers back again, unnecessarily, to the reader.

The assessment criteria in A1 differentiate between an understanding of the question and an understanding of the work. The assessment criteria for essays, for example, are divided up into five areas:

- knowledge and understanding of works
- response to the question
- appreciation of literary features
- presentation
- formal use of language.

Each level, then, has its own level indicators. The assessment criteria have short headings, which make the task of referring to the criteria when assessing work that much easier. This memory aid is good note-taking practice in any effective learner's skills repertoire. A level's A2 has four assessment objectives; if we look at assessment objective 2, we find nestled among seven quite contrasting criteria:

- sound knowledge and understanding of text
- crucial aspects of a question clearly identified.

This mixture in assessment objective 2 means that teaching and learning need to be more closely geared to the requirements of the objective if students are to receive high marks. In A1 Paper 2, by contrast, it is easier to give credit to students who show an understanding of the work, but answer the question badly. This is because A1 standard- and higher-level questions tend to be considerably more open than A-level questions. Assessment B 'Response to the question' is more allied to constructing an argument than at A level, where answering the more closely guided question is more indicative of understanding the work. An example will serve to illustrate this.

> *Higher level*: 'Playwrights employ specific techniques to lead an audience to respond either positively or negatively to particular characters. How far and by what means have playwrights in your study made clear their vision of individual characters?'

> *Standard level*: '"A chronological sequence is only one way (though a powerful one) of telling a story." Discuss novels which you have studied in the light of this statement commenting on how the "story" is told and what effects are produced by the way the narrative is conducted.'

> *A-level*: Doctor Faustus: 'What is the importance of the speeches of the chorus in the play as a whole?'

In the higher-level question, students are invited to define:

Table 5.4 Number and weighting of works/texts in A1 English and A-level English literature

	A1 higher level	AS/A2 level
Number of works/texts studied on course	15	10
Number of works/texts assessed in final written examination	4	5 or 8, depending on coursework options
Weighting of examination works/ texts on final grade	50%	70%

- the techniques authors use, and how many characters they use, to illustrate their points
- how they respond as readers
- their understanding of 'authorial vision'.

At A level, the crucial aspects of the question are fewer, and the question is in a sense more straightforward to answer.

The range of examination questions in the A-level course, however, is more varied than in the A1 course. This is because more of the set works/texts are assessed by a final written examination. Table 5.4 compares the number of works/ texts needed to complete the courses and sit the final examinations, as well as their overall weighting, and so illustrates this point.

More essay questions in the final A-level examination, together with more testing of students' understanding, mean that the range of questions is also wider:

Unit 3: C20th drama

The Glass Menagerie: 'In a letter to a friend, Williams once wrote: "I have one theme – society's destruction of the sensitive, non-conformist individual." To what extent does this claim apply to *The Glass Menagerie*?'

Unit 4: Section A (Drama pre-1770)

Othello: '"If you omitted the scenes on Venice in Act 1 and began the play in Cyprus in Act 2, you would have a much better play."

"Without Act 1, the audience would never understand the evil of Iago or the shaky foundations of the relationship between Othello and Desdemona."
Which case would you argue for both these opinions?'

The questions are formulated excellently. However, they require only written articulation on the part of the student, not oral articulation, and only two of the five or eight works assessed are compared.

Lastly, an important element of the A1 course is to promote international under-standing through the teaching of literature in English. In the preface to the *Language A1 Guide*, we find that A1 'is envisaged as having the potential to enrich the international awareness of IB students and to develop in them the attitudes of tolerance, empathy and a genuine respect for perspectives different from their own' (IBO 1999: 4). A-level English literature's aims are to introduce candidates to 'the traditions of English literature', in the same way as Key Stages 3 and 4 introduce students to the major developments or 'highlights' of English literature. The IBDP's literature course is simply titled 'A1 in English'. However, one does not need to be well travelled or from a multicultural background to enjoy a variety of literature in English. To quote Ian Hill, deputy director of the IBO, 'it is not needed to have international staff to teach the IBDP but staff who are internation-ally minded.' This aspect of the A1 course is arguably more in the spirit of the National Curriculum, and goes a long way towards reflecting the exhilaration of the variety of cultures that can currently be felt in the media, in the bookshops and on the street in many parts of the country.

Teaching and learning styles

The IBDP offers a linear five-term course of studies. The college's level of teaching on the course is high, and there is no room for streaming due to the small year cohorts, so high entry requirements for the IBDP must be firmly enforced. Overseas and locally recruited students tend to be bright, but all have to adapt to a new way of learning and be able to keep up with the demands of the IBDP. Five terms' work gives them the time they require to adjust, but they need to do so early on in the course.

The comparative framework of literature study, which is emphasised in the *Language A1 Guide*, together with the comparison of the five world literature works positioned throughout the programme, means that ideally one lecturer should deliver the A1 course. An obvious reason for this is that, during the teaching, links can be continuously made between texts, something that increases the students' understanding of the works they are studying. These links can also serve as the basis of their world literature assignment 2.

The IBO offers A1 as a self-taught option. In cases where students do not have access to 'an external teacher on a frequent and regular basis' or 'where no teacher of the language is available' (IBO 2005: 6), the self-taught A1 option gives the more literary students the chance to integrate the culture of their best language into the body of their IBDP studies. This option is just as useful for UK students with English as a second language as for those students studying at international centres whose best language is not the working language of the centre, usually English.

The college offers students mixed higher- and standard-level English classes, because of the small numbers – there are on average 20 IBDP students per year. This is not an ideal arrangement, but seems to work well in practice. Higher-level students study the standard-level works in the main class time, twice a week, and the higher-level texts are studied in an extra weekly lesson. With two to five students currently opting for A1 higher-level English, this arrangement is quite workable.

Correct referencing conventions, and methods of recording background reading, are important elements of the A1 course. We use the Harvard system, because it is quick to read, since it avoids the use of footnotes. We have extended this to all IBDP subject areas, and especially to the presentation of the extended essay. Differentiating between lists of references and bibliographies, and correct referencing of websites, are important skills of IBDP coursework, which students require special help with. The IBO's curriculum and assessment service is, moreover, particularly good at intercepting cases of suspected plagiarism.

Due to the pressures of time and the larger number of works to be studied, A1 lessons require more prior reading of the selected works than their equivalent at A level. Knowing the works, at least to GCSE level, before the class discussions start is more critical, as the time is simply not available to coax students through the basics of the works, or interest the students in them, during the lesson. The A1 higher-level course is for students who are of proven academic (and good English) ability, and who are also self-motivated and organised learners at the start of the course.

Assessment

The orally assessed Parts 2 and 4 are positive features of the A1 course, as students learn a great deal about conducting effective presentations in the classroom. The assessment criteria remain constant throughout the five-term course, making it easier for students to internalise the requirements. The highest levels, though, are very difficult to attain, and for writing tasks, harder to get than grade A at A level, as the range in student performance is narrower and more demanding.

World literature can be covered at any point on the course. As it is an innovative, demanding and exciting element for many UK-trained literature teachers, world literature is arguably best left to the second year of the course. This gives teachers the opportunity to read around the prescribed world literature list, and also provides students with the chance to undertake the required reading over the summer holidays of the first year of the course. The world literature assignments can then be set during the autumn term of the second year, soon after teaching commences and before the other coursework deadlines start to arrive thick and fast. This is a common strategy at IBDP centres, but the teacher, in conjunction with the IBDP coordinator, is free to choose their own preferred approach to this issue.

Administration and resource implications

Students should study their strongest language at A1 level. However, finding a language teacher to teach those whose mother tongue is, say, Bemba or Hindi can be difficult outside main UK cities. Moreover, if foreign students need the highest marks in the IBDP in order to attract UK university scholarships, then this becomes even more of a pressing problem that needs to be addressed.

Group 2 subjects

Group 2 languages comprise a family of three courses with many elements in common. They encourage students to:

- understand and use another language
- understand their associated cultures and how they relate to their own way(s) of life
- discover and actively use the target language
- enjoy and be stimulated by the creative and playful use of that language.

Overall, the IBDP language courses provide a modern and effective programme by which learners can acquire high levels of competence in another language. The principles of language acquisition, evaluation and development are therefore highlighted, something that A-level syllabuses would do well to emulate.

Syllabus content

As students at ab initio level will have had little or no contact with the target language – and have two years to acquire an appropriate level of proficiency in it – the *Language Ab Initio Guide* (IBO 2002a) sets out clear topic areas and target language items to be covered. These are:

- the individual
- education and work
- town and services
- food and drink
- the environment
- health and emergencies.

The vocabulary and grammatical items that need to be learnt are also described in the language-specific syllabuses. Those for Spanish, for example, include the main tenses, the subjunctive, the conditional and imperative modes, reflexive verbs and negative formations, to name just a few of the principal language items.

The *Language B Guide* (IBO 2002b), however, in my opinion lacks the useful structure of the other two guides, which make them useful as handbooks for teachers. It has no compulsory topics, and simply recommends 'possible areas of study' such as:

- social groupings
- political institutions

- international issues
- the media
- the arts' traditions
- distinctive leisure activities.

The course content is thus broad, and assessment is based entirely on unseen and unprepared works. The IBDP's A2 course, though, offers an interesting mixture of cultural and literary options. Out of the four options that comprise the course, students have to study a minimum of one of each. The cultural options include:

- language and culture
- media and culture
- future issues
- global issues
- social issues.

As far as the literary options are concerned, the works to be studied are left to the discretion of the teacher.

By way of comparison, if we now look at an A-level French specification (AQA 2003), we see that the module titles are quite different:

- young people today
- aspects of society
- people and society
- contemporary issues
- the cultural and social landscape in focus
- yesterday, today and tomorrow.

Frankly, such headings seem uninspiring and outdated. For example, if we take a closer look at the subject content of the unit entitled 'Aspects of society', the topics that are recommended for study include the mass media; pollution, conservation and the environment; immigration and multiculturalism; France and Europe; and, finally, the French-speaking world. At GCSE level, it is arguable whether this range of subtopics could be satisfactorily covered in a term, but it becomes extremely unlikely that they could be given much justice in a term's work at A level.

Whereas the A-level specification needs at least one annual local area meeting to interpret the content of the course and to establish any recent assessment changes, the IBDP subject guides are generally agreed to be self-explanatory. The syllabus detail of IBDP courses has neither compulsory nor exhaustive prescription. The guides are formulated as precisely that: booklets that contain interesting and workable subject-specific ideas for practising teachers. Specimen course outlines are presented, along with examples of each type of task required, and types of questions likely to appear in the examinations. (In other words, the guides include the sort of information that teachers of AQA syllabuses can normally expect from local board meetings.) IB Africa, Europe and Middle East, the regional office with responsibility for the UK, also lays on courses for beginner teachers in Latvia every July, and for more experienced teachers near or during holiday periods or weekends throughout the academic year on a regional basis. The AQA all-day meetings are for all teachers of a given region, and are held once a year during term time. While the former remain optional, the latter are compulsory.

Aims, objectives and outcomes

An important aim in all three IBDP courses is to focus on the culture of the target language. This is not an end in itself, but devised in order to ensure that students can communicate more effectively in the language, so that in turn they can be better understood. Students are also given the opportunity to explore links between the target language/culture and the language/culture with which they are more familiar. In fact, they are positively encouraged to make inter-linguistic and intercultural connections at the level of awareness and, hopefully, understanding.

The Theory of Knowledge (TOK) course is intended to reinforce the kind of cross-cultural understanding introduced in the group 2 subjects. As far as A-level syllabuses are concerned, the AQA's French specification, for example, also addresses the issue of culture in practical ways in nearly all its units. However, it does not really address the comparative element through the student's own culture, vital if learning is to make sense of another language. Language and culture, in other words, are treated as discrete topics within the student's knowledge of the world.

At ab initio level, the focus is very much on vocabulary and basic tense acquisition, overall understanding and fluency, but as we go to B and then to A2, the focus shifts from language acquisition to language evaluation and more sophisticated uses of language for the purposes of debate, discussion and critical thought. Allied to this, increasing use is made of that language's *literature*, so that by A2 level, students should study at least some literature at standard level and up to nine works of literature at higher level, if so desired. On the other hand, at A level, students must study four texts, with no literature provision if they decide to conclude their studies at AS level.

It is clear that IBDP courses thus address:

* the needs of the student of a second language
* the role of literary study.

From ab initio to A2 the topics change too, from being concrete ones for transactional use to more abstract and conceptual ones for use in transformational language activities, such as creative-writing tasks involving the composition of speeches or letters by literary characters in the works studied. As the introduction to the *Language A2 Guide* so clearly puts it:

the ab initio student should be able to give clear directions to someone looking for the beach, and understand the information in a tourist brochure. The language A2 student, on the other hand, should be able to describe in detail the beauty of the waves, and critically analyse the misleading use of language in the brochure.

(IBO 2002c: 3)

The IBDP language guides emphasise the type of tasks that are appropriate for each course. For instance, on the ab initio course, basic generalised topics are identified with the corresponding situations the language would be used in, and the text types or specific registers normally associated with them. A whole-class project is outlined, where the cultural aims are once again highlighted. At A level, on the other hand, one is instructed to cover the subjunctive, or a tense, but the questions always remain 'Where do I start and where do I stop teaching the subjunctive?' or 'What is a good use of tense?' or 'How do I best teach the past perfect (continuous) tense in Spanish?'

In short, the IBDP language courses adopt functional and interactive approaches to learning a second language, rather than a grammatical one. How you *use* the language with a degree of confidence is more important than how you *translate* it, and understanding the gist of a fast-spoken realistic dialogue is valued more highly than perfect understanding of rather controlled language. It is untidy and threatening at first for students, who need to overcome these responses. When their attitude to language learning becomes more playful and relaxed, the real learning of a new language starts. The most convergent thinkers, though, will continue to ask for tables of the different tenses.

The IBDP's levels and methods of second-language learning are thus very flexible, modern and stimulating, in order to accommodate the students' previous experience of the target language and their intended goal for learning it, as well as their current competence and general academic interests.

Teaching and learning styles

The IBO's language-specific syllabuses are in the target language, and, as these should be passed on to the student, they encourage an 'immersion' approach to learning languages. By comparison, just one page of the AQA's A-level French specification is in French – and, perhaps more astonishingly, Unit 6:1's stimulus material for the oral examination is in English and not in French. The IBDP's courses are currently available in English, Spanish and French, and so group 2 students can be given the assessment criteria in these target languages. As the ab initio Spanish course progresses, Spanish can be delivered in an increasingly monolingual environment. This is something that has to be achieved early on in language B, and from the outset of language A2, courses.

Group 2 is an area where different programmes can be reasonably combined, if class sizes are not too large. Thus, A2 and B teaching, or B and ab initio teaching, is possible in the right conditions. Different levels of stimuli are not so clearly defined in IBDP languages, as they promote an immersion, rather than a 'structured blocks', approach to learning vocabulary and grammar, and developing reading and listening skills. This means quite different students can be put into small groups to study the same language. This kind of combined-course approach only works effectively, however, if teaching is targeted at those requiring language acquisition. Where class sizes are small, weaker students can overcome the hurdle of a 'new-language-as-intimidating' attitude and adopt a 'new-language-as-challenging-and-fun' approach.

Out-of-classroom learning and student participation in the selection of topics, works and resources are key elements of the IBDP's course rationale. Group 2 learners are encouraged to maintain dossiers or portfolios of their work in progress, so that they can use them for comparative purposes, for example, as a preliminary step to preparing for oral activities, or as a springboard for written coursework tasks. The maintenance of dossiers or portfolios is an integral part of the 'learning-to-learn' ethos of the IBDP, helping students to organise their many competing demands, and providing them with opportunities to organise complex resources for subsequent university work.

Colleges that offer language evening courses – for instance, in German, Greek, Italian or Russian – will normally have the staff available to offer these subjects in the IBDP. These will attract a secondary market to their IBDP course, if the promotional literature offers such peripheral options unequivocally and freely. At my college, for example, students who have already acquired the second language attract funding of 15 hours per year of extra tuition. This is the rate for distance learning, which allows capable 'other language' learners to train for the A2 examination with a lecturer familiar with the course requirements.

Assessment

At A level, a specific style of assessment, rather than the target language, seems to be at the heart of the course. The approach is very much one of covering the textbook in order to meet the objectives of the examination. With the IBDP, it is the *process* of target-language learning in its fullest sense that is constantly emphasised. (Recording of achievement, through internally assessed coursework, will be looked at below.)

As A level's AS and A2 are one-year courses, teaching after about a term and a half needs to be focused on examination skills, such as key vocabulary, the tenses in the specification or the module topics – what one might call, in other words, 'teaching to the examination'. As this happens once in the IBDP, the extra term and a half's teaching plus the summer holidays allow the language to be explored even further in all its complexity and novelty.

The oral assessments for languages A2 and B, and for A level, are fairly similar. The A-level mark schemes are detailed, and emphasise the end product. Achievement and performance are the main criteria. On the other hand, assessment in the

IBDP is more open, in the sense that there is generally more help offered to the student with the learning and assessment processes leading up to the oral. In fact, students develop such a sense of control of the learning and assessment processes that they can be tempted to insist on re-examination of internal coursework elements. The lecturer needs to be firm about sticking to the marks awarded and moving on quickly to new coursework requirements. However, mock oral assessment of other work is allowed, and is a realistic option. As the criteria are more challenging and meaningful, both student and lecturer feel greater ownership of the learning experience.

A brief outline of the assessment procedures of the various courses in group 2 and at A level (Table 5.5) will perhaps usefully highlight the main differences between them.

Administration and resource implications

IBDP beginners' workshops are an excellent place to learn to use the online curriculum centre (a teacher-support website run by the IBO), to mark accurately according to the assessment criteria provided and to share language-teaching experiences and views with other teachers. As mentioned earlier, these are held annually, and offer good opportunities for staff to learn the ropes of teaching a group 2 course very quickly. There are cost implications for the institution, but, like any course, much is learnt during the first two years of teaching the programme. The crucial issue is whether this learning experience can be maximised through attendance at a training workshop before programme delivery commences, or after the first year of course delivery, before students sit their final examinations.

Group 6 visual arts

The group 6 option in the IBDP hexagon exists to allow centres to offer students either another subject from groups 1–5, or visual arts as part of the central curriculum. This flexibility allows schools and colleges to offer either a fairly specialised or a broad-ranging IBDP course. This, in turn, enables a wide range of students to receive IBDP recognition and, therefore, have access to higher education in different countries.

Syllabus content

The IBDP visual arts and A-level art and design programmes have many elements of course design in common. These elements may be summarised as follows:

- similar breadth in range of topics
- insistence on high standards (the courses being designed as pre-university tracks)

Table 5.5 Comparison of assessment procedures for group 2 and A-level language courses

Course	Assessment type	Activity	Type of work	Time allocation	Percentage of final mark
ab initio	External	Paper 1	Text handling	1 hr 30 min	40%
	External	Paper 2	Two written productions; min. 180 words	1 hr 30 min	30%
	Internal	Two different oral tasks	Interview with teacher; interactive oral	10 min, excluding preparation time; other free	30% for both
Language B	External	Paper 1	Text handling	1 hr 30 min	40%
	External	Paper 2	Written production; min. 250 words	1 hr 30 min	30%
	Internal	Two different oral tasks	Interview with teacher; interactive oral	9–12 min, excluding preparation time; other free	30% for both
Language A2	External	Paper 1	Comparative commentary	2 hrs	25%
	External	Paper 2	Essay on any aspect of course	2 hrs	25%
	External	Two written tasks	One on cultural option; one on literary option; max. 1,500 words	—	20% for both
	Internal	Two different oral tasks	Individual oral commentary or analysis; interactive oral	15 min, excluding preparation time; other free	30% for both
A-level French (AQA)	External	Unit 1: Listening, reading and writing	Short- and long-answer comprehension	1 hr 30 min	17.5%
	External	Unit 2: Writing	Two questions on pre-release booklet	1 hr 30 min	15%

Continued

Table 5.5 Continued

Course	Assessment type	Activity	Type of work	Time allocation	Percentage of final mark
	External	Two written coursework assignments	Max. 1,400 words	—	15% for both
	Internal or external	One listening task; two oral tasks	Question-and-answer oral; conversation	7 min; 15 min, 15 min	52.5% for all three

- aims of developing the student's voice
- limits to the amount of critical studies that can be undertaken in the subject.

Differences include the following.

- Specialisations, usually as discrete topics, are encouraged at A level, for example, graphics, textiles and photography. The IBDP encourages 'an integrated approach towards visual arts' (IBO 2000: 4). Furthermore, the subject is expected to contribute to the Creativity, Action, Service and TOK programmes, as well as serving as a possible extended essay area.
- The visual arts programme makes no significant mention of the word 'design'.
- Art and design would appear to be better integrated into Key Stage 4 of the English National Curriculum.

Let us now take a look at the common features. Visual arts is broad-based and requires students to explore issues such as art's relationship with society, and to become familiar with current trends and exhibitions. Art and design also requires students to understand how 'images and artefacts relate to ... their social and cultural contexts' (Edexcel 2000: 5). In addition, both courses underline the high ability levels of the student's work. Art and design, for instance, has as its highest A2 assessment criteria 'personal, coherent and highly competent' realisations of intention, 'thorough and sustained research' and 'mature response and interpretation'. The IBDP course rewards mostly 'exceptional understanding of the conceptual and technical underpinnings of artistic expression' and 'highly sophisticated exploration of ideas appropriate to the visual arts' (IBO 2000: 27). The assessment criteria of both courses clearly demand work of the highest calibre. Finally, the A-level course offers critical and contextual studies only as an AS, while the IBDP allows 70 per cent of the course to be dedicated to the research workbook, but only at standard level.

The differences between the courses reveal some interesting divergences. A level offers students the choice to study two or three areas, or 'dimensional approaches', in art and design. The bulk of the A-level specification (Edexcel 2000), however, outlines the requirements of each topic in some detail. The *Visual Arts Guide* states 'work in the studio may combine several techniques and any medium may be used' (IBO 2000: 9). Permitted media are mentioned and examples are given, such as conceptual art, computer graphics and puppetry. On the other hand, if we look at the A-level specification, the range of allowed media is clearly spelled out (there are 17 in total). In the IBDP course, 'conceptual art' might be covered under 'advertising'; 'computer graphics' under 'product design'; and 'puppetry' under 'theatre design'. The IBDP course thus emphasises the medium, the A-level course, the vocation.

'Design' is an important word in the A-level course's title; the manufacturing, advertising and functional requirements of industrial design therefore figure largely in the syllabus. The element of design, as it is related to artwork, is not presented as a discipline in its own right in the *Visual Arts Guide*. Rather, it is presented as a topic alongside craft, electronic media, printmaking and sculpture, to mention just a few examples. Art within the IBDP course is once again seen to be less vocationally directed.

Key skills are clearly mapped in the art and design specification. IT and communication learning objectives are included in its appendices (Edexcel 2000: 47). This part of the specification comes as a welcome reassurance to lecturers keen to integrate these key skills into their schemes of work. Being international in scope and intent, it is not viable for the visual arts programme to incorporate this level of detail into its subject guide. The details of course design are rather left up to the resourcefulness and expertise of teachers and lecturers within their departments.

An overview of the visual arts programme may be useful here to help us understand the requirements of the course. The two modes of working within this subject are through studio work and through the research workbook. As is the case with group 1 subjects, and most group 2 subjects, visual arts is offered at higher and standard level. At higher level, 70 per cent of students' work is weighted towards studio work. However, at standard level, students have the option of spending 70 per cent of their time either on studio work or on their research workbook. The quality and maturity of visual arts work, however, may not always be greater at higher level than at standard level, as other academic demands are made on students' time and energies within the overall IBDP. Students can thus choose to spend more time studying not what they are most proficient at, but what they are most interested in. The relationship between academic ability and subject options, on the other hand, becomes much tighter at A level, as commonly only three subjects are offered.

The two-year visual arts programme is made up of the following components:

Higher level – two compulsory parts

A. Studio work 168 hr (84 p. a.)

B. Research workbook 72 hr (36 p. a.)

Standard level – two compulsory parts
A. Studio work 105 hr (52 p. a.)
B. Research workbook 50hr (24 p. a.)

As stated previously, the hours allocation of components A and B can be reversed at standard level. The core elements, which are common to both higher and standard level, include:

- the practice and experimentation with various media and the acquisition of studio techniques
- an introduction to basic art concepts
- the use of research to support practical work
- an introduction to the practice of art criticism and analysis
- the relation of art to its sociocultural and historical contexts.

Studio work provides students with the opportunity to explore the aesthetic qualities of the visual arts, to discuss the relationships between form and meaning and to explore their social and cultural functions. By the end of the course, students should have developed an integrated understanding of conceptual content, of form and of technical skill, and be able to demonstrate this in appropriate research workbooks. The workbooks should reflect the students' personal interests and include sketches, diagrams, notes and other areas of investigation. There should be a balance between analytical research and open-ended enquiry in the illustration of their interests.

Aims, objectives and outcomes

In overall terms, arts courses both at A level and in the IBDP show considerable similarity, since in the most general sense each is designed to encourage students to:

- develop informed art (that is, develop the skills of process and the resulting outcomes)
- develop as young artists as well as young critics
- become involved in learning about a variety of times and cultures.

None the less, some specific distinctions between the courses belie their different origins and the different directions that they take. The first departure is that the assessment criteria of the A-level syllabus are more prescriptive (or more tightly worded, depending on one's point of view), whereas the wording is freer (or looser) in the assessment criteria of the IBDP course. Some illustration of this distinction will make the point clear.

For example, taking 'the sustained exploration of an artistic idea' as a theme, the art and design specification's assessment objective 3 reads as follows:

'[Students should] develop ideas through sustained investigations and explorations, selecting and using materials, processes and resources, identifying and interpreting relationships and analysing methods and outcomes.' The highest band, 24–30 points, states that students will demonstrate 'creativity and consistent exploration and development of ideas', 'the selection and exploration of appropriate resources, materials, processes and techniques skilfully' and 'high levels of understanding and application of the integrated formal elements'.

By contrast, the wording of 'purposeful exploration' in the *Visual Arts Guide* is as follows:

> At the highest level of achievement there is evidence that the candidate's explorations of ideas are clearly and strongly integrated with his/her life and cultural context. The candidate includes both analysis and synthesis in the investigations, resulting in a powerful and significant body of work.
>
> (IBO 2000)

Another aspect of the programme design that is evident from the above extracts is that the wording of the IBDP aims is more learner-orientated than that of the A-level aims. The gap between the development of ideas and the development of the learner seems to be smaller in the *Visual Arts Guide* than in the art and design specification. Whereas the IBDP measures student growth in a more learner-based way, A level measures it in a more criteria-based way, in which the criteria focus on understanding, abilities and knowledge rather than on the acquirer and interpreter of those competencies.

A level requires individual study of art and design in its unit outlines (Edexcel 2000: 25), assessment outline (Edexcel 2000: 43), and assessment objectives (Edexcel 2000: 6). That students' work is assessed independently of other students is not made explicit in the specification, but has been a principle of secondary education in England for some time. Key skills C3.1a, C3.1b, LP3.1, LP3.2, LP3.3, WO3.1, WO3.2 and WO3.3 require group interaction, and all bar 'own learning and performance' require peer group work. This is presented in the form of an appendix to an A-level course, but is not an integral part of it, nor indeed does it form part of the formal grade assessment. In some ways, this is similar to English GCSE, which awards one mark for written and reading work, and another for oral and listening skills, while only the former guides universities and employers. Written information seems to be valued over spoken information, and individual achievement over group achievement. Collaborative project work is also prescribed within the *Visual Arts Guide*, and needs to be catered for in the programmes of study. The guide states, 'The course structure devised by the teacher should contain in Part A and Part B … individual and collaborative exploration' (IBO 2000: 8). It goes on to say, however, that 'the final assessment is an individual one, so students' work overall must show evidence of their individual achievements' (IBO 2000: 9).

Other differences exist. A-level specifications, for instance, put particular emphasis on the identification of a problem in each of their units (Edexcel 2000: 12), together with equal opportunities, the morality debate, access to spirituality, group and individual psychologies and the desire to reduce bigamy and racism (Edexcel 2000: 9). On the other hand, the *Visual Arts Guide* makes no mention of these areas. That part of its educational philosophy that tackles rights and wrongs, or values – the *Homo Faber* area of the Middle Years Programme – is not dealt with, it would seem, specifically within the individual subjects of the IBDP. (One suspects, however, that the IBO would argue that it is dealt with under the aims of the course – and more specifically, within TOK.)

Teaching and learning styles

The flexibility of the IBDP course allows for a wide range of teaching styles within secondary schools and colleges. The general definitions and indications for suitable areas and methods of study allow teachers and lecturers from very different backgrounds to deliver an effective pre-university arts course. The IBDP outlines a course that is amenable to adaptation within each institution, and the preface to the *Visual Arts Guide* points this out: 'Teachers design their courses of study according to ... the cultural background of the school ... the situation of the school ... and the teacher's own training and special skills. Because these factors vary considerably, the precise syllabus content is not specified' (IBO 2000: 7).

Once again, it is the presence of relatively small distinctions that point to the different types of courses being offered. Teachers who see the development of individual students' abilities as being inextricably linked to human development and maturity may not appreciate the more modular structure of A-level art and design. The IBDP visual arts course, on the other hand, is designed as a student-led foundation course. However, the visual arts programme has less time for the career artist, as it is one of six subject choices rather than one of three or four, as is the case with art and design. This important difference allows A-level students more time to work on the art for their portfolio in preparation for entry to colleges of art.

The greater amount of 'directedness' in their modules, for example, thematic study, arguably makes A level a more attractive proposition for students training for specialised arts-based degrees. On the other hand, if we take into account the looser structure, the later assessment, the lesser insistence on drawing and the way that growth is measured, then the visual arts programme can be seen to be more attractive to students who may not have had prior experience of the subject.

Assessment

Both courses reward equally specific aspects of process and outcomes. It can be seen that the art and design assessment objectives 1 ('Record observations') and 4 ('Present a personal, coherent and informed response') are targeted towards final results, whereas assessment objectives 2 ('Analyse and evaluate critically sources') and 3 ('Develop ideas through sustained investigations and exploration') are more targeted towards developing skills in the discipline. Similarly, the visual arts course includes a spread of assessment criteria, from the process-biased general criterion 'Growth' to results-orientated criteria such as 'Technical and media skills' and 'Formal qualities' of the studio work.

The main difference is that in the visual arts course the 'Growth and holistic judgement' assessment criteria are not externally assessed until the end of the course, while in art and design the assessment is carried out at specific stages of the course. This is due to its modular structure. The A-level specification states that it is so structured that teachers can 'construct a course of study which can be taught and assessed' via 'distinct modules of teaching and learning, related to units of assessment taken at appropriate stages during the course' or 'as a linear course which is assessed in its entirety at the end' (Edexcel 2000: 3).

However, the fact that the units can all be terminally assessed does not make the course linear in its delivery. For example, a number of issues have to be taken into account when AS criteria are considered at the same point on a student's progress as their A2 equivalents, since AS- and A2-level criteria are obviously different in terms of their level of difficulty.

1   If A-level units are marked separately, progression becomes more difficult to assess (Edexcel 2000: 7).
2   There is more differentiation by task, and less emphasis on differentiation by outcome, a notion that becomes more problematic with the open-endedness that characterises many aspects of arts learning. By rewriting assessment criteria from AS to A2, what seems to be *assessment by outcome* is really *assessment by task*, as the nature of the tasks change (Edexcel 2000: 24).
3   Having to teach to lower-level criteria before moving on to higher-level criteria risks impeding the pace at which students achieve.

(Note: The three points above are applicable to the assessment of all subject areas, and not just art and design.)

Another factor that needs considering is that the assessment criteria for art and design are more tightly related to the actual marks awarded than the assessment criteria for visual arts. This makes achievement at A level easier to justify. In visual arts, where it is more the student's personal journey that is being assessed, the process can be more problematic. For example, exhibitions and student interviews are a part of the external assessment process to help establish quality of work. A level is moving this way, too, and now involves examiner visits even for viewing one student's work. However, all work must be sent off in case of grade-award issues arising. While A-level assessment tries to be more objective, in visual arts assessment has long been a part of the overall educational process.

AS/A2 work journals are fuller than research workbooks on account of the increased time given to art and design. Allied to this point, A level requires more writing in a certain format and of a certain register. Students must write a total of between 4,000 and 12,000 words, depending on which endorsements they choose, whereas the requirements are not so specific for the IBDP's research workbooks. The reduced emphasis on assessed writing in the visual arts course probably reflects the increased workload an average IBDP student has to do during the two years of the IBDP as a whole. These assessment requirements reflect the difference in homework time available to students. IBDP students have less time per subject than A-level students. In visual arts, IBDP students tend to do less homework than their A-level counterparts, although across the board they seem to do more. This is partly due to the fact that the wider range of assessment methods encourages students to work consistently, and with greater motivation, throughout the duration of the course.

If we look at external assessment requirements, we see that 40 per cent of all A-level work is externally set, as compared to none for IBDP. Studio work accounts for either 70 or 30 per cent of the total marks awarded, the figure for A level being 50 per cent.

Administration and resource implications

The range of resources students will need in both courses is similar, and includes a selection of basic equipment and tools, such as A3 spiral-bound sketchbooks, pencils, charcoal, acrylic paints, brushes and a folder to keep work in. With small numbers of IBDP arts students, a college may wish to combine A-level and IBDP teaching, as only the assessment methods vary in any significant way. Teaching and learning activities can be combined if class sizes are not too large.

Conclusion

Readers who have got this far should be in no doubt that I believe the IBDP has considerable advantages over A levels. This is largely due to three factors. First, the IBDP is modern in its design and conception: the curriculum reflects the actual needs of university-bound students, and succeeds in developing mature and independent thinkers. Second, the IBDP does not change except under a very controlled schedule, and only then if it is deemed necessary by a syndicate of selected educators. (Grade inflation is thus never an issue with the IBDP.) Third, the assessment of students, though arguably more inexact, is far more wide-ranging.

UK students today have increasing access to a world of new ideas, through air travel, university exchange schemes and the Internet, to name just a few recent developments. They are reading more Canadian, West Indian, Irish, Nigerian and South African literature than before, listening to music that is more varied than before and being asked by the EU commission to prepare for greater worker mobility than before. An internationally minded qualification will exploit these changes, and when it is realised that a modern education means an internationally minded curriculum and not one for international students, then English 16–18 education can take a real step forward.

The IBO is the provider of a qualification and also of an educational ethos. It does not seek to regulate the activities of its centres. A-level examination boards provide a qualification and regulate activities more tightly, arguably at the expense of a more holistic view of the candidate. In pinning down the achievements of the learner, one could argue that much of the learning experience is thus being lost, which begs the question – is this what universities really want?

Group 1 and 2 subjects, together with visual arts courses, all have common design features: to allow teaching to flourish in its many different ways; to give students the freedom to test out their academic curiosity; to develop an international perspective that has more than just a European dimension; to invest trust in the judgement and integrity of the lecturer; and, finally, to allow students to formulate their own questions and then answer them. The IBDP as a whole refuses to prescribe detail in its subject guides, and thus relies on the expertise of the teachers. It demands an amount of teaching time that many level 3 pre-university courses do not match. Because there is so much knowledge content for students to acquire, so many skills to develop and so much understanding to build up, attending lessons becomes vitally important. Most UK-trained students will also need time to adapt to the new ways of working and learning that the IBDP demands. A further issue has to do with the individual school or college ethos. Examination boards provide curricula, but no ethos; the IBO, on the other hand, provides both. Schools and colleges provide staff, and also create their own ethos, and arguably their own curricula. The central issue that remains, therefore, is to what extent should UK institutions adopt the ethos of the IBO, and how far should they adapt the qualification for their own ends?

References

AQA (Assessment and Qualifications Alliance) (2003) *A-level French Specification*, AQA, Manchester.
Edexcel (2000) *A-level Art and Design Specification*, Edexcel, Mansfield.
IBO (International Baccalaureate Organisation) (1999) *Language A1 Guide*, IBO, Geneva
IBO (2000) *Visual Arts Guide*, IBO, Cardiff.
IBO (2002a) *Language Ab Initio Guide*, IBO, Geneva.
IBO (2002b) *Language B Guide*, IBO, Geneva.
IBO (2002c) *Language A2 Guide*, IBO, Geneva.
IBO (2005) *Vade Mecum*, IBO, Geneva.

Chapter 6

Mathematics and the sciences

Sharon Dunkley, Dave Banham and Alex Macfarlane

MATHEMATICS, COMPUTER SCIENCE AND THE IBDP

Mathematics

E T Bell described mathematics as 'the Queen of Science', reflecting the dual nature of mathematics as both a service to other subjects and a study in its own right. Increasingly, mathematics is seen as a fundamental body of knowledge in our modern society, whether it is used as an essential skill for many professions or a language that can be used to analyse our natural surroundings. Some topics that initially appeared to be abstract, and studied only by those who enjoy the challenges posed by the logical techniques of mathematics, have proved to be crucial as our technology has advanced. (For example, complex numbers were classed as 'pure' mathematics until the 1940s, when their use in electronics became apparent.) Others appreciate mathematics as an aesthetic experience, or even as a basis for organising our existence into a set of coherent logical concepts. Given the widespread applications of mathematics, it is not surprising that the study of this subject is one of the six key strands of the International Baccalaureate Diploma Programme (IBDP), and is compulsory for all students on the programme.

Syllabus content

To reflect the differing abilities and interests of the students, the IBDP offers four levels of mathematics, consisting of mathematics at higher level and three options at standard level: mathematics, mathematical studies and further mathematics. Several factors need to be taken into account when students are deciding which course they wish to follow. These include their ability and interest in mathematics; which other subjects they are going to study within the IBDP and in their future studies; and, in some cases, which universities they are hoping to apply for, particularly if they intend to study abroad.

Mathematics at higher level is a challenging course. It covers many areas of A2-level mathematics, as detailed later, as well as some topics from the further mathematics syllabus, such as complex numbers and matrices, so it is aimed at those students who wish to study mathematics as a main component of their university subjects. Students who have taken this course recently, for example, have moved on to study mathematics, architecture, medicine and engineering. To be successful, students should have already demonstrated a high degree of mathematical insight and competence, and should be confident in their algebraic manipulation skills. The students also need to have a genuine enthusiasm for the subject, as well as the tenacity to meet the challenges posed. At Impington Village College, Cambridgeshire, we generally recommend that students have at least a grade A at higher-level GCSE or equivalent, although increasingly students are starting the course with higher qualifications, such as additional mathematics or some of the core modules from the AS-level course. Given the fast pace, and the rigorous development of concepts, that this course requires, these extra qualifications are clearly advantageous.

The mathematics standard-level course covers the same core topics as the higher-level course, but omits some of the more complex ideas, so it is similar to an AS-level course, albeit with a few extra topics. The course focuses on introducing key mathematical concepts that may be required for future studies in subjects such as chemistry, psychology and economics. The ideas are approached from a more practical than theoretical perspective, so students are given greater opportunities to solve realistic problems set in appropriate contexts. To be successful on this course, students also need a strong mathematical background; again, we would recommend a grade A at GCSE, as well as enjoyment of the subject and a good work ethic. In some countries – Germany, for example mathematics at standard level is the only standard-level course that can be taken if the IBDP is to be accepted as a university-entrance qualification.

Mathematical studies is the second standard-level course, and is aimed at students with more varied backgrounds and abilities. The course covers many topics similar in standard to those at higher-level GCSE, so a grade C or equivalent is desirable, but also fosters new skills by introducing the basic elements of calculus. The ideas of logic are investigated, too, helping students to develop their ability to present information in a coherent form. The aim of the course is for students to increase their confidence, and to encourage them to appreciate the fact that mathematics can be used as an important tool in a wide range of fields. Those students who have also studied GCSE statistics have an advantage, as the course covers similar topics, such as the normal distribution, regression lines and the chi-squared 'goodness of fit' test.

The further mathematics standard-level course is the course for the real enthusiast, with topics from the further mathematics A2-level course, as well as some skills from a first-year degree course. The topics are demanding, suiting those with flair and a real confidence in their skills. Some students take it as an alternative to a group 6 arts standard-level subject, whilst others tackle further mathematics as a seventh subject, certificated separately. It is not an essential requirement for studying mathematics at university, as many of the universities recognise that the higher-level grade 6 is comparable to an A2-level grade A, but it is a bonus when applying to most prestigious universities in the world.

Aims

The aims of all the courses in group 5 are to enable students to:

1 appreciate the multicultural and historical perspectives of all group 5 courses
2 enjoy the courses and develop an appreciation of the elegance, power and usefulness of the subjects
3 develop logical, critical and creative thinking
4 develop an understanding of the principles and nature of the subject
5 employ and refine their powers of abstraction and generalisation
6 develop patience and persistence in problem solving
7 appreciate the consequences arising from technological developments
8 transfer skills to alternative situations and to future developments
9 communicate clearly and confidently in a variety of contexts.

(IBO 2004)

The stated aims 2–9 of the IBDP mathematics courses are similar to those of AS- and A2-level courses. Aim 1 is emphasised by an additional statement on 'Internationalism', which specifies that students should be given opportunities to discuss differences in notation; the cultural contexts of mathematical discoveries; the ways in which specific mathematical discoveries were made; and the technologies used to make them.

Objectives

Having followed any one of the mathematics courses in group 5, students are expected to know and use mathematical concepts and principles. In particular, students must be able to:

1 read, interpret and solve a given problem using appropriate mathematical terms
2 organize and present information and data in tabular, graphical and/or diagrammatic forms
3 know and use appropriate notation and terminology
4 formulate a mathematical argument and communicate it clearly
5 select and use appropriate mathematical strategies and techniques
6 demonstrate an understanding of both the significance and the reasonableness of the results
7 recognize patterns and structures in a variety of situations, and make generalizations
8 recognize and demonstrate an understanding of the practical applications of mathematics
9 use appropriate technological devices as mathematical tools
10 demonstrate an understanding of and the appropriate use of mathematical modeling.

(IBO 2004)

Comparisons between IBDP and A-level syllabuses

Mathematics at both higher and standard level covers the same seven core topics, although the standard-level course does not cover the full depth of each topic. The core topics are as follows:

- algebra
- functions and equations
- circular functions and trigonometry
- matrices
- vectors
- statistics and probability
- calculus.

In addition, at higher level, students are required to take one of the four option topics:

- statistics and probability
- sets, relations and groups
- series and differential equations
- discrete mathematics.

At Impington, we chose the statistics and probability option, as this links well to other subjects, particularly when students are analysing their data for their group 4 experimental science project or in psychology. Also there are plenty of resources readily available in this field, as it covers many of the skills included in the A2-level courses.

The further mathematics course covers all four option topics of the higher-level syllabus. As it is taken as an additional subject, this essentially means that the three remaining options are covered during the two-year course. In the first year, we cover the sets, relations and groups topic, together with some of the discrete mathematics topic, as these topics are not dependent on higher-level skills.

The eight topics covered in mathematical studies are all compulsory, and they are as follows:

- introduction to the graphic display calculator (GDC)
- number and algebra
- sets, logic and probability
- functions
- geometry and trigonometry
- statistics
- introductory differential calculus
- financial mathematics.

Below is a brief outline of the topics covered by the current higher- and standard-level mathematics syllabuses (first assessment 2006); the links with the current OCR AS and A2 syllabuses (first assessment 2005) have been identified.

- *Core: Algebra.* This covers the subtopics arithmetic and geometric progressions, and binomial expansions with natural indices. Other concepts from the AS and A2 module C2 (core module 2) include exponents and indices. Additional subtopics for the higher-level course are proof by induction and complex numbers, corresponding to the AS and A2 modules FP1 and FP2 (further pure mathematics modules 1 and 2).
- *Core: Functions and equations.* This topic has broadly the same content for both higher- and standard-level mathematics. The basic ideas of functions are developed, graphs are investigated and the different transformations are explored using a GDC, including reciprocal and absolute functions, so this section of work matches that in C3. The key features of the quadratic function are developed, including the use of the discriminant, as in C1, and exponential and logarithmic functions are covered, as in C3.
- *Core: Circular functions and trigonometry.* Both the higher- and standard-level courses cover circle measures, such as the area of a sector, and the primary trigonometrical functions, their graphs, the solution of trigonometrical equations and their applications to solving problems for non-right-angled triangles, so matching the work in C2. In addition, the higher-level syllabus includes the secondary trigonometrical ratios, as well as compound angle formulae and more complex equations, thus linking to the work in C3.
- *Core: Matrices.* Overall, the higher- and standard-level courses both cover the same material on the basics of the arithmetic of matrices, including finding the inverse of a 3×3 matrix using a GDC, and their use in solving equations with three unknowns (although only the higher-level course covers non-unique cases using the augmented matrix). All of this material is covered in the FP1 module.
- *Core: Vectors.* The higher- and standard-level courses broadly cover the A2 module C4, by developing the basic concepts of vectors, finding vector equations of lines and using the scalar product to find angles between lines.
- *Core: Statistics and probability.* Both the higher- and standard-level courses develop the basic statistical techniques for displaying data and calculating central measures and measure of spread. The probability laws are covered and discrete distributions considered, including the binomial distribution, so much of the work is similar to that in S1 (statistics module 1). The higher-level course includes continuous distributions, but both courses cover the normal distribution, concepts that appear in S2.
- *Core: Calculus.* This topic covers all the expected basics of calculus, including the differentiation and integration of the main families of functions, turning points, and the area under curves (as in C1, C2, C3 and C4), although some of these are tackled by using the GDC functions. Kinematics problems of a similar

standard to those in M1 (mechanics module 1) are also covered. In addition, the higher-level syllabus includes differentiation using the product and quotient rules (as in C3), integration by parts and by substitution, and the solution of first-order differential equations by separation of variables (as in C4).

Option topics: Higher-level and further mathematics only

- *Option: Statistics and probability.* This covers the different types of discrete and continuous probability models, including more unusual ones such as the negative binomial, the hypergeometric and the exponential distributions. The distribution of the sample mean and the central limit theorem are included, leading into confidence intervals and significance testing for both means and sample proportions. The chi-squared test is also covered, but the emphasis throughout is on using the GDC to calculate the statistics. This option ties in with S1, and largely with S2 and S3.
- *Option: Sets, relations and groups.* The first two parts of this topic cover the basics of set theory, including De Morgan's laws, and equivalence relations and classes, but have no equivalent at A level. However, the third part of this topic is very similar to the work covered in FP3, covering the different types of groups, and including La Grange's theorem and its corollary.
- *Option: Series and differential equations.* Again, the first part of this topic has no equivalent in the A2 courses. Different tests for identifying whether a series converges absolutely or conditionally are developed, as well as work on alternating and power series. There is some work on the Mauclaurin series, which is to be found in FP2, but this is extended to include Taylor's series and l'Hôpital's rule. The ideas of first-order differential equations are extended in this topic to include homogeneous differential equations and those requiring an integrating factor (as in FP3), and Euler's method for finding a numerical solution.
- *Option: Discrete mathematics.* The graphs section of this topic covers similar material to D1 (discrete mathematics module 1). Basic graph terms and forms are covered, leading to Hamiltonian and Eulerian paths and circuits. Prim's, Kruskal's and Dijkstra's algorithms are included, as well as the travelling salesman algorithm and the Chinese postman problem. The other section of this topic does not have an equivalent in the A2 course, covering matters such as the Euclidean algorithm, linear Diophantine equations and Fermat's little theorem (resources can be quite difficult to find for this section).

Traditionally, those following an A-level course in physics would usually take an A level in mathematics, opting for the mechanics papers, an added bonus that helped the students to consolidate their understanding and could boost their grades in both subjects. Apart from the small section of work on kinematics in the calculus core, the IBDP higher-level course curiously offers no option for the study of mechanics, although students opting for physics will cover some aspects of applied mathematics.

Teaching and learning styles

The higher-level syllabus is large and, with a time allocation of 240 hours stipulated by the International Baccalaureate Organisation (IBO), the course does rather become shoehorned into our curriculum time of four 50-minute lessons per week. This does have an effect on the style in which the course is delivered, when compared with the A-level course. The rigorous approach, where the development of each topic often requires justification and proof, coupled with the time constraints, does tend to result in a more traditional style of delivery. Students need to be confident in their algebraic manipulation, so that they can apply these key skills in more advanced situations. When compared with the traditional linear A-level course, the time differential between the courses is considerable but, interestingly, one of the main issues raised with the modular course is the reduction of teaching time, making it more difficult to cover the A2 syllabus in both width and breadth.

The standard-level courses all have a time allocation of 150 hours over the two-year course, but the teaching and learning styles vary considerably to match the differing abilities of the students. The further mathematics classes consist of a small number of outstanding mathematicians, so the delivery is almost that of a tutorial, with lively debate and the development of concise logical arguments. The discrete mathematics option lends itself well to research on the Internet, with many sites offering interactive applications for investigating algorithms, such as Dijkstra's and Prim's. The mathematical studies groups cater for many differing abilities, ranging from those who have a high standard of mathematical ability, who do not wish to develop their skills further, to those who have a grade C at GCSE, sometimes at intermediate level. The teaching style needs to cater for these differences, providing challenges for those who are already confident in the techniques, whilst covering the basics for others. However, the inclusion of topics such as sets and logic, does give all students the opportunity to acquire new skills on this course.

The overall aim of the IBDP does come across in the lessons, particularly at the higher level, as the students do ask questions about what the limitations might be, or they hypothesise about how the ideas might be extended or combined. The coursework element of the IBDP builds on this, giving the students the opportunity to work in a more investigational style, and to use and apply mathematics in real-life situations. The time allocation for coursework is ten hours of lesson time for higher-level, standard-level and further mathematics, with additional time spent at home. In mathematical studies, a more substantial project is carried out over a period of 20 hours, similar in standard to coursework at GCSE higher level.

The use of a GDC is an integral part of all the IBDP courses. Indeed, at higher level, some questions are set that are only answerable through the correct use of a GDC, such as a definite integral of the function $e^{\sin x}$. In addition to the graphing features and their associated functions, students are also expected to use the other functions, for example, to find the inverse of a 3 × 3 matrix, so it is not necessary to work through the traditional method using the adjoint matrix. However, the use of the augmented matrix is still used to solve systems of linear equations in three unknowns where the solution may not be unique. Where the statistics option is chosen, students are expected to have a GDC that will perform calculations for the key distribution types and calculate test statistics. They are expected to set up the problem mathematically, but include the calculated results from the GDC, using the correct mathematical notation, rather than calculator-specific terms. Students may also store programs on their GDCs, and common ones that are shared between the class are programs for solving quadratic equations, and for finding the angle between two vectors using the scalar product. The IBDP philosophy is a good one, but to be really successful in an IBDP examination you still need to have a good under-standing of the basic concepts. In our experience, competent use of the GDC can boost a student's performance by approximately one grade in the IBDP examination, but would have less of an effect at AS and A2 level.

At Impington, a high proportion of our IBDP students are from abroad, and are usually highly confident in the traditional skills. However, there are differences in their experiences. For example, many students have not covered statistics in the same depth as those who have taken GCSE. This topic forms a key part of our syllabus, so students need to assimilate these skills pretty rapidly and they need to be prepared to work independently. The students who have chosen the IBDP tend to be well motivated and do respond well to these challenges, provided that they have the necessary mathematical experience. For those whose skills are not secure enough, the pace can be too much, and these students may swap subjects to move to a standard-level course, or change to an A-level programme.

The new internationalism aim of the course does tend to occur fairly naturally within our teaching. The wide cultural mix of our students means that we regularly come across variations in approaches to a topic. For example, when we review how to solve a quadratic equation, some of the European students use an alternative to the traditional quadratic formula used at GCSE, so it is interesting for students to derive these and compare the different approaches. The fact that mathematics is an international language is readily apparent. Students who arrive with a weaker level of language at the beginning of the course are able to join in successfully with the classes, although topics with a high ordinary language content, such as those involving statistics, probability and logic, can cause some difficulties, and these are left until later in the course.

Assessment

For the IBDP higher level, the external assessment consists of three written papers contributing 80 per cent of the final mark (Table 6.1).

The questions in Paper 1 are of varying levels of difficulty, and are usually designed to test a particular skill from the core syllabus. The questions are

Table 6.1 External assessment of higher-level mathematics

Paper	Time in hours	Weighting	Nature of the paper	Comments
1	2	30%	20 compulsory short-response questions based on the core syllabus	The questions are intended to test a student's knowledge across the breadth of the core syllabus.
2	2	30%	5 compulsory extended-response questions based on the core syllabus	The emphasis in this paper is on problem-solving, with responses requiring extended reasoning. Normally, the questions begin with relatively easy tasks, and progress to more challenging ones.
3	1	20%	4 sections based on the option topics	Each section consists of a small number of extended-response questions. Students are expected to answer one section only.

typically quite routine, but there are also interesting ones that test the creative ability of students. Each question is worth 6 marks, but it is sometimes quite difficult to see how to allocate the marks, as a solution may involve a few simple steps or several more complex skills. Some questions, such as those concerning a numerical integral, can be solved directly by using a GDC, and the only working may be a sketch of the graph displayed on the GDC.

The questions in both Papers 2 and 3 are lengthy and involved, frequently combining several elements of the course. The core and the probability section have a real emphasis on problem-solving, and often branch into ideas from just past the edge of the syllabus, requiring the student to think creatively whilst under the pressure of an examination. Students are required to know all the topics covered by the core and their chosen option, but not all the topics are assessed, and it is difficult to predict which skills are likely to be included. This contrasts with the AS and A2 examinations, which invariably show an excellent syllabus coverage, weighting topics according to teaching allocation. After completing several past A-level papers, it is possible to spot patterns and identify questions that are likely to arise in the examination.

Certainly at higher level, the phrasing of the questions does test students' understanding. For example, an IBDP question may simply ask a student to integrate a particular function. Because the examination covers the whole of the syllabus, the student then has to identify which technique is required or whether to use the GDC, whereas the modular style of the papers at A level narrows down the possibilities. Also, the wording in the A-level papers does tend to direct students more to the right technique. This is particularly true of the statistics topics – there is almost a sense that if it is S2, then it must be a Poisson distribution, and the need to look for the key identifying features does not arise.

Table 6.2 External assessment of standard-level mathematical studies and mathematics

Paper	Time in hours	Weighting	Nature of the paper	Comments
1	1.5	40%	15 compulsory short-response questions based on the core syllabus	The questions are intended to test a student's knowledge across the breadth of the core syllabus.
2	1.5	40%	5 compulsory extended-response questions based on the core syllabus	The emphasis in this paper is on problem-solving, with responses requiring extended reasoning. Normally, the questions begin with relatively easy tasks, and progress to more challenging ones.

The external assessment for both the standard-level subjects of mathematical studies and mathematics follows the same pattern (Table 6.2).

Coursework

Unlike the AS and A2 courses, all the IBDP courses include a coursework element, accounting for 20 per cent of the final mark. This gives students opportunities to explore mathematical ideas in depth, increasing their understanding and questioning skills, as well as developing their ability to write a technical report.

For higher-level mathematics, standard-level mathematics, and further mathematics, a portfolio comprising two pieces of work is submitted. One of the pieces is a mathematical investigation; the other is on mathematical modelling. Ten hours of the course time are allocated to this work, so the ideas can be discussed in class, but students are expected to work on the tasks independently over a period up to two weeks. The tasks are based on areas of the syllabus, but could be an investigation to introduce a new concept, or could be used to reinforce the students' understanding. For example, the first piece of coursework that we do at higher level is an investigation to derive the chain rule. Another consolidates the unit of work on vectors, by comparing different methods for finding the distance between a point and a plane. Examples of a modelling task are statistically based ones involving the use of the chi-squared test or the representation of population growth, such as the relationship between the growth of populations of rabbits and foxes.

The tasks are marked by the teacher, against similar criteria to GCSE coursework, for example, the communication of ideas, including the use of notation and terminology; the mathematical processes carried out; and the generalisation or interpretation of the results. In addition, the students are assessed on their use of technology, which may include the use of a computer, and the overall quality of their work. The marks are submitted towards the end of the course, and a sample is then selected by the IBO for external moderation.

As students have had different experiences of producing an extended piece of mathematical work, it is important that they are given the opportunity to complete more than two tasks. We also have a bank of previous students' work, which gives students some ideas about what is expected. Our scheme of work incorporates one coursework-style piece of work each term, and students are given feedback after each one, so that they can strengthen their skills. The best two pieces of work can then be submitted for their portfolio.

The coursework requirement for the mathematical studies element of the IBDP is a more substantial project, involving 20 hours of class time plus homework. Students choose their own theme, and the project can vary in type, for instance, it could be an investigation, a modelling piece or a statistical project, but it should relate to their own interests, whilst being mathematical in nature. Recent examples have included investigations into the number of lines on a noughts-and-crosses-style grid or the patterns in Pascal's triangle, as well as statistical investigations into the widths of guitar strings or journey times to college. The coursework is started in the summer term in Year 12 and finished towards the end of the following Autumn term, with the lesson allocation spread out over this interval to allow for the development of the ideas. Students need to look at previous examples of coursework, and one possible introductory activity is for students to mark a previous piece against the assessment criteria.

Summary

Overall, there are many favourable aspects to the IBDP mathematics courses. The examination structure, including the coursework element, does give students the opportunity to think creatively, counteracting recent criticisms that the more traditional courses are not preparing students adequately for the workplace or university. The IBDP students find the course hard work, but extremely rewarding, and they complete the course with a strong sense of achievement. Further to this, their study skills are first rate, and many are able to make the transition to post-18 studies with ease. However, to cope with the demands of higher- and standard-level mathematics, which tie into A2- and AS-level mathematics respectively, students usually require at least a grade A at GCSE. Even then, the pace at which the courses are delivered and the challenging style of the questions may mean that students, who would have been reasonably successful at AS or A2, become disheartened and are unable to cope with the course demands.

It is difficult to compare the IBDP mathematics examinations directly with the AS and A2 examinations, as their differing formats tend to favour differing types of students. The IBDP is an umbrella-type qualification, encompassing a broad curriculum and incorporating a number of non-assessed enrichment activities such as Theory of Knowledge, the development of creative skills and an element of community service. The students who opt for this course often have strengths in many curriculum areas, and they frequently respond well to the challenges that the programme offers.

Although the IBDP offers some flexibility in the course by providing a choice of four option topics, in practice there is only time to tackle one of these. In smaller sixth-form colleges, there is usually only one higher-level group, so it is not practicable to offer any choice in the option topic. The new AS and A2 modules are designed to offer greater flexibility, allowing students to select applied units that match their interests and abilities, or that support other subjects (although smaller sixth forms, by necessity, may not be able to offer such variety). Students who choose the A-level route tend to have a narrower curriculum profile, so it is perhaps unsurprising that, in our experience, proportionally more students move on to degree courses incorporating further mathematical study.

Computer science

Computer science is a group 5 subject that can be taken at either higher or standard level. However, it cannot be offered instead of a mathematics option – it is an elective subject, so it can be used as a replacement subject for the group 6 arts option. The emphasis of both higher- and standard-level courses is to foster a logical approach to problem-solving and to develop analytical-thinking skills. Students learn how to identify and define problems using a computerised system, breaking the task down into a series of manageable units and constructing appropriate algorithms.

Aims and objectives

The aims of the computer science courses are identical to those of the other group 5 subjects. The objectives for students on both the higher- and standard-level courses are as follows:

- Demonstrate an understanding of: terminology, concepts, processes, structures, techniques, principles, systems and consequences (social significance and implications) of computing.
- Apply and use: terminology, concepts, processes, structures, techniques, principles and systems of computing.
- Analyse, discuss and evaluate: terminology, concepts, processes, structures, techniques, principles, systems and consequences (social significance and implications) of computing.
- Construct: processes, structures, techniques and systems of computing.

(IBO 2004)

Syllabus content

The higher- and standard-level courses have a common core, which covers the following:

- *Systems life cycle and software development.* This topic includes systems design and analysis, software design and development, as well as the social implications of computer systems. These units are similar in standard to those covered in the AQA AS and A2 courses.
- *Program construction in Java.* The implementation of algorithms and data structures in the Java programming language form a key part of the program dossier. Students following AS and A2 courses, however, can choose to program in any language.
- *Computing system fundamentals.* This includes computer architecture, language translators and network systems. Data representation and error-handling methods are also investigated. The depth of coverage is generally similar to the AQA courses, except that language translators are not included and the AQA courses place a much greater emphasis on computer systems and utility software.

Both IBDP courses carry out a case study based on a real-life problem that can be solved using computer systems. A scenario is issued by the IBDP well in advance of the examination, so that teachers may enhance the materials with background information and give students the opportunity to carry out independent research into the application. Examples of case studies include the development of computer-aided engineering or management systems. The same case study is used for a period of two years, and contains material relevant to all sections of the syllabus, but the level of questioning for the two different levels is differentiated. There is not an equivalent section in the AS and A2 courses.

In addition the higher-level course covers the following topics.

- *Computer mathematics and logic.* This topic incorporates differing methods of number representation, also covered in both AS and A2 courses, and Boolean logic, which is included in the A2 syllabus.
- *Abstract data structures and algorithms.* This includes static and dynamic data structures. The ideas of recursion are developed, and the efficiency of algorithms is evaluated. These units are mainly in the A2 modules, but only at pseudo-code level, and are used within the projects where appropriate.
- *Further system fundamentals.* Processor configuration, operating systems and utilities, and computer/peripheral communications are covered, although not to the same depth as in the A2 modules.
- *File organisation.* This topic covers sequential and indexed file organisation, and identifies efficient techniques. It is similar in standard to the coverage within the AS modules.

Assessment

At both standard and higher levels, 65 per cent of the assessment is based on exter-nally marked written examinations (Table 6.3), which is similar to the assessment of the AQA AS and A2 courses.

Table 6.3 External assessment of higher- and standard-level computer science

IBDP computer science	Higher level	Standard level	Format
Paper 1	2.25 hours	1.5 hours	A mix of short-answer and longer structured questions. All questions are compulsory.
Paper 2	2.25 hours	1.5 hours	Compulsory extended questions, one of which includes algorithm construction. One case-study question.

The remaining 35 per cent of the IBDP assessment is based on a program dossier. The project should be an in-depth study of a single problem. On the higher-level course, 35 hours of teaching time is allocated to this project, as compared with 25 hours on the standard-level course, but students are expected to work on their project outside lesson times, too. The dossier should include four key elements:

- analysis of the task to be tackled
- a detailed design, including modular organisation and algorithms
- the program
- documentation.

The dossier is assessed by the teacher, and a sample is then selected for moderation by the IBO.

AS students also carry out a project, but, unlike on the IBDP standard-level course, all students produce solutions for the same task. It is only on the A2 course that students select their own project, and this accounts for 20 per cent of their total mark.

EXPERIMENTAL SCIENCES AND THE IBDP

Experimental science methodology involves some or all of the following:

- putting forward a hypothesis or idea
- planning a valid way of testing the hypothesis
- collecting results or data, in a variety of forms
- analysing and drawing conclusions from the available data
- making a critical appraisal of each stage of the process.

This process is an integral part of the development of the informed individual. It gives students the knowledge and understanding to assist them in making sense of what they hear and read, and in making decisions on issues of importance. An experimental science, or group 4 subject, thus has a key role as part of the International Baccalaureate Diploma Programme (IBDP).

Syllabus content

The group 4 subjects in the IBDP consist of biology, chemistry, physics and design technology, at higher and standard level, together with environmental systems, at standard level only.

The syllabus content includes a core of material, studied by both higher- and standard-level students in all subjects, and this is supplemented by the study of two options. For both the core and option material, higher-level students study additional material. Higher-level students are required to spend 60 hours out of a total of 240 hours, and standard-level students 40 hours out of 150 hours, on practical work. This includes 10–15 hours on the group 4 project, which is internally assessed.

Although the International Baccalaureate Organisation (IBO) states that it does not support the joint teaching of students at different levels, the curriculum model does make this possible. At Impington, where we have relatively few students studying physics, at any level, and chemistry, at standard level, we have found that combining the teaching of the two levels enables us to offer a full range of subjects to the students. Standard-level students are timetabled to attend all lessons in the subject. When additional higher-level material is being taught, standard-level students may be given an alternative project or examination questions to work on, or they may simply be given study time. In biology, we have run mixed groups, as well as groups consisting of higher- or standard-level students only. Although the standard-level students may slow the pace of the lesson a little, the mixed groups tend to create a more stimulating learning environment, as students with a greater breadth of interests share their ideas. Students studying at standard level benefit, as they are encouraged to take a more serious approach, and to appreciate the depth of the subject and the level of interest that other students have.

With dispensation, it is possible for students to study three experimental sciences in the IBDP. In practice, this happens rarely. In our experience, two or three students in the past 12 years have opted to take biology, chemistry and physics. A far greater proportion will study two experimental science subjects, and, of those, most will take either biology or physics with chemistry (all students do mathematics, and so have the necessary subjects for going on to study medicine). Curiously, and for no obvious reason, the students who opt for environmental systems tend to be those who have strengths in other areas, or have very little scientific background and have not opted to study a second experimental science. One former student has gone on to develop her interest in environmental issues at university, and then with the United Nations.

The topics covered by students studying biology, chemistry or physics at higher level will broadly match those covered in any A-level class. The syllabus content for the IBDP may be slightly reduced, as the time allocation for each subject is less than that at A level. However, the demands placed on IBDP students for the under- standing of key concepts and principles, together with the emphasis on practical skills, ensures that they are very well prepared for university study in any science subject. Students who study at standard level are taking the subject to a level roughly equivalent to AS level. In my experience, it is unusual for students with no background in a particular science discipline to pick up, and be successful at, an experimental science at higher level.

Although the modular A-level courses do have some advantages in terms of reducing large amounts of content into manageable chunks for revision and exami- nation, we have found that it can force us into compartmentalising our teaching. Teaching the linear IBDP course enables us to make links between topics more easily, and allows for the intellectual development of the students.

Aims and objectives

Many of the aims of the IBDP experimental science courses are similar to the aims you would find in the specifications of any of their current A-level equivalents. The differences, however, are key to our understanding of the philosophy of the IBDP course, and how it relates to experimental science. For example, whereas the aims for A-level chemistry are subject-specific, the aims for all of the IBDP experimental science courses are generic. Experimental science is placed in a global context, and students are expected to recognise the importance of collabo- ration in the development of scientific ideas. It is rare that these ideas are devel- oped independently; the majority of scientists will combine their own strengths and expertise with those of others. With the advancement of science comes the understanding that there are limitations and restrictions in what can be achieved. On a very small scale, students themselves have an opportunity to recognise this in the group 4 project. Finally, students are encouraged to appreciate the fact that science has a key role to play in the acquisition of knowledge. The 'scientific method' involves the formulation, testing and modification of hypotheses through observation and measurement under controlled conditions. This links, closely, with how the Theory of Knowledge (TOK) programme debates the whole concept of 'truth'.

Aims

Each course aims to:
1 provide opportunities for scientific study and creativity within a global context which will stimulate and challenge students
2 provide a body of knowledge, methods and techniques which charac- terise science and technology
3 enable students to apply and use a body of knowledge, methods and tech- niques which characterise science and technology

4   develop an ability to analyse, evaluate and synthesise scientific information
5   engender an awareness of the need for, and the value of, effective collab-
    oration and communication during scientific activities
6   develop experimental and investigative scientific skills
7   develop and apply the students' information technology skills in the
    study of science
8   raise awareness of the moral, ethical, social, economic and environmental
    implications of using science and technology
9   develop an appreciation of the possibilities and limitations associated
    with science and scientists
10 encourage an understanding of the relationships between scientific disci-
    plines and the overarching nature of the scientific method.

(IBO 2001: 6)

Points 2–6 are the principal aims that are formally assessed in all of the group 4
subjects. From these are derived the objectives for each course.

Objectives

Students are expected to:

1   Demonstrate an understanding of:

    a   scientific facts and concepts
    b   scientific methods and techniques
    c   scientific terminology
    d   methods of presenting scientific information.

2   Apply and use:

    a   scientific facts and concepts
    b   scientific methods and techniques
    c   scientific terminology
    d   methods of presenting scientific information.

3   Construct, analyse and evaluate:

    a   hypotheses, research questions and prediction
    b   scientific methods and techniques
    c   scientific explanations.

4   Demonstrate the personal skills of co-operation, perseverance and responsi-
    bility appropriate for effective scientific investigation and problem solving.

5   Demonstrate the manipulative skills necessary to carry out scientific
    investigations with precision and safety.

(IBO 2001: 7)

It is interesting to note objective 4, which emphasises the importance of personal skills within a science programme. This is the only post-16 science course of which I am aware that assesses these skills as part of the practical programme, where they account for 6 per cent of the final examination mark.

A comparison of syllabuses

Tables 6.4 to 6.9 outline the IBDP syllabus topics for chemistry, biology and physics, together with the notable differences between these and the A-level syllabus topics that we teach.

Chemistry

A-level syllabus: Edexcel, chemistry (Nuffield) 9086

The Nuffield A-level chemistry course offers students a very practical experience, and many of the practicals from this course have been adapted for use within our IBDP scheme of work. Unless students take the further organic chemistry option, the IBDP syllabus misses out a significant section of organic chemistry. With the exception of IBDP organic chemistry, all of the core topics help to develop a student's awareness of the applications of chemistry.

Biology

A-level syllabus: Edexcel, biology 9040

In the past few years, the syllabus content has been reduced in order to make teaching more manageable, and the emphasis has changed in order to accommodate some of the major advances in biotechnology and genetics that have taken place over the past 25 years. As a result, some of the traditional biology, like classification and evolution, is not well covered in the core syllabuses.

Physics

A-level syllabus: Edexcel, physics 9540

As our numbers for A-level physics tend to be low, we will be teaching A-level and IBDP physics in a combined group from the start of the next academic year. This will be possible as students studying each course will be taught separately for some time each week, and the IBDP course outline will dictate the order in which topics are taught. The A-level students will take a practical examination to cover that component of their course.

Table 6.4 Comparison of IBDP and A-level chemistry (Nuffield) syllabuses with reference to core topics

IBDP core topic	Comparison with A-level syllabus
Stoichiometry	No real differences, although the requirement for IBDP students to carry out calculations without the use of a calculator proves challenging for some students.
Atomic theory	No major differences.
Periodicity	In the IBDP syllabus, trends in physical and chemical properties of groups in the periodic table are studied through the group 1 metals. In the A-level syllabus, students do a detailed study of the physical and chemical properties of the alkaline earth metals.
	The reactions of the halogens are covered in more detail at A level, for example, the hydrogen halides, the action of sulphuric acid on the halides and the reaction of the halogens with sodium hydroxide.
Bonding	In the IBDP syllabus, students are expected to predict the shape and bond angle for 5- and 6-negative charge centres. Dative covalency is not required by the IBDP syllabus, although it is often discussed.
States of matter	Application of the ideal gas equation is not required at A level.
Energetics	No major differences.
Kinetics	No major differences.
Equilibrium	Liquid–vapour equilibria are not part of the A-level syllabus, although links between boiling point and intermolecular forces are discussed.
	K_p is not required by the IBDP syllabus. Students with a good understanding of K_c have no problems in applying their understanding to K_p.
Acids and bases	IBDP students are expected to calculate pOH, and to use the expression for K_b, as well as K_a. They are also required to state and explain whether salts form acidic, neutral or alkaline solutions.
Oxidation and reduction	No major differences.
Organic chemistry	This topic shows the greatest difference between the IBDP and A level. The content in the IBDP core syllabus is considerably less than in the A-level core syllabus. However, the IBDP option of further organic chemistry covers most of the subject matter detailed below.
	The mechanism for nucleophilic substitution reactions is the only mechanism required by the IBDP syllabus. The mechanisms for the photochemical halogenation of the alkanes, electrophilic addition reactions, electrophilic substitution reactions, elimination reactions and addition-elimination reactions are not required by the IBDP syllabus.
	Other topics not on the IBDP syllabus are preparations of halogenoalkanes; reactions of the arenes and phenol; carboxylic acid derivatives (although formation of polyamides is discussed); amines, amino acids and proteins other than formation; and the properties of synthetic polymers.

Table 6.5 Option topics in chemistry at IBDP higher level and at A level

	IBDP higher level (two options are chosen)	A level (one option is chosen)
Available options	Medicine and drugs	Biochemistry
	Human biochemistry	Chemical engineering
	Environmental chemistry	Food science
	Chemical industries	Materials science
	Fuels and energy	Mineral process chemistry
	Modern analytical chemistry	
	Further organic chemistry	

Table 6.6 Comparison of IBDP and A-level biology (Edexcel) syllabuses with reference to core topics

IBDP core topic	Comparison with A-level syllabus
Cells	Metabolic processes in prokaryotic cells are required in the IBDP syllabus; the A-level syllabus expects a knowledge of centrioles and microtubules.
Chemistry of life	Less detail is expected by the IBDP syllabus on the structures of hexoses, including β-glucose, pentoses, cellulose and glycogen.
	The IBDP syllabus does not require the difference between saturated and unsaturated fats, or the structure of a phospholipid.
Genetics	The structure of histone proteins is required by the IBDP syllabus.
Ecology and evolution	This topic has a superficial coverage in the IBDP core syllabus. However, the IBDP option of ecology and conservation tackles the topic in greater depth than at A level.
	The A-level syllabus requires the detailed effects of eight human influences on the environment; the IBDP syllabus requires an outline of only two.
	Topics not on the IBDP syllabus are holozoic nutrition; saprobiotic nutrition; mutualistic nutrition; productivity; the water or nitrogen cycle; energy resources; control of growth; succession; factors affecting population size and conservation; selection pressures; allele frequency; types of selection; and speciation mechanisms.
Human health and physiology	The A-level syllabus requires vital lung capacity and histology of the gut wall, but does not require the detailed digestion and absorption of proteins and lipids.
Nucleic acids and proteins	More detail is expected by the IBDP syllabus on DNA replication and transcription; replication in 5'–3'; post-transcription modification; and the role of reverse transcriptase. However, content on enzymes is similar – the IBDP syllabus does not require immobilised enzymes.
Cell respiration and photosynthesis	The IBDP syllabus requires the chemiosmotic theory to explain adenosine triphosphate synthesis. The function of specific minerals is not required, nor is the mechanism of stomatal opening.

Continued

Table 6.6 Continued

IBDP core topic	Comparison with A-level syllabus
Human reproduction	IBDP students need to know the histology of ovaries and testes; the structure of sperm and eggs; details of fertilisation, including the acrosome reaction; and the role of human chorionic gonadotrophin.
Defence against infectious disease	The IBDP syllabus contains a lot of additional information about the immune system.
Nerves, muscles and movement	Phytochrome pigments are not part of the IBDP syllabus.
Excretion	A-level students are required to know the histology of tubule cells.
Plant science	Reproduction in flowering plants is only found in the A-level syllabus.

Table 6.7 Option topics in biology at IBDP higher level and at A level

	IBDP higher level (two options are chosen)	A level (one option is chosen)
Available options	Evolution	Microbiology and biotechnology
	Applied plant and animal science	Food science
	Ecology and conservation	Human health and fitness
	Neurobiology and behaviour	
	Further human physiology	

Teaching and learning styles

As experimental science teachers of IBDP students, we appreciate some of the added benefits that the students bring to our lessons. First, the nature of the students who choose the IBDP – rather than the more traditional, and therefore safer, A-level route – is very different. Typically, students who come to us from the English system have been expected to study A levels. On learning about the IBDP, they often decide that it is the programme for them, even if it means refusing to follow friends, undertaking long daily journeys or living away from friends and family. These students are risk-takers, and they revel in the challenges of the demanding courses offered. Second, the students bring skills and ideas to their study of the experimental sciences that they use in other lessons. The best example is that all students, at some level, are still practising and developing their numeracy and literacy skills. In comparison with students studying A-level sciences, without mathematics, the IBDP students tend to have fewer problems with stoichiometric and equilibrium questions in chemistry, or with data interpretation and statistical analysis in biology. Third, in TOK classes, students are encouraged to question and challenge assumptions. This affects the way students respond in class. For example, Ofsted inspectors, having observed classes at

Table 6.8 Comparison of IBDP and A-level physics (Edexcel) syllabuses with reference to core topics

IBDP core topic	Comparison with A-level syllabus
Physics and physical measurement	This topic is unique to the IBDP syllabus. Some aspects of the topic will arise at A level during practical work.
Mechanics	The IBDP syllabus deals quantitatively with gravitational potential and escape velocity.
	Orbital motion is covered in more detail in the IBDP syllabus.
	Statics appears only on the IBDP syllabus; simple harmonic motion appears only on the A-level syllabus.
Thermal physics	The IBDP syllabus is more detailed than the A-level syllabus, and has a section on the second law of thermodynamics.
Waves and wave phenomena	With regard to travelling waves, polarisation is not part of the IBDP syllabus.
	With regard to wave properties, IBDP students will consider reflection, refraction, the Doppler effect and beats.
Electricity, magnetism and electromagnetism	The IBDP syllabus contains a separate section on alternating current.
	Capacitance only appears on the A-level syllabus.
Atomic, nuclear and quantum physics	Work on quantum and particle physics is covered in the A-level options.

Table 6.9 Option topics in physics at IBDP higher level and at A level

	IBDP higher level (two options are chosen)	A level (one option is chosen)
Available options	Biomedical physics	Astrophysics
	The history and development of physics	Solid materials
	Astrophysics	Nuclear and particle physics
	Relativity	Medical physics
	Optics	

Impington, have commented favourably on the extent of questioning, student involvement and independent learning apparent within IBDP biology lessons.

As teachers within an international school, with up to ten nationalities represented in our lessons at any one time, it is important to recognise and embrace the extra dimension that this gives, whilst appreciating the array of scientific experience that the students have. Teachers should therefore be sensitive to the contributions made by scientists of different nationalities; the use of language; culture; and background. Below are some of the teaching strategies we have used that exploit multinational differences.

- As a simple introduction to an experimental science course, ask each student to produce a poster, explain to another student in the class or give a brief presentation about the achievement of a scientist from their country.
- Ask students to label key structures or diagrams in their own language, as well as in English. There are many words that sound similar.
- Be aware that we may use the same or different words for similar things, and that usage may be different in other languages. For example, 'hair' and 'fur' can produce a spectrum of responses.
- Acknowledge the reasons for differences in opinion or viewpoint.
  - In chemistry, for example, during a discussion about the siting of a chemical plant, students may differ in their viewpoints. Their view on a particular issue is based on input from the past, such as the media, politics, religion, parents and friends. Students from other countries are likely to have received a different input and, hence, to place a greater importance on one factor, such as jobs, than on another, such as the impact on the environment.
  - In biology, the discussion of controversial issues such as cloning, IVF, genetic counselling and contraception is particularly interesting, as differences in law and religious beliefs, in particular, lead to differences in knowledge and understanding.
- Compare these differences with the importance of constancy in so many aspects of science: the need for standard values, a common language and repeatable experiments.

As I have already pointed out, practical work is an important element of the IBDP experimental science courses. The practical programme should relate strongly to the syllabus content and develop investigative skills. Time taken on practical work is stated, and should account for 25 per cent of the total teaching time of higher-level subjects. Practical work is internally assessed, and accounts for 24 per cent of the final examination. This is a greater proportion than in the majority of A-level science courses.

In practice, we find that the GCSE investigations prepare students well for the IBDP practical assessment criteria, but many of our overseas students have very little practical experience. Much of the practical work they have seen has involved

Table 6.10 A series of experiments on enzymes, demonstrating how practical skills can be developed

Experiment	Comments
The effect of temperature on the ability of rennin to clot milk	Rennin is one of the commercial enzymes specified in the syllabus. This investigation is used as a training exercise in:
	• discussion of independent and dependent variables;
	• simple manipulative techniques, but which still require accurate measurement of volume and temperature – students will have to set up their own water baths;
	• discussion of individual and class data;
	• graphic processing of data;
	• evaluation of the experiment, including discussion of the end point of clotting, which is not obvious.
The effect of substrate concentrate on enzyme activity (hydrogen peroxide on catalase activity in potatoes)	Students measure the volume of oxygen produced by the displacement of water from inverted burettes; an ideal opportunity to practise, and perhaps assess, manipulative skills.
	Students should be encouraged to record the raw data, rather than the volume of oxygen produced.
	Skills assessed: data collection; data presentation and processing; conclusion and evaluation.
A study of the enzyme pectinase	Pectinase is one of the commercial enzymes specified in the syllabus. It is possible to look at the action of pectinase on different apples.
Observing the breakdown of egg white by the enzyme pepsin at a different pH	This experiment can be used to reinforce the idea of variables, and also to link with work on digestion.
An investigation to study the action of amylase on starch	Students study the extent of starch breakdown, using iodine as an indicator. This is carried out as a full investigation; students are able to select a suitable variable to study.
	Skills assessed: planning; data collection; data presentation and processing; conclusion and evaluation.

teacher-led demonstrations to show a particular property or example of scientific behaviour. They have a minimum of experience in investigative science and basic skills (even lighting a Bunsen burner). It is therefore important that the practical work, particularly at the start of the IBDP course, trains the students in good practical techniques. We have actually mapped a practical induction course that, as part of the scheme of work, will introduce students to all of the key manipulative skills that would be expected of them as they embark on a post-GCSE science course.

Table 6.10 provides an example of how experiments on enzymes, for example, can help to develop practical skills. The first experiment is viewed entirely as a training exercise. Subsequent experiments focus on specific criteria, leading to a full investigation into the action of amylase on starch.

These experiments would also form part of an A-level practical course, which might lead to an assessed investigation on enzyme activity. The IBDP practical assessment criteria encourage the emphasis on practical skills, as well as outcome, in a way that is not always present at A level.

Assessment

Assessment of A-level and IBDP courses includes elements of knowledge, understanding, analysis and practical skill. Once again, there is a common format of assessment for all of the IBDP experimental sciences, but at A level the mode of assessment will depend on the course being taken. As A-level examinations are modular, many of the papers test a discrete section of the syllabus, and it is only the questions on the synoptic paper that draw the understanding together. This is not the case with the IBDP. Key features in the assessment of the AS and A2 chemistry courses we teach are outlined in Table 6.11.

For the IBDP, at both standard and higher level, the external assessment consists of three written papers. Higher-level students are examined for a total of 4.5 hours, and standard-level students for 3 hours. Key features in the assessment of the higher- and standard-level chemistry courses we teach are outlined in Table 6.12.

Table 6.11 Key features in the assessment of the Nuffield chemistry courses at AS and A2 level

	Edexcel chemistry (Nuffield) AS GCE	Edexcel chemistry (Nuffield) A GCE
Total time for written assessment	2 hours 45 minutes	7 hours (including AS)
Practical assessment	30% of course	22.5% of course
	Students complete four practicals, covering skills of design, execution and data processing	AS assessment, plus one extended investigation
External assessment	Unit 1 – structured questions (topics 1–5)	Unit 4 – structured questions (topics 11–15)
	Unit 2 – structured questions and comprehension (topics 6–10)	Unit 5 – options
		Unit 6 – structured extended-response questions (synoptic paper, as part of open-book examination)

Table 6.12 Key features in the assessment of the IBDP chemistry courses at higher and standard level

Paper	Weighting		Nature of the paper	Comments
	Higher level	Standard level		
1	20	20	Multiple choice	Tests knowledge and understanding of core and additional higher-level material. Includes calculations.
				Calculators are not allowed.
2	36	32	Short-answer and extended-response questions	Tests knowledge, understanding and analysis of data.
				Section A consists of one data-analysis question, plus another short-answer question.
				Section B consists of extended-response questions. Students are guided through each question, and are required to write a few paragraphs on a topic, solve calculations or analyse data. (Higher-level students choose two from four; standard-level students choose one from three.)
3	20	24	Short-answer and extended-response questions	Students answer compulsory questions on the two options.

As mentioned earlier, compared to A levels, there is an emphasis on practical work in the IBDP. The internal assessment of practical work is worth 24 per cent of the final assessment. This is a greater percentage than in any of the A-level courses that we offer. Higher-level students are expected to carry out, and produce a record of, a 60-hour practical programme (40 hours for standard-level students). This programme should comprise an interdisciplinary project (the group 4 project), as well as investigative and small practical tasks. Students are marked on eight different practical skills, which are judged against published criteria. The possible achievement level for each skill area is 0–3 marks. In practice, students are assessed many times to ensure they improve their practical skills, since some start with a low level of competence. Two marks in each skill area will count in the final assessment.

Tables 6.13 and 6.14 show part of the practical programme that students studying chemistry and physics follow at Impington. Students studying at standard level will not do the practicals on topics outside the common core. The skill areas that could be assessed in each practical are highlighted in the grid.

Each of the eight skill areas are divided into two or three aspects (Table 6.15), and the subject teacher will then decide how well each has been addressed by considering the guidelines laid down in the syllabus. If all aspects of a skill have

Table 6.13 Part of the IBDP chemistry-practical programme at Impington

				Practical skills assessed							
Date	Practical	Hours	Topic	Planning (a)	Planning (b)	Data collection	Data presentation and processing	Conclusion and evaluation	Manipulative skills	Personal skills (a)	Personal skills (b)
	The effect of an electrostatic field on a jet of liquid (determining the polarity of molecules)	1	4	▓							
	An investigation to determine the bonding in ten unknown substances	3	4		▓	▓	▓	▓			
	Determining the molecular mass of natural gas	1	5			▓	▓	▓			
	The gas laws	3	5			▓	▓	▓		▓	
	Measuring enthalpy changes	2	6	▓		▓	▓	▓			
	Enthalpy change neutralisation	2	6	▓		▓	▓	▓			
	Chance in chemical reactions; a look at entropy changes	2	15			▓	▓	▓			
	Group 4 project	12							▓		▓
	Looking at the factors affecting the rate of a chemical reaction	4	7	▓	▓	▓	▓	▓	▓	▓	▓
	The effect of concentration on rate (two methods) – the reaction between iodine and propanone	2	16		▓	▓	▓	▓	▓	▓	▓

ontinued

Table 6.13 Continued

Practical skills assessed

Date	Practical	Hours	Topic	Planning (a)	Planning (b)	Data collection	Data presentation and processing	Conclusion and evaluation	Manipulative skills	Personal skills (a)	Personal skills (b)
	The effect of concentration on rate (continuous method) – the reaction between hydrochloric acid and calcium carbonate	1	16			▓	▓	▓			

Table 6.14 Part of the IBDP physics-practical programme at Impington

Practical skills assessed

Date	Practical	Hours	Topic	Planning (a)	Planning (b)	Data collection and processing	Data presentation	Conclusion and evaluation	Manipulative skills	Personal skills (a)	Personal skills (b)
	An investigation to determine how water cools (surface area, evaporation, container insulation)	3		▓	▓	▓	▓	▓			
	Energy transfer between any two forms			▓	▓	▓	▓	▓			
	The wavelength of a laser using Young's slits	4				▓	▓	▓	▓		
	The number of sheets on a toilet roll (errors and uncertainties)	1									
	The penetration of alpha, beta and gamma radiation (half-life)	6								▓	

Table 6.15 Example of how a skill is divided into its specific aspects

Skill	Aspects	
Planning (b)	1	Selecting appropriate apparatus or materials
	2	Designing a method for the control of variables
	3	Designing a method for the collection of sufficient relevant data

been demonstrated fully, then 3 marks are awarded. If one or more aspects are not demonstrated fully, 2, 1 or 0 marks are awarded.

For example, if a student being assessed for planning (b) partially demonstrates all aspects of the skill concerned, they will be awarded 1 mark. The student may have selected *some* appropriate apparatus and described a method that makes *some* attempt to control variables, but their method may not have allowed collection of *sufficient* relevant data.

During external moderation, the IBO will require evidence for the allocation of marks for the following practical skills: planning (a); planning (b); data collection; data presentation and processing; and conclusion and evaluation.

Unless students choose to complete their extended essay on an experimental science subject, they do not, ordinarily, have the opportunity to conduct an extended investigation. This often forms part of practical assessment at A level. In practice, this probably does not matter, as students learn how to carry out investigations anyway, and, whatever the subject of the extended essay, they will also learn how to write up a piece of extended research. For those students who do opt for an extended essay in the experimental sciences, the titles tend to be similar to those used in A-level investigations. For example:

- behaviour in woodlice
- a comparison of natural and synthesised antibacterial agents
- abiotic index, abiotic factors and the water quality of the River Cam
- analysis of aspirin tablets
- analysing the copper content of brass
- a comparison of methods to analyse the vitamin C content of fruit drinks.

The following is an example of an abstract of an extended essay in chemistry, recently completed by a student at Impington:

Investigating chemiluminescence

Chemiluminescence is a process in which light is emitted from matter as a result of a chemical reaction; an excited molecule returns to its ground state releasing photons.

As the preparation of an oxalic ester in the lab was deemed to be too expensive, triboluminescent crystals were synthesised as a preliminary experiment. These crystals are not chemiluminescent. They emit light when ground.

Factors affecting the luminescence of luminol were then investigated using specifically designed apparatus. Although it was not possible to determine maximum intensity of light produced, it was found that the higher the temperature, the shorter the duration of the reaction, and the greater the concentration of hydrogen peroxide, the shorter the duration of the reaction.

The length of luminescence and the intensity of light emitted are important factors in the use of chemiluminescence in analytical chemistry to determine presence of metal cations and different compounds. These two factors are also important in the military and emergency services as they use chemiluminescence to provide emergency lighting. The chemiluminescence required for this has to be long-lasting and intense in order to provide efficient lighting.

The group 4 project

In my experience, this type of exercise is unique to the IBDP experimental science courses. Students from all of the experimental science disciplines work together to undertake investigations, smaller experiments, surveys and research on a topic with an overarching title. Although the actual science is not necessarily of the highest level, the potential benefits are considerable. Students develop an understanding of the nature of investigative science, and have the opportunity to research and plan safe experiments on a topic they wish to study. (They often learn that experiments may not actually work or be possible.) They are also encouraged to collaborate in teams, and to recognise both strengths and weaknesses in their peers. At Impington, we require all students to share their experience and results in a final group presentation. Each presentation lasts approximately 20 minutes, and gives students an opportunity to demonstrate information technology, artistic and communication skills.

To be a success, the project has to be planned very carefully. The timing and format will depend on the number of students taking part, and any timetabling restrictions imposed by the school or college. At Impington, the group 4 project is carried out annually in May. Our programme is outlined in Table 6.16.

Although, it is possible to assess all skills during the project, we use it as an ideal opportunity to assess students' personal skills.

Table 6.17 shows how a group 4 project title, in this case 'City life', may be split into suitable exercises for teams of students to work on.

Summary

In summary, the IBDP experimental science courses, at higher level, prepare students well for science courses at university. Although taught in less time than the equivalent A-level subject, the content of the courses is sufficiently detailed that students will, on the whole, develop an excellent understanding of how topics within a subject tie together. In my experience, this tends to be the case for only

Table 6.16 Programme outline for the organisation of the group 4 project at Impington

Initial preparation	Dates are arranged and put in the school calendar a year in advance.
	Students are placed in teams and allocated a partner to work with. Each team comprises students from each subject discipline. A member of staff is assigned to that team.
	A list of suitable titles is drawn up.
Planning (one afternoon)	All students are gathered together and fully introduced to the project. They are told what is expected of them and given copies of the programme of dates.
	Students gather in their teams and discuss a suitable title for the school project. A vote is then taken.
	Each team elects a leader, and then starts to discuss aspects of the title, which will be investigated. Staff from all disciplines are on hand to offer suggestions and provide guidance.
Subject-specific planning and practical work (roughly five hours)	Students discuss plans with their subject teacher, and produce detailed lists of equipment and material for the technicians. Some practical work or research will be done during lesson time.
Investigation (all day)	All students are off timetable for a day to get the bulk of their work done. They also have an opportunity to meet in their teams to plan their presentation.
Final preparation (one afternoon) and presentation (after school)	Students will spend the afternoon putting together their displays and equipment.
	Each team then gives its 20-minute presentation, outlining the work completed. Students need guidance with this, as they tend to want to say everything that they have done. Other staff are invited to the presentation.

Table 6.17 Example of how the group 4 project title 'City life' may be split into exercises

Group title	Biology	Chemistry	Environmental systems	Physics
City infrastructure, energy and transport	What is jet lag? Deep-vein thrombosis – the cause, and how to avoid it	Energy from fuels – making gasohol	Parking surveys – use of park and ride The growth of yeast near roads as a measure of pollution	Car-crumple zones The effect of earthquakes on buildings
Health and beauty	Exercise and smoking The growth of microbes – the spread of disease; antibiotics; natural antibacterial agents	The extraction of essential oils Making soap and cold cream	Packaging	Hair dryers Levers – backs and arms

Continued

Table 6.16 Continued

Group title	Biology	Chemistry	Environmental systems	Physics
Food and drink	Energy in foods The effect of caffeine on the body Various enzyme experiments	Analysis of food colourings The extraction of caffeine Making wine	Litter and recycling Sewage	Insulation in food packaging Containers for carbonated drinks
Entertainment and leisure	The effect of drugs on the body	Fireworks – emission spectra	Leisure facilities in the local area Noise pollution Analysis of the local river	Bungee jumping – elasticity An effective rollercoaster

the most able A-level students, given the more fragmented nature of their modular courses.

In addition, the IBDP as a programme prepares students for independent study at university or tertiary level, by providing them with a range of skills that enable them to become accomplished critical thinkers. Students tend to be confident, having practised key skills in literacy and numeracy, and, thanks to a range of assessment formats in different subjects, having written essays and given talks and presentations. At Impington, many of the students live in host families within our catchment area, where they learn how to live with the additional freedom that most students only experience at university.

References

Mathematics, computer science and the IBDP

IBO (International Baccalaureate Organisation) (2004) *IB Diploma Programme Guide: Mathematics*, IBO, Geneva.

Experimental sciences and the IBDP

IBO (2001) *IB Diploma Programme Guide: Chemistry*, IBO, Geneva.

Chapter 7

The core components

Sue Austin

The International Baccalaureate Diploma Programme (IBDP) curriculum model, as represented in the hexagon (see Preface, Figure 1), has at its core three additional components: the Theory of Knowledge (TOK) course, the extended essay and the Creativity, Action, Service (CAS) requirement. The importance attached to these elements by the founding fathers in the 1960s is just as great today in fulfilling the stated objective of the IBDP: that alongside developing academic potential, it should also offer opportunities for young people to become well-rounded, imaginative and compassionate individuals.

TOK

What is it? 'An interdisciplinary requirement intended to stimulate critical reflection on knowledge and experience gained inside and outside the classroom'(IBO 2002: 5).

As a unique mandatory component of any 16–18 programme in the UK, the TOK course has aroused considerable interest from academic institutions as well as the wider public. It is not, as the name might suggest, a course in philosophy, which has its own subject options, but rather an invitation to every student to reflect on and question what they know and how they know it. In the words of Edward de Bono, world-renowned thinker and inventor of the term 'lateral thinking', our reluctance to recognise the importance of thinking skills is:

> sad and extremely disappointing … The British tend to believe that intelligence is enough. That if you are an intelligent person then any thinking you do must be good thinking … That is definitely not true. Some mighty intellectuals are extremely bad thinkers (*Independent* 2002).

With all IBDP students required to include each of the principal domains of knowledge in their diploma, it is possible for all to take part in informed discussions about the nature and purposes, as well as the strengths and limitations, of particular knowledge systems. Thus, not only the breadth, but also the coherence, of each student's course of study is ensured. So, how to embark on this audacious voyage of discovery? The approach adopted is a Socratic one, with an extensive array of questions to confront the 16-year-olds, and jolt them out of any hint of complacency they might harbour about the nature and certainty of knowledge claims. Questions taken from prescribed lists of essay titles in recent years include the following.

- 'Does knowledge come from inside or outside? Do we construct reality or do we recognise it?'
- 'What are the differences between information, data, belief, knowledge and wisdom?'
- 'Are there technologies specifically designed to impart each?'
- 'The word "know" does not translate easily into all languages. In what ways do various languages classify the concepts associated with "to know"?'
- 'What constitutes a "good reason" for belief? Is a persuasive reason necessarily grounded in truth?'
- 'To what extent is intuition to be taken seriously in the different Areas of Knowledge?'
- 'Does knowledge always require some kind of rational basis?'
- 'Is it possible to experience an emotion, a feeling, an attitude or sensibility that cannot be expressed in language?'
- 'How does a mathematical proof or a scientific law differ from a historical judgement, an aesthetic opinion or a moral value?'

How do you teach TOK? In grappling with questions like these, students need to draw both on their familiarity with academic subjects at school, such as history, natural sciences and literature (English and foreign), and on their personal experience, so as to consider the role of emotion or moral values, for example. Once the concepts and terminology underlying the course have been clarified, there is scope for wide-ranging discussion and original ideas, always provided they are backed up with specific examples. This is the time for lateral thinking and challenging statements. Clarity of expression, in both verbal and written form, is required for the final assessments, but in the early stages there should be plenty of opportunity for exploration of ideas and linking themes.

In order to investigate the central question 'How do we know what we know?', students have to develop critical-thinking skills, which will probably not have formed part of their education to date. Prior to the sixth form, apart from perhaps general studies or religious education classes, they will have been fed a syllabus consisting mainly of 'facts' to be absorbed, or previously digested 'expert' opinions to be regurgitated for examination or coursework purposes. While asking questions is not actively discouraged in the UK, as in some parts of the world, the scope of such questions is usually circumscribed, and likely answers might be 'You must have done something wrong in setting up the experiment' or 'Because we say so.' Being launched on to the open sea of intellectual uncertainty can be a daunting experience, especially for those who have succeeded very well so far by staying within the tramlines and passively accepting the words of their teacher.

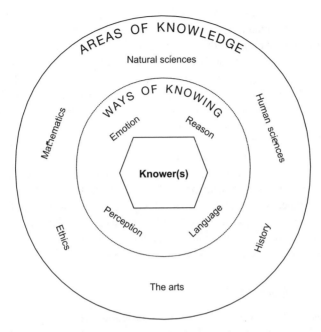

Figure 2   The TOK curriculum model, showing Areas of Knowledge and Ways of Knowing

The syllabus

Asking questions forms the basis of the TOK programme, indeed the 'syllabus' contains page after page of searching questions, to which there are no simple answers. Here are some examples.

- 'How does the social context of scientific work affect the methods and findings of science?'
- 'Could it be argued that mathematics is simply the application of logic to questions of quantity and space?'
- 'Is it correct to think that what constitutes a good reason varies from discipline to discipline and from culture to culture?'
- 'Is emotion an essential ingredient of scientific or artistic knowledge? Can there be creativity without emotion?'

Such a vast and ambitious undertaking requires a well-defined structure for deconstruction. A visual representation of the TOK curriculum model, as in Figure 2, is helpful here.

It will be seen that 'Knowledge' is classified in a conventional, though contestable, manner into the areas of mathematics, natural sciences, human sciences, history, the arts and ethics. The inner circle includes four 'Ways of Knowing', seen as a means of exploration and interpretation of the world: the receipt of sensory stimuli through 'perception'; response guided by 'emotion'; expression through 'language'; and the attempt to seek order and clarity through 'reason'. It is important to clarify this terminology with students at the start of the course. They will be familiar with the words, but not always with the specific interpretation of them that is required. 'Perception' gives rise to particular difficulty, because of its alternative colloquial meaning of 'viewpoint'. The philosophical basis of perception is *a posteriori* knowledge, or knowledge through experience. In TOK, it refers primarily to sensory perception, the signals sent to the brain by the five senses. The other three Ways of Knowing are more obvious, but still need definition and explanation. It is helpful to schedule this for the start of the course, in order to give students some benchmarks. They can then consider issues relating to the various 'Areas of Knowledge' with some tools at their disposal. The 'Knower(s)' at the heart of Figure 2 refers to the students, both at an individual and a collective level, and to particular interest or cultural groups, such as doctors and scientists. The central position is deliberate; the emphasis in this course is on individual discovery and reflection, in which the personal experience of each student is especially valued.

Critical thinking and TOK

The emphasis on the student at the centre, as the Knower, marks the course out from the AS-level course in critical thinking, where the emphasis is on a more theoretical interpretation of 'reasoning'. The stated objectives of two of the five modules in this course are 'to identify the elements in a reasoned case or argument' and 'the analysis of argument using principles of logic and philosophy' (OCR 2002).

Practice in identifying, criticising and developing a concise and coherent argument is a valuable skill, developed, it is hoped, in the preparation of TOK essays and presentations, but it is not taught in a vacuum – rather, it is related to a specific theme and grounded in the students' personal experience.

Of course, the great philosophers, as well as more modern pundits, have their place in the subject matter studied. It would similarly be foolhardy not to refer to the work of Richard Dawkins in the science section, or to Steven Pinker when discussing the role of language in thought. In fact, with current dramatic developments in research on the brain, the rapprochement between 'arts' and 'sciences' is becoming evident, and the old boundaries are losing relevance.

Further reading lists should also be an essential feature of lesson notes. However, the bulk of the TOK course is concerned with a broader exploration of the acquisition of knowledge, with 'reason' remaining quintessential, but with greater weight being given to consideration of other paths to 'the truth', for example, through emotion or intuition. There are clearly overlaps in subject matter with the AS course, especially noticeable in the presentation section of the TOK course, where current issues of public concern, such as global warming or euthanasia, form the topics. Essential skills of assessing the credibility of sources, investigating assumptions and evaluating claims feature in both courses, but the TOK approach is towards the students coming up with their own examples, from personal experience in or out of school, while in the AS course the texts for analysis are preselected and ready-made for them.

The type of assessment of the two courses differs distinctly. The TOK student is encouraged to evaluate their learning so far, and to investigate the assumptions and value judgements behind what may hitherto have been regarded as 'the facts'. The emphasis remains firmly with the individual student, and with their appreciation of the knowledge they have to date, its validity and possible limitations. This distinction is highlighted by the different forms of assessment. The AS is examined in two short papers, one involving multiple-choice questions and short structured texts for analysis, and the other requiring the writing of a reasoned case using material provided, and the critical evaluation of an argument, also provided. While the course content, as stated in the syllabus, bears a similarity to aspects of the TOK course – 'aspects of culture and morality, scientific horizons; social perspectives and cultural expression' – the practical opportunity to explore all these areas in a two-term course, as well as preparing students for examinations that demand quick, and thus fairly superficial, evaluation of texts, is necessarily restricted. The end-of-module examination chosen for the AS level has been consistently rejected by those responsible for the TOK course, who have preferred the reflective essay, written without time restrictions, on one of a small list of prescribed titles, to a precise word count (1,200–1,600 words), and marked according to a set of criteria focused on the effectiveness of analysis of 'the problem of knowledge' concerned.

An integral part of the IBDP

One point to be stressed is that the TOK course is not a 'bolt-on', which can be taught independently of an IBDP course, as has been suggested by some who recognise its value. Its role is not as a stand-alone course; it is an integral part of the IBDP, dependent on the participants taking a prescribed range of subjects from which they have an opportunity to reflect on the nature of the different bases of knowledge. However worthy the intentions of the architects of the AS course in critical thinking, it cannot hope to fulfil the same role of drawing together and assessing the validity of various 'claims to knowledge' made in different subject areas. TOK thinking should ideally become a mindset for the whole staff; indeed the spin-off into other classes has been promoted even more vigorously in recent years, with TOK sessions being held at all subject workshops run by the International Baccalaureate Organisation (IBO). All those involved in IBDP teaching should have an awareness of the kind of questions about the nature of 'truth' in their specialist field of knowledge that they can raise and discuss with their classes.

Delivering the course

There is no magic formula for running a TOK course. What works in one school may not in another. As mentioned earlier, the guidelines in the syllabus deliberately leave considerable scope for interpretation. These state that 'Many effective approaches are possible and, while being sensitive to the needs of their students, teachers are encouraged to be adventurous' (IBO, 1999: 3). One can focus on the Ways of Knowing, and see how each applies to the various Areas of Knowledge. One can use linking questions, such as those given above, to challenge traditional thought patterns. One can work through the Areas of Knowledge, using specialist teachers to tease out assumptions and linguistic issues, dilemmas and limitations. Naturally, constraints of staffing, timetabling, resources and allocation of rooms will all affect delivery of the course in school.

Initially, it makes sense to introduce the course, in order to explain the terminology and demystify the concepts to the whole IBDP group. The value of holding plenary sessions should not be underestimated, even when the IBDP cohort is quite large. This is best done by the staff member in charge of TOK; such a person needs to be appointed in advance of the IBDP being offered. At the very least, they must be fully cognisant of the demands of the course, and have established how the teaching and work for assessment is to be delivered. A TOK coordinator may come from any subject specialism. Natural scientists, mathematicians, social scientists and linguists all make for excellent team leaders; the main prerequisites are an open mind, intellectual curiosity and organisational ability.

The personal voyage of discovery by each student is at the heart of the course, and the role of the teacher is significantly that of an animateur. It requires quite a mental and psychological leap for students, who at first will be keen to ask for 'the right answer', and will be disturbed to learn that there is no right one, and that the teacher admits to knowing as little, or as much, as they do. The temptation to conclude that any conclusion is of equal validity, however, must be addressed early on. The value of clear rational thinking, or at least a recognition of the forces at play behind a certain decision, is one of the key points of the course. This is where the Ways of Knowing come into play, and it is important to anchor them firmly in the students' minds at the start. A seminar approach works well here; general introductory talks are often more effective when they are concluded with small-group sessions working on specific questions arising out of them. Subsequently, more detailed investigation of the premises on which knowledge is based in the various fields can be carried out within the small groups, under the guidance of specialist or non-specialist teachers. In either case, study materials in the form of books dedicated to this purpose, articles from newspapers and periodicals, and videos can all provide a valuable stimulus for discussion and analysis. It is particularly important to try to draw out the less articulate students at this stage, so that they begin to feel more comfortable with expressing their views in a TOK format.

It is not only students, but also teachers, who can feel somewhat uncomfortable about challenging the status quo in the approach to their subject discipline.

One way that has proved successful in bringing in colleagues not already part of the TOK team is to invite them to give a talk on a topic that fascinates them. Most subjects can be given a TOK slant, with a little forethought. Recent examples from Sevenoaks School that come to mind are talks on 'Maps', 'Victorian architecture', 'The original Shakespeare', 'The number zero', 'The enigma of cold fusion' and

'Women artists through history'. In another school starting the IBDP, the head volunteered to give one of the first talks, establishing a high profile for TOK from the start; subsequently, members of his staff were queuing up for a slot. One should emphasise, however, that this is not simply a form of general studies under another name. Material presented must subsequently be subjected to the TOK classification and analysis. The normal procedure would be regularly to break up into small groups with teachers for the second part of the session, so as to consider the subject matter in the context of particular Areas of Knowledge and Ways of Knowing.

The delivery of a successful TOK course relies, to an extent, on variety and a lively approach. As well as inviting in colleagues on the staff, contributions from outside speakers can also prove valuable, and shed fresh light on aspects of TOK. In one recent example, a local MP explored the UK system of political representation, initially in a historical and geographical context, leading into an examination of the issues currently facing the House, on which he would have to vote the following week. There were particular scientific and ethical issues, as well as discussion of the relative roles played by reason and emotion, not to mention the language employed in Parliament. The more specific TOK discussion that followed this stimulating talk would have had far less impact had the material been read from a worksheet. On another occasion, a parent working for a large PR firm volunteered to lead a session on the ethics of advertising. Having done his homework thoroughly, he was able to relate his material very effectively to the curriculum model shown in Figure 2, linking it to the arts, ethics and human sciences Areas of Knowledge, showing how language in particular – but also how the other Ways of Knowing, perception, emotion and reason – are involved in our reactions to advertisements.

None-the-less, the danger of such outside talks being seen as light relief should not be underestimated. Two preconditions need to be met: first, the speaker should be carefully briefed on the nature of the TOK terminology and concepts, and be asked to provide a brief résumé of the main points; second, the regular TOK teachers need to be present at the talk, so that they can lead an informed discussion afterwards.

Continuing the theme of adding spice and variety to the course, here are two suggestions, perhaps for the end of term. The first, a balloon debate, is relatively simple to organise: a panel of teachers from the spread of disciplines, with some prior knowledge of TOK ideas, answers 'big' questions, mainly pre-prepared, from the perspective of their subject, and the audience of students then votes out the least convincing. Examples of questions might be as follows.

- 'Establishing cause and effect is the basis of progress in society.'
- 'An appreciation of beauty is what separates man from the animal world.'
- 'Understanding human nature enables us to predict future behaviour.'

The second TOK 'event' suggested requires more forward planning. This is to stage a TOK day or weekend, on a broad theme, in which several schools take part. Recent examples have been 'Determinism' and 'Hearts and minds'. The theme can be considered from different perspectives (science, literature, ethics, social sciences), and a variety of active exercises can be incorporated, on which groups of students from different schools work together. The interchange of ideas amongst fresh faces can be very stimulating. The onus should, of course, be placed on the students to absorb and digest whatever material is presented to them, and to collect and digest notes handed out by speakers or written during talks. These should be added to the dossier of TOK materials that each student should be amassing. Also included will be any articles from newspapers, periodicals or the Internet that they find to illustrate a particular aspect of TOK. Teachers may advise in this area, and may offer their own material, but ultimately the students themselves should be responsible for collecting material that can later be used in their essays or presentations. In some schools and colleges, TOK diaries are kept, in which students make notes of examples relevant to TOK concepts from other classes or topical events. For instance, an element of uncertainty in a scientific theory, or discussion of one now discredited, would provide practical evidence of the scientific method, while a Romantic poem might illustrate the role of emotion in the search for ideals of beauty.

At this point, there is an important distinction to be made between TOK and general studies; in the former, the focus on an end product, the essay and the presentation is there to keep students on task, while in the latter, although much stimulus to the imagination may be provided, without a clear structure and terminology, sustained motivation is hard to achieve.

Practical considerations

The TOK course is a compulsory part of the IBDP, and thus, although the teaching time per student per week may not be very great, the entire cohort is involved, which can present timetabling and staffing difficulties. The most common form of delivery of the TOK programme in English schools and colleges is through a weekly slot over four to five terms. The IBDP requirement is for 100 teaching hours of TOK. Some schools choose to run the entire programme in the first year of the IBDP, sometimes ending up with a TOK week away together. This approach would seem, however, to be out of line with the overall ethos of TOK, which is intended to be a constant underlying theme throughout the IBDP. The luxury of a TOK week out of school is, in any case, not normally available in UK schools, where academic demands, as well as pressure from other traditionally 'extra-curricular' demands – language exchanges; Model United Nations sessions; musical, dramatic or sporting events; and so on – is intense. Within the IBDP, these activities can be readily justified for CAS (to be described later in this chapter), but they militate against even more time spent out of school for a TOK programme 'in the field'. Nonetheless, smaller scale one day conferences are more feasible.

The staffing allocation will depend on how it is decided to deliver the course. In some institutions, a single teacher is largely responsible, calling on the services of colleagues as and when desired. Where the IBDP group is of one class size only, this can work effectively, always provided the potential polymath teacher is to hand. Where the cohort is large, the usual approach is via a multidisciplinary team:

a mathematician, a scientist, an English and/or foreign-language teacher, a specialist from one of the social sciences, an art or music teacher and someone who is willing to discuss ethical issues, probably a religious studies teacher, would provide a suitable nucleus. The normal procedure would be for each teacher to be assigned what is in effect a seminar group, and, wherever possible, to follow these students through their entire TOK course, with occasional sessions being run partially or wholly in plenary.

At Sevenoaks we have experimented with a carousel system, involving 'experts' running sessions on their particular specialism. However, a degree of staleness began creeping in by about the fifth repeat performance, and, perhaps more seriously, no one was monitoring the individual students' progress through the course sufficiently. Considerable guidance is needed by many students in what is essentially a new approach to studying. Feeling at ease with one's teacher is especially important for students in the presentation section of the course, which is carried out in class and entirely internally assessed. One way of minimising the discomfort that may be felt by, say, a linguist being faced by a session on mathematics is to ask for lesson materials from the specialist, with even a guest visit from the department concerned, if it can be arranged.

Making it possible for all these staff to be available at one time in the week offers a timetabling challenge. At Sevenoaks, it has been necessary to move from one block to two, and then to four, as the numbers taking the IBDP have risen. There are obvious disadvantages to fragmenting the delivery of the course in this way; general sessions to introduce the Ways of Knowing, for example, or sessions run by outside speakers, must be repeated, or special exceptions be made to students' normal weekly schedule.

Staffing

Recruiting staff on to the TOK programme may require a little PR within the school, in addition to the sessions offered by the IBO at their subject workshops. Once the aims and objectives are outlined, a number of colleagues generally show interest. For teachers new to the TOK perspective, the IBO offers a series of exemplary lessons, which describe tried-and-tested sessions with titles like 'The power of names', 'Does it matter if what we believe is true?' and 'Nothingness'. These normally provide materials for active class participation, to be followed up by small-group feedback and discussion. An effective introductory lesson to 'Language as a Way of Knowing', for example, uses situation cards for students to mime, pointing up the impossibility of conveying complex explanations or abstract ideas without words. Another, entitled 'The map is not the territory', uses different types of maps to explore different conceptual schemes around the world, the legacy of history in our knowledge of today and the association of knowledge with power. The TOK magazine *Forum* also includes valuable ideas for taking up in the classroom.

Conveying the excitement of shared exploration in the worlds of knowledge and truth is heady stuff. Encouraging students to search through newspapers and periodicals, as well as the Internet, for articles and features that can be considered from a TOK perspective is a good means of involving them early on, and of preparing the ground for presentations.

Assessment

At this point, it is worth looking in more detail at the assessment of the TOK programme, in order to discover the objectives of the programme. It takes two very different forms, although the criteria look similar. In both cases, 'problems of knowledge' are sought, and students are given credit for the way in which they use the terminology described above, and for the clarity of their analysis. There is no final examination, but one essay on a title chosen from a prescribed list of ten is submitted for external marking. The mark given here, out of 40, represents two-thirds of the final mark. The remaining 20 marks are available for the oral presentation, delivered to the class and internally assessed, without external moderation.

The presentation

Some clarification of the latter, somewhat unconventional, method of assessment, is necessary. The objective is for students to 'illustrate ways in which contemporary issues or events may be linked with knowledge issues, providing a prompt for reflective thinking' (ibid.: 41). The scope is very wide, and although some guidance is given as to potentially fruitful subject areas, the ultimate choice of topic is left to the student to decide, in consultation with their teacher. The syllabus guidelines state that 'students should nominate the topics which most interest them' (ibid.: 40). This is a welcome departure from the set-text format, and an invitation to real participation appreciated by most students. Caution needs to be exercised in the choice, however. Favourite topic areas are medical ethics and 'popular' science, such as genetic modification; these need to be treated with caution, and refined to produce a specific 'problem of knowledge', otherwise there is a tendency for the discussion to lack focus or to be over-emotional in content.

An awareness of the nature of the various approaches to the subject matter and an evaluation of the evidence found – whether in the form of statistics, official statements or newspaper headlines – are important, but so too is the form in which the analysis is given to the group. How far is the audience involved in the issue? In considering the question 'How can we know that judicial decisions are right?', one student offered the group a diagram of the scene of the crime, and asked them to be the jury. The use of video clips, PowerPoint software, diagrams and other visual prompts can all contribute to the vitality, and thus the effectiveness, of a presentation. The skills required are somewhat different from those required in reasoned analysis of a text on paper. Putting forward a logical and balanced argument orally presents a challenge to the average sixth-former, but demands skills of oral delivery and persuasion that will serve him or her well in later life. Exposition, explanation and justification of points of view to a live audience are areas of expertise highly valued in universities and the working world. The formal evaluation of presentations can be a little problematic. The subjective nature of the content, together with the natural tendency to inflate the scores of students well known to the teacher, are recognised pitfalls, but the value of delivering a well-prepared and lucid exposé of a 'knowledge issue' to a small and familiar group is taken to outweigh the negative factors. In England, public speaking tends to be underdeveloped in school, and many students show a considerable lack of confidence. In a non-IBDP sixth form, a few already articulate students will take on debating societies of various types, but the majority will stay well out of the limelight. Such anonymity is not possible for an IBDP candidate. Of course, the more diffident students will need coaxing, both in choosing a title and preparing their presentations. A particular news story can provide a good starting point – the fight of a terminally ill woman to be allowed to decide the time of her own death, for example. Rather than an investigation into 'the death penalty', a very successful presentation took the case of a prisoner who went to the electric chair having been convicted of murder, and examined the murder rate in the US state concerned, alongside that of a comparable neighbouring state without the death penalty; as well as looking at media coverage, ethical considerations and historical and cultural perspectives. Another student looked at the Arab–Israeli conflict from the perspective of 'How do we know we are right?' An extract from a recent student's self-evaluation report reads:

> We addressed several different aspects of the subject; religion, history and science … we showed how many arrive at the conclusion that polygamy is 'wrong' by using emotion, reason and intuition. It was vital that both sides of the argument were displayed, showing that trying to reach the truth is often more difficult than first anticipated.

Schools will vary in the internal organisation of the TOK programme, but it clearly makes sense for the concepts and terminology to be set out first, and for some time to be given to exploration of the assumptions and value judgements behind the different Areas of Knowledge, before any forays are made into the worlds of essays or presentations. It seems useful to set practice essays, perhaps of a shorter word limit, once this exposition has been completed. Such drafts can then be returned to after the presentation exercise has been completed. It is important to note that the maturity of students in their approach to TOK tends to develop markedly over the two-year course, and thus setting an early date for receipt of final essays, although tempting in view of other pressing deadlines, is unwise if candidates are to give of their best. With careful organisation, presentations may be spread evenly over the course. Another method is to devote the autumn term of the second IBDP year to students' presentations, by which time they should feel comfortable within their group and, one hopes, with their teacher, who will be responsible for the assessment. Students are also required to write their own self-evaluation of their presentations; a special form is issued for this purpose, to be completed immediately after delivery of the presentation.

The essay

Towards the end of the Autumn term, the essay can be reintroduced, with full-length drafts being set for the early weeks of the Spring term, and a final deadline for midway through this term. It is to be hoped that by this stage of the course most students will have attained the level of maturity needed to compose a critical essay that addresses a selected title utilising concepts and ideas in a TOK context. It is no mean task.

First, let us consider the subject matter of the essays. As stated in the syllabus, the scope is wide-ranging. The prescribed titles 'entail generic questions about knowledge and are cross-disciplinary in nature' (ibid.: 38). Some recent examples are as follows.

- 'Is there knowledge we should not seek? Or is all knowledge inherently a good thing, and can only persons be harmful?'
- 'Is it possible to justify a hierarchy of disciplines, or types of knowledge? If so, on what basis?'
- '"A belief is what we accept as truth" (J W Apps). Is this a claim that you could defend?'
- '"Art upsets, science reassures" (Braque). Analyse and evaluate this claim.'
- 'Must all "good explanations" allow for precise predictions?'
- 'How can we know, if at all, that our behaviour is ethical?'

Some guidance on the approach to be taken in embarking on the essays is given in the syllabus, which states that the titles:

> … may be answered with reference to any part or parts of the TOK programme, to specific disciplines, or with reference to opinions gained about knowledge both inside and outside the classroom … they are not meant to be treated in the abstract. In all cases claims should be justified and relevant, and where possible, counter claims and original examples should be cited to illustrate the argument (ibid.).

The phrase 'counter claims' requires some explanation, since students are often tempted to present an excessively one-sided argument in defence of a strongly held view. 'Original examples' are not that easy to come by, and it is tempting to fall back on some familiar old chestnuts, such as the universally held belief, before Copernicus, that the earth was at the centre of the universe. Here a 'dossier' of TOK examples collected over the course can really come into its own.

In the preparation of a TOK essay, as in the presentations, cross-cultural considerations should not be neglected. Cultural issues are significant throughout the TOK course. For example, one of its stated objectives is for students to be able 'to demonstrate awareness of the virtues and the limitations of both their individual outlook and the views common to the communities and cultures to which they belong' (IBO 1994: 4). Referring to the recently revised assessment criteria for the essay, to obtain a high score on one criterion, examples must 'reflect a degree of cultural diversity' (ibid.: 49). In the multicultural society of the UK today, not to mention in this time of global tensions, such considerations are vital.

It is a tall order for most 17- to 18-year-olds, and the proportion of students gaining an A grade each year is small. It represents a real challenge, however, to the high achievers – an opportunity to stretch their intellect and show that they can think outside the box. As stated earlier, the assessment criteria are weighted towards the identification and evaluation of 'problems of knowledge', which account for half of the marks, with the rest available for breadth in TOK terms, clarity of expression and range of examples given. Sources must be acknowledged in a recognised manner, and a bibliography provided.

Clearly, some practice is required by most students in writing a succinct, original, thought-provoking essay of no more than 1,600 words on a title such as those mentioned above. Students might be encouraged to try their hand at one or two of the titles before deciding which works best for them. Although it would be counter to the spirit of TOK to focus too heavily on the one final essay sent off for external marking, one or two drafts submitted to teachers for comment would be commonplace; these should not, however, be 'marked' but simply commented on, following the usual procedure for coursework. Ultimately, however, the value of the TOK course is not to be sought in the marks obtained but in the development of independent reasoning, self-awareness and critical reflection that it fosters.

The extended essay

The second component of the core within the IBDP hexagon is the extended essay. Another feature of the IBDP that has enlisted much support from higher-education bodies, this offers students the opportunity to pursue in some depth a specific topic of enquiry within a chosen field. In the introductory words of *The Extended Essay Guide*, 'Emphasis is placed on the process of engaging in personal research [and] … on the communication of ideas and information in a logical and coherent manner' (IBO 1998: 7).

While the general criteria for assessment and the format of the essay are prescribed, the choice of topic is left deliberately wide, in the hope of nourishing a passion or facilitating a personal discovery. The list of subject areas available includes not only all those disciplines within the IBDP, but several more, such as politics and world religions. All IBDP students select their topic area, and then decide on the specific research question to be addressed, in conjunction with their supervisor.

The 4,000-word essay must be the student's own original work; the IBDP stipulates that a maximum of four hours should be given in supervision, and thus the supervisor must take a backseat role, however fascinating the subject. Their role, as in higher-level academic research, is to direct students to fertile sources, and advise on selection of material and organisation of the essay.

The general criteria need to be studied in some depth at the start, as they account for two-thirds of the final assessment marks. They are concerned with presentation of the essay as a serious piece of academic research, and relate to the appropriateness of the research question and 'the way in which the material is handled, the level of analysis and the quality of the argument' (ibid.: 15). In practical terms, this means that a proper abstract, a complete bibliography and a closely argued text, adequately supported by data, are essential ingredients.

Many, but by no means all, students will choose to write their extended essay within the field of one of their higher-level subjects, especially if they have already decided on their course of study in higher education. It can be of particular value in applying for certain highly subscribed courses, such as English or history. Although A-level students with whom they are competing will have produced coursework, the subject matter will have been predetermined, and the personal input consequently diminished. Nor will the same degree of academic rigour have been expected. An extended essay represents a step up the ladder towards tertiary education, where the capacity for independent study and personal research skills are essential attributes. As one university admissions tutor commented: 'I would fall over backwards for more IB students' (IBO 2004).

Supervision

Allocation of students to subject areas can be a little sensitive in schools with larger IBDP cohorts, since popular areas, notably history, psychology and business studies, can quickly become oversubscribed. Less focused students may need to be steered towards the less popular subject areas, which may require delicate negotiation. Teachers in the more popular departments are liable to become overloaded, and this needs to be watched, as initial enthusiasm may not materialise into the weekly checks necessary to keep students on task. The easiest way to ensure regular contact is for a student to be supervised by their own subject teacher. Clearly, it is helpful if the supervisor has some prior knowledge of the topic chosen, but this is not always possible. In any case, the background research needed to guide students may be time-consuming, and it is advisable to set a limit on the number of essays to be supervised by any one teacher, even though this may sometimes have to be overridden. In general, teachers seem to be reasonably happy to take on the supervision, which offers a chance of a fresh and detailed investigation within their subject area. It is a way of helping students to take control of their own learning, and in this sense it complements the TOK course, where again the teacher's role is to point the student in the right direction, and then to step back.

The choice of title is crucial – it is hard to write a good essay on a poor title, but similarly hard to write a poor essay on a good title. Worn-out topic areas ('Hitler' springs to mind) are to be avoided; the title should be specific enough for research to be focused, but not too specialised for there to be too little information available. Supervisors need to advise here, and guidance is also offered in the subject-specific criteria section of *The Extended Essay Guide*. To take an example from physics: '*Does the frequency of light affect the resolution of the eye?* is better than *How well do we see in different lights?*' (ibid.: 107). Science essays are a special case, in that they often demand the collection, analysis and evaluation of experimental data. Clearly, a school laboratory cannot be transformed into a research facility at the level of a university medical school, and students' aspirations may have to be tamed. It is important to keep in mind that the main purpose of the essay is to offer an opportunity to produce the student's first truly academic paper; to this end, the majority of the marks are given to the general criteria described above. Only one-third of the assessment is subject-specific, a point that students and staff alike find hard to grasp. This needs stressing at the start of the course, at the stage when the extended essay is introduced, generally during the first term of the IBDP. It normally gives rise to considerable excitement in the student body, and while one would not wish to dampen students' enthusiasm, a note of caution needs to be sounded to make sure that they set off on the right track. Since the time between this introductory session and the final submission of the essay may be as much as a year, clear guidelines over how to go about producing it are required. A flow chart, such as that shown in Figure 3, can be useful.

Some students will be well organised as well as highly motivated; others will need more guidance and reminders. At Sevenoaks, each student receives an in-house brochure, which gives practical advice and guidance on the various stages of the process, including detailed information on how to present a bibliography. We have also experimented with an appointments card to be signed by the supervisor as each stage of completion of the essay is reached. This enables supervisors and parents to keep track of progress, and should help to reduce panic as the final deadline approaches. In particular, a period of time must be set aside for the uninterrupted writing of the first draft. In many schools, the only time available for the sustained commitment required for a piece of work of this nature is the summer break between the first and second years of the IBDP. If this is designated as the main writing period, the preparation of the student's research investigation and a detailed plan must have been approved before the end of the summer term.

The wide range of interests students are able to explore through this opportunity will be evident from a small selection of titles recently submitted.

- 'To what extent could the Russian literary intellectual perceive Soviet ideology to be the totalitarian hijacking of a romantic creed?'
- 'What have been the extent and the consequences of second home ownership in north-west Norfolk?'
- 'The Ruskinian concept of changefulness'
- 'What influence did the intelligence agencies have on shaping the development of the Cuban Missile Crisis?'
- 'How catalysis affects reaction kinetics'
- 'How are Salman Rushdie's novels *Midnight's Children* and *The Satanic Verses* influenced by cinema?'

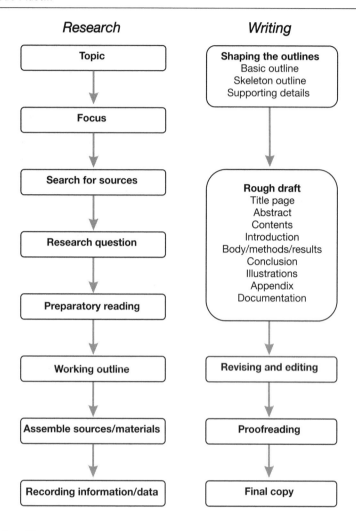

Figure 3 The extended essay: Suggested writing schedule

- 'What is the effect of sulphur dioxide pollution on the diversity, distribution and abundance of lichens across churchyard walls in Godstone and Oxted?'

Once the specific title has been approved, background reading established and a clear structure for the essay determined, students can be let loose for the summer on what one hopes will prove to be an exciting voyage of intellectual discovery. As in the TOK course, the best extended essays will demonstrate considerable critical thinking: the ability to distinguish between various accounts of the lead-up to the Gulf War, for example, or to work out why experimental results did not fit the original hypothesis. For most students, this is the first chance they will have had to produce truly original work, and the results are often impressive. Fascinating essays, well researched and meticulously presented, are often the outcome. As one student commented:

> Once I had chosen a title that really interested me, being able to focus on it and build up a complete data bank of material, so that I became the expert in that one small field, was stimulating and very satisfying.

The completed essays are not marked by supervisors, who will simply be asked for a grade prediction in the normal coursework manner. They are sent off to subject-specialist examiners around the world, who then award grades on an A–E scale. Taken together with the TOK grade, this can result in up to 3 bonus points to add to the aggregate IBDP score. However, the intrinsic value to most students extends beyond the points score; it can and should represent a considerable personal achievement, not only in the form of the completed essay to display to university personnel, but also of the successful execution of the research process, meeting norms of academic rigour. On many occasions the extended essay has formed the focus of a university interview, and it undoubtedly adds substantially to a personal profile.

CAS

'Developing enquiring, knowledgeable and caring young people who help to create a better, more peaceful world' is part of the IBO mission statement. The 'caring' aspect is addressed by the CAS programme. All students following the IBDP are required to undertake a programme of activity in the three areas of creativity, action and service (from which the acronym CAS is derived). There are no IBDP points for these activities, but the requirement to complete a minimum of 150 hours across the three areas is unequivocal, and the IBDP can be, and has been, withheld if a student fails to meet these obligations. The philosophy here is evident; the IBDP is intended to offer not only academic balance, but a well-rounded education in the wider sense, to foster the development of fit and healthy young people able to think imaginatively for themselves, and to demonstrate their responsibilities towards others, either in their local community or further afield.

Creativity

The value of extra-curricular activities has long been appreciated by teachers and higher-education institutions. Schools have always tried to provide as many opportunities for activities outside the classroom as possible, conscious that appetites are both varied and insatiable. Sadly, the recent increase in modular examinations in the UK system, with most AS subjects taken in the first year of the sixth form, has squeezed out many laudable extra-curricular initiatives, as staff and student energy is focused on jumping through yet another examination hoop. The casualties in this process-driven world are drama productions, concerts, photography clubs, dance groups, school magazines – all distinctly creative outlets, and wonderful learning environments for those they attract. The difference with the IBDP is that such activities form an integral part of the course, and thus can be defended against other contenders for that block of school time. IBDP schools can be justly proud of their theatrical productions, their musical ensembles and their ceramics or weaving sessions, since all can count towards a student's final diploma. An obvious proviso is that there must be no overlap with creative subjects taken within the IBDP; a student taking theatre arts, for example, would have to find another outlet for their creative talents for CAS purposes, perhaps by demonstrating musical or photographic skills. It is interesting to note that, although initially there may be some diffidence about the creativity lurking in each 16-year-old embarking on the course, the vast majority surprise themselves and sometimes their teachers by producing remarkably original work on a wide variety of themes in a number of media. The prerequisite here, of course, is resources, both in terms of staff and materials. Some fine-tuning of the timetable may be needed in order to match student and staff availability, and part-time employment of teachers in the creative departments can compound the problem. None-the-less, the obligatory nature of this component means that it should be taken into consideration when planning a budget for the IBDP.

Fertile ground for CAS possibilities within school can be found in the ethnic background of the students themselves. A cultural-awareness society can provide an opportunity for less confident students to share their different cultures with their UK peers, demonstrating exotic and intriguing customs, dress, food and music. One participant in such a programme wrote:

> I feel that I captured the essence of my country's culture. The difficulty lay in exposing others to customs that seem archaic and exotic ... Members of my team helped me to see the bias of my views and hence to look at the world from a more objective point of view.

Action

The action component of CAS presents little difficulty for the majority of students in UK schools, where sports programmes are strongly encouraged, if not compulsory, after the age of 16. At this stage, however, enthusiasm for team sports has often waned, and alternative forms of physical exertion may need to be explored. Financial constraints, and lack of facilities and coaches, may deter schools from offering 'luxury' sports like squash or golf, but basketball, aerobics and dance can be popular options. The recent alarm over the lack of physical exercise taken by increasing numbers of young people, who run the risk of obesity and its associated health risks, needs to be taken seriously.

The Duke of Edinburgh's Award mirrors CAS to a large degree, and the expeditions that form part of the bronze, silver and gold awards suggest the kind of action component envisaged by the authors of the IBDP. IBDP students have not only to prove that they have undertaken a programme of physical exercise, but also that they have set themselves personal goals, described in the self-evaluation reports, the official compulsory form of reporting for CAS, in which each student is asked to describe what they have learned from the specific activity about themselves, and about working with others. Participation in teams develops skills of cooperation and 'team spirit'; meeting the challenge of learning a new sport, or setting a personal target in an individual sport like swimming or running, develops endurance and persistence. As in the case of the extended essay, students are encouraged to take control of their own learning, by coming up with their own CAS ideas, inside or outside the school walls.

Service

Evidence of students' active involvement in service to others is always going to be viewed favourably by university admissions officers and future employers. Many schools support local community activities, some organise their own volunteer programme while most encourage students to take part in community service. However, this has to be extra-curricular; only in IBDP schools is service an integral part of the curriculum. The choice of service activity remains in the hands of the student; once chosen, there is an obligation to complete it.

Providing opportunities for service hours, especially in a school with a relatively large IBDP cohort, puts a heavy demand on school resources. The time involved in setting up community service projects is commonly underestimated. It tends to fall on the shoulders of one or two dedicated members of staff who already have, or are prepared to make, contacts with outside agencies, whether local branches of charities, working with the elderly, a local hospital or an environmental project. One needs to bear in mind that each new placement will involve many hours of preparation, and will most likely benefit only a handful of students. And yet the most valuable experiences are those where the young people have to think for themselves and act responsibly, perhaps taking risks away from the safety of their peer group. Making contacts with non-governmental organisations or local volunteer groups is fraught with frustration; the personnel tend to work variable hours and rarely to be at fixed office bases. Some service opportunities can be found within school, of course. Local community groups, from primary schools or sheltered housing for those with learning difficulties, can be invited in for computer training, concerts or art activities. Such events can provide effective service opportunities for students in a less threatening environment; staff supervision is also easier to arrange on campus. However, the visitors will usually still need transport to and from the school.

The administration of the service aspect of CAS is demanding, and requires the appointment of a CAS supervisor responsible for allocation of students and detailed monitoring of their individual CAS programmes, and for overall surveillance of the school's CAS provision. Each activity undertaken has to be authorised by the school, and an adult supervisor, not a parent, must be identified.

Registration can be something of a headache, since attendance at out-of-school activities is harder to register than in class. Some form of CAS record card is a good idea, with spaces for adult supervisors to sign for hours completed in the three sectors. An objection commonly raised is that once service is counted in obligatory hours clocked up, it is no longer voluntary, and, even worse, may be seen as conscription. The clock-watching, hour-counting mentality has to be discouraged. Then again, it is significant how many of the most reluctant 'volunteers' actually come to enjoy and gain a lot from their 'forced' volunteering. Examples from the self-evaluation forms described above, in which students reflect on their service, bear witness to this.

- 'I discovered the importance of perseverance and sharing ideas within a group.'
- 'It has inspired me to apply more creativity to fund-raising in future.'
- 'I learned how important it is to convey one's knowledge and feelings to others, on all levels, in an interesting way. I found it rude and hurtful when a (primary) student's concentration slipped too obviously despite my efforts.'

Nowadays, volunteering is beginning to take on a more acceptable image in mainstream employment circles; many graduates are actively encouraged to take up temporary voluntary work, with increasing possibilities of longer-term employment.

The service element of CAS shares characteristics with, and can be seen as a logical development from, the GCSE course in citizenship. At AS level, one of the stated aims is 'to critically evaluate … participation within school and/or community activities'(AQA 2004). Suggested areas of involvement for this assignment are:

Involvement in a local voluntary/community group (e.g. to bring about change – slum clearance or community regeneration; to help local groups – coaching a sport/activity to young people); or working with young children (e.g. a reading/mentoring scheme for a younger age group).

Such activities are precisely the areas of involvement sought for CAS service. The take-up for this course, introduced only in 2002, is as yet uncertain, but the political call to develop 'citizenship' qualities is increasingly being heard. In fact, since August 2002, all students in England have been required to study citizenship as a national curriculum subject. Input from schools here would bring the UK into line with other European countries, where education in this area has long been part of the national curriculum. CAS programmes could well provide the blueprint for such developments.

As far as the running of a CAS programme within the IBDP is concerned, students clearly have to be allowed enough time in the week for their CAS activities. Depending on the nature of the school, in particular how wide the catchment area is and, thus, how long the average journey to school takes, it may be feasible to arrange placements at the end of the school day. Typical projects at Sevenoaks have included running an after-school club for children from a neighbouring estate, and visiting a respite home for disabled children when they return from school. Some placements, such as helping in primary schools, have to occur during the school day. Here the possibilities are varied: developing ICT skills, listening to reading, assisting teachers wherever this is needed – just bringing a taste of secondary-school life in a friendly, unthreatening way – all these can be immensely valuable, but there needs to be careful preparation beforehand, and regular monitoring by CAS staff of the relationship between helper and helped. Service to people involves building up trust, and this can take some time.

Other service opportunities can be found with elderly residents in the area. Apart from practical help with shopping or gardening for those living on their own, valuable time is spent just visiting, listening and befriending. Loneliness is one of the greatest problems for many elderly people; a regular young visitor may show a refreshing interest in, and patience towards, them. A number of reminiscence schemes have been set up around the country; there is an obvious role here for volunteers, recording individual memories and adding to the databank of oral history. Other students may want to work in local hospitals, where they will often need to show determination, for the red tape (medical checks, health-and-safety regulations and so on) will defeat all but the most determined. Schools and homes for disabled young and older people are more accessible, and offer extremely rewarding service opportunities. A fairly common nervousness and apprehension about handicap is readily overcome in most cases, once the contact is made, and gentle encouragement is often well rewarded. Such voluntary work can also provide valuable experience to would-be doctors, as the following comment from a student who spent time with patients in a paediatric clinic suggests: 'I learned that patience is required in dealing with patients, as well as the ability to listen, even for a short time.'

Running a CAS programme

The fact that CAS is not only an integral part of the course, but linked with the possibility of failing the IBDP, should a student not complete their CAS component satisfactorily, gives it much more weight within the curriculum than is normally the case for such activities. The *Creativity, Action, Service Guide* states that 'The IBO expects the school administration to share its belief in the educational value of CAS, acknowledge the central role of CAS within the Diploma programme and encourage staff support and participation as far as possible' (IBO 2001: 11). The school's management team must be on board, not only in arranging adequate funding to ensure the smooth running of the programme, but also in recruiting motivated staff, especially those with any relevant previous experience, and in ensuring that they are released from other duties for CAS supervision. Recruiting staff to run creative activities – art, music and drama – tends to be less of a problem, since one can call on the services of specialist teachers already known to the school. Reimbursement for such services can be more difficult, since many will be peripatetic and self-employed. Organisation of community service does not demand 'experts' in the same way, and staff may be reluctant to come forward, or management reluctant to release them from other duties. Some form of contractual obligation is probably best, for instance, requiring staff to contribute to sport or voluntary service once or twice a week.

At Sevenoaks, one afternoon is entirely devoted to non-academic activities for the older students, offering a valuable period of quality time for CAS activities. The voluntary service programme is, in fact, open to students from Year 10 upwards, giving them a chance to 'taste' the various service outlets, and, in the most successful cases, providing a source of volunteer help for several years, rather than just the usual one and a half years through the CAS programme. Ideally, older IBDP students should be able to supervise this younger group; this is workable if the IBDP students concerned have already been in the school for some years, although they may wish to continue with the community service they have been involved with so far. One disadvantage of sending students out into a community project for just the period of their IBDP course is an inevitable lack of continuity, and a three- or four-year commitment by a student is worth a great deal to the recipients.

Yet another fertile area of community involvement is that of environmental issues. Local councils are currently active in promoting 'green' policies by force of EU necessity. Many young people are ecologically aware, and local campaigns to raise consciousness may attract interest. Organisation of campaigns is extremely time-consuming though; the most viable way to support green power is to join an already established group, and offer manpower as well as ideas. The design of posters and leaflets, or help with websites, all require creativity, of course, and CAS hours gained in this way can be categorised as either creative or service contributions.

Given the restraints described above, finding enough hours in the school week for each student to complete their CAS commitments can present difficulties. One way of surmounting these is to promote creative or service activities during the holiday periods. These need not be run by the school; they might include helping at a local authority play scheme or with riding lessons for the disabled. Provided that the CAS supervisor sanctions the activity and that an adult supervisor can be found to confirm the participation, such involvement can provide a valuable learning experience.

Designing CAS schedules

Making decisions on the creativity and action components of CAS is generally relatively easy for students, although some may need advice and guidance on the creative side. Service is a little trickier. Choosing the right student for the right project, and vice versa, is a difficult business, and mistakes will be made. Comprehensive information about the options available should be provided before students make their choices at the start of the IBDP. Some enterprising students may come up with their own ideas, and, wherever possible, these should be encouraged. A student who has found their own placement will probably make it work. On the other hand, no one should be forced to continue with an activity they feel uncomfortable with, and the CAS supervisor needs to be there to sort out problems.

One essential consideration in selecting community projects is logistics. Transport to and from projects can present headaches, and should be addressed from the start. Public transport may be inadequate; using it will often take up a disproportionate amount of time. Some schools have minibuses; these will soon be used to full capacity during the time allocated to CAS. Parents may be persuaded to drive, but there is no guarantee of the reliability of all but a few. Ideally, students will walk to their placements – at a charity shop, a day centre for the elderly or a home for the elderly, say – but the availability of such openings will depend on the locality. Moreover, all placements will have to be subject to a risk assessment. Insurance and health-and-safety requirements need careful consideration at the planning stage; any involvement with the outside world brings with it the potential risk of litigation. The safety of young people, as well as those they work alongside, must be paramount, and yet the parallel objective of offering chances to show initiative, care and concern for others must be met. Finally, in designing the programme, it is important to bear in mind a basic CAS tenet: 'CAS is a framework for experiential learning, designed to involve students in new roles. The emphasis is on learning by doing real tasks that have real consequences and then reflecting on these experiences over time' (ibid.: 4).

Teamwork

It is worth stressing that the totalling-up of hours should *not* be the main objective of the CAS programme. Similarly, rigid division of activities into the three categories does not represent the spirit of CAS. The *Creativity, Action, Service Guide* states:

> Although there are three elements to CAS, it is important not to consider them as mutually exclusive. CAS is about the education of the whole person, and the three elements are therefore interwoven … Together, they enable a student to recognise that there are many opportunities in life, away from formal academic study, to grow in knowledge of life, self and others (ibid.: 3).

There are many examples of projects that involve all three components, and thus embody the true spirit of CAS. Many schools have a link with a partner school in another country. At Sevenoaks, there is one such link with a special school in Romania, and another project with HIV-positive children in a hospital in Moldova. Teams of students go out to these venues each summer to run educational programmes designed to bring fun and fulfilment, but most of all friendship, to the children. In the process, the students learn a lot about themselves and their interaction with others. As one student who participated in this project commented:

> I learned that under tough conditions the people I was working with relied on each other more and more … I can now cope much better in dealing with disabled people, and I know more about how they like to be treated.

Such schemes are, of course, extremely costly in terms of planning hours, but are effective vehicles for the delivery of CAS on a larger scale, if one takes account of the teams back in school involved in fund-raising and publicity. Such activities may appeal to the less confident students, who would prefer to find their CAS opportunities in school rather than outside. This area needs exploiting, and not just because it eases the pressure on transport. There is huge value in inviting the local community into the school, whether it is offering computer training to those with learning difficulties, running an art club for local primary children or organising a 'Make a difference day' that offers fun with art, music and pets, together with tea and a disco, to physically or mentally handicapped people in the area. Whether the target is individuals needing care here and now, or at a distance – for example, support for prisoners of conscience or, again, concern for the future of the whole planet with green campaigns – the real value to students lies in their personal involvement, as well as their participation in a team. Cooperation with others, or teamwork, recognised as a key skill by the government, is at the heart of the CAS philosophy.

Finally, despite all the practical and bureaucratic obstacles that may be encountered in planning the CAS programme, a school should always bear in mind the mission statement in the *Creativity, Action, Service Guide*: 'CAS should extend the students. It should challenge them to develop a value system by which they enhance their personal growth. It should develop a spirit of open-mindedness, life-long learning, discovery and self-reliance' (ibid.). Considered in this light, the core components of the IBDP can thus be seen to represent the true 'value-added' element of the course.

References

AQA (Assessment and Qualifications Alliance) (2004) *Specification for AS-level Science in Citizenship*, www.aqa.org.uk

IBO (International Baccalaureate Organisation) (1994) *Theory of Knowledge Guide*, IBO, Geneva.

IBO (1998) *The Extended Essay Guide*, IBO, Geneva.

IBO (1999) *Theory of Knowledge Guide*, IBO, Geneva.

IBO (2001) *Creativity, Action, Service Guide*, IBO, Geneva.

IBO (2002) *Schools' Guide to the Diploma Programme*, IBO, Geneva.

IBO (2004) *Perspectives of the Diploma*, IBO, Geneva.

Independent (2004) 'Edward de Bono: Lateral thinker in despair at the wasted state of British schools' by Sarah Cassidy, 28 October, *Independent*.

OCR (Oxford, Cambridge and RSA Examinations) (2002) *Specification for AS-level Critical Thinkings*, www.ocr.org.uk

Chapter 8

Marked for life? Progression from the IBDP

Gary Snapper

Introduction

I would not hesitate to recommend the IBDP, despite the heavy workload ... The time I spent doing the course helped shape me into who I am as an adult. University was almost a let-down by comparison.

Student B

I have never regretted taking the IBDP – on the contrary, I have always felt privileged to have had the opportunity to take it ... When I first went to university I found it disappointing after my time [in the sixth form]. Classes were not as stimulating and certainly not as focused, other students were not as comfortable in taking part in discussions, and many showed little interest in any subject other than their own as it was narrowly defined by the syllabus.

Student D

I firmly believe that the range of subjects I took as part of the IBDP made me better prepared for my later life in every way than A levels would have.

Student H

I find it almost impossible to be objective about the IBDP as it was a wholly positive experience for me, and I still firmly believe that in terms of preparation for life after the sixth form, whether in academia or otherwise, the IBDP has far more to offer than A level ... The roundedness of the IBDP ... gives, in my opinion, a far better grounding than separate A-level courses, and I certainly felt when I got to university that I was significantly advantaged by my sixth-form experience.

Student I*

*These and subsequent quotations are taken from a written survey that I carried out with nine ex-students who studied for the IBDP between 1993 and 1999. Students were asked 'to write briefly about why [they] decided to do the IBDP instead of A level', and 'in some detail about how [they] felt the IBDP may have helped to prepare [them] for university, for employment and for what might be described as citizenship – functioning effectively as an individual in society.'

The International Baccalaureate Diploma Programme (IBDP) provides a characteristic set of experiences, which contrast in fundamental ways with those of A-level students, and which inevitably set IBDP students apart from A-level students, as they progress through to their life beyond the sixth form. The strong ethos and tightly structured nature of the IBDP, with its integrated cross-curricular and extra-curricular elements, and the intensity of its approach to breadth of knowledge and skills, as well as cultural awareness and critical thinking, mean that an IBDP student is taking on a great deal more than a selection of separate subjects under the loose umbrella of a national qualification system. In addition, the very fact of 'doing the IBDP' marks IBDP students out, and this difference can in itself be a distinctive element of the experience of both IBDP students and IBDP teachers. Indeed, such is the distinctiveness of the IBDP that it has a habit of becoming a way of life for those who teach and study it, often appearing to be something of a mission for those involved, and frequently engendering evangelical zeal in its participants.

Nevertheless, once the IBDP is over, its graduates are, in terms of 'the system', exactly where their non-IBDP peers are: ready to progress to higher education or employment, and to find their way as citizens of the nation and the world. How, then, are IBDP students different from others? What benefits do these students gain from their distinctiveness, and are they better placed to deal with the next stage of their lives than those who have followed a more mainstream route? To attempt any comparative evaluation of the IBDP in terms of progression would be fraught with difficulty, since it is clearly impossible to establish whether any student would have behaved differently or become a substantially different person if they had taken A levels (or other national qualifications) instead of the IBDP – although a study of similar students taking different qualifications within the same institution might, of course, prove interesting. However, there is a good deal of evidence to suggest that the IBDP is perceived by its graduates – and those who teach and work with them – as a comparatively strong and reliable starting point for progression, and one that confers clearly distinguishable characteristics on those who have undertaken it.

Most existing data on this topic comes from semi-formal and anecdotal accounts by university students and teachers. Ian Hill, the deputy director general of the International Baccalaureate Organisation (IBO) since 1993, for instance, writes:

> At conferences and meetings in different parts of the world IB students almost invariably emphasise that they found their first year of university less onerous than they had anticipated because they had already developed independent research skills, had learnt to structure essays and reports, had learnt to organise and prioritise their study activities, had learnt how to study (not just how to memorise) – how to assimilate and study critically, and had approached issues with an open mind.
>
> (2003: 63)

During the period 1993 to 1999, this writer was regularly in touch with university admission tutors and lecturers in a number of countries in Europe and elsewhere. They said frequently that IB students were consistently:

- self-confident and independent
- mature and tolerant towards the opinions of others
- open to challenges and willing to take risks
- critical readers and thinkers
- participating actively in local and global events.

This is not to say that the above qualities are not to be found in other students to varying degrees; clearly they are. The point is that IB students are perceived almost always to demonstrate these attributes (Hill 2003: 63).

A small but solid body of formal data, some quantitative and some qualitative, also exists. Hill, for example, gives details of four surveys of differing scale and type, the results of which, published between 1991 and 2002, show consistently high levels of satisfaction with the IBDP as a starting point for progression to university (2003: 63–5). Such findings are again confirmed by the most recent survey of this type, published in October 2003 and carried out by the IBO itself, among 71 UK universities and colleges (IBO 2003).

In his introduction to *The International Baccalaureate*, Alec Peterson, the founding father of the IBDP, is categorical about the intended relationship between the IBDP and preparation for university education and life in general. Outlining five key skills of critical thinking, he declares that 'to subject to university education those who do not have them does no service to either the university or to the students who are forced through the growingly irrelevant academic mill.' But he continues:

> The potential scholars are also human beings and share with all their fellow human beings capacities and needs for the physical, moral and the aesthetic life, which are not related to their comparatively rare academic gifts. It has been one of the failings of European education in the lycée, Gymnasium, or grammar school that ... the development of their common humanity has been starved (1972: 35).

My own experience, over ten years, as an IBDP English teacher and sixth-form tutor, certainly suggests that many students (and teachers) are positively affected, both by the characteristic content of the IBDP and by their identity as participants in it, in significant and influential ways, and in ways that may continue to mark them out from many A-level students long after the completion of the IBDP, whether in future study, employment or in their personal and social lives. This chapter, therefore, presents a commentary on the testimonies of nine of my ex-students, which point to ways in which studying for the IBDP may distinctly affect their later lives, and which offer a closer look at the nature of the IBDP as it is experienced by students, and at how IBDP students form a distinct identity.

Student perceptions of the IBDP

It is the nature of the IBDP itself that is the main contributory factor in the IBDP student's progression. However, it is important to remember that, given the current post-16 system – in which the IBDP is a choice, in practice, available only to a small minority of students – the decision to study for the IBDP at all is a significant and formative element in the experience of an IBDP student, and a key moment in the way such a student thinks about purpose and progression. The process of building an identity as an IBDP student thus begins before the sixth form. All potential sixth-form students make choices, of course: given the largely compulsory nature of pre-16 education, the move to the sixth form represents the first major life choice most students have had to make – whether and where to undertake further education, which subjects to take and so on. But students who are offered a serious choice between two quite different, perhaps even oppositional, models of education in the sixth form have a strong additional focus for their decisions about the future, and for their thinking about their lives, education and careers. For these students, the move to A level is no longer automatic, as it is for the vast majority of students intending to attend sixth form in England.

At the school where I taught the IBDP for some years – a suburban state comprehensive with an international sixth form, where students can choose to do either A levels (which they might also choose to do at one of two nearby sixth-form colleges) or the IBDP – it is interesting to observe the annual decision process, with students weighing up the relative benefits of different institutions and qualifications. A relatively small proportion generally make the decision to stay at the school for the IBDP – normally students who know that they are 'all-rounders' and wish to keep their options open, or socially and intellectually curious students who recognise that the IBDP might offer them a distinctive experience, not least because of its international ethos and because of the presence of international students. In addition, a small number of students each year might opt for the IBDP because it promises a happy environment for their own ethnic difference or international profile. As well as the 'home-grown' students, another category of students makes even more drastic decisions – students who choose to come to the sixth form to study for the IBDP from other schools in the local area, the region or the country (in some cases from quite far-away schools, necessitating either long daily journeys or boarding in local homes). Such a decision usually means that the students in question have struck out in a highly idiosyncratic way, choosing not to follow the vast majority of their peers; clearly, these students are highly motivated by the distinct experiences the IBDP has to offer. (There is also, I should add, a further category of students: a large number of overseas students for whom the choice of doing the IBDP is often secondary to the choice of attending school in the UK.)

In my survey of nine ex-students, all UK students who had taken GCSEs at the school or nearby schools, these reasons for choosing the IBDP were frequently given, and there was evidence that students made their decisions with a very sharp awareness both of the ways in which their decision might affect their future choices, such as university entrance, and of the kinds of qualities they wanted their learning experiences to embrace. (Table 8.1 gives details of their IBDP grades, university degrees and subsequent study or employment.)

Regarding university, Student D 'was considering applying to study medicine at university, but did not want to stop studying arts subjects'; in the end, she read English and Russian at university. Student F 'knew that [he] wanted to study history at university' (and indeed went on to do so) 'but didn't want to narrow down studies overall.' Student A felt that she 'was still unsure what [she] wanted to study at university and didn't want to close any doors.' Student H felt that the IBDP 'would help [her] stand out from other applicants when applying to university', a reflection that is frequently borne out in the comments of university tutors.

Most of the students were attracted by the breadth, ethos and integrated nature of the IBDP, often making explicit comparisons with A level. Student C, for instance, explained that 'he had the option of either studying four subjects in isolation (A level) or studying a far wider range of subjects with embellishments,' whilst Student H pointed to the 'reputation for in-depth learning' that the IBDP had, and Student B 'loved the idea of studying Theory of Knowledge to help me to understand the roots of all the other subjects I was taking.' Two students actually started studying A levels at a nearby sixth-form college with an excellent reputation for academic achievement, but returned to do the IBDP having been disappointed by the learning experience offered to them. Student E 'disliked the learning system at [the sixth-form college], which involved being fed a lot of information in preparation for exams, as it wasn't interactive or in any way to do with the process of learning'; and Student I 'didn't enjoy the way the subjects were taught so independently, that there was no real attempt at integration of the courses and that there didn't seem to be any desire to provide an holistic learning experience over the two-year period.' Student H, who decided not to attend the sixth-form college, also pointed to its 'poor reputation for pastoral care and the encouragement of non-academic achievement', compared with the holistic and extra-curricular provision of the IBDP.

Finally, the internationalism of both the course and the sixth form proved attractive to several, such as Student B, who 'was already curious about travel and different cultures as well as languages' (and is now principal flautist in a top Chinese symphony orchestra!). In an environment such as this, then, where choice is available, many students make a conscious and highly formative decision to take the IBDP because it offers them something different from and, perhaps, better than the mainstream alternative; and the making of this choice – the choice to be different and to commit to a challenging and unfamiliar minority – is, at present, an important part of the identity of IBDP students, and an early indicator of the way in

Table 8.1 Progression of nine IBDP students

Student	IBDP results	University qualifications	Employment and postgraduate study
A	En 7, Ma 7, Bi 5, Ec 5, Ch 4, Ge 4	Aberdeen, biomedical science BSc (1st class)	Research assistant and PhD, physiology, University of Bristol
B	En 6, Mu 6, Ru 6, Bi 5, SA 5, Ma 4	Leeds, music BMus (1st class)	MMus, Royal Northern College of Music; principal flautist in professional orchestras
C	Bi 6, Ma 6, Ph 6, En 5, Sp 5, SA 4	Keele, social anthropology and biology BSc (2:1)	Network administrator for large company
D	Bi 7, En 7, Ru 7, Hi 6, SA 6, Ma 5	Oxford, English and Russian BA (2:1)	PhD, Russian literature, University of Oxford; private Russian teaching
E	En 6, Fr 6, Hi 6, Ma 6, SA 6, Bi 5	Oxford, English BA (1st class)	MA, creative writing, University of East Anglia; senior editor in academic publishing
F	En 7, Hi 7, Ma 6, Fr 5, Ph 5, Ru 5	LSE, history BA (1st class)	PhD, history, University of Cambridge; lecturer in history, University of London
G	En 7, Ma 7, Ru 7, Bi 6, Fr 6, Psy 6	Oxford, human sciences BA (2:1)	MPhil, medical sciences, University of Cambridge
H	Hi 7, En 6, Ru 6, Bi 5, Ma 5, Psy 5	LSE, social anthropology BA (1st class)	PhD, social anthropology, LSE
I	Ec 7, En 7, Ma 7, SA 7, Fr 6, Bi 6	Sussex, social anthropology BA (2:1)	PhD, international relations and gender politics, University of Bristol

Notes
Ec = economics
En = English
Bi = biology
Ch = chemistry
Fr = French
Ge = German
Hi = history
Ma = mathematics
Mu = music
Ph = physics
Psy = psychology
Ru = Russian
SA = social anthropology
Sp = Spanish

which these students will be alert to aspects of their progression. Even where choice is not so readily available or where it is less likely to be considered (as, for instance, in a number of mainly independent schools, where the IBDP is the only option available), the institution and the students within it will still inevitably define themselves formatively, to a certain extent, by their difference from the majority.

However, although the differential between the IBDP and A level can at present be a valuable element of the IBDP experience, this ought not to suggest that the benefits of the IBDP and the identity of the IBDP student should not, or could not, be available to all: far from it. Ultimately, it is the content, structure and ethos of the IBDP itself – rather than its oppositional status – that are important, and that give the IBDP its progressive and distinctive shape, and make it radically different from A level.

Of course, life in the post-compulsory sector inevitably has a progressive and distinctive feel to it. It represents the first definitive new start most students have experienced since the move to secondary school at 11. For many, this new start will be reinforced by the move to a sixth-form or further-education college; for others, the sixth form will almost certainly be a separate unit within the larger school, with its own routines, buildings and staff. And, of course, the separateness and structure of the sharply delineated two-year course, and the urgency of university applications or other career decisions, as well as the newly acquired independence of students at this stage, with all its attendant opportunities and its need for self-motivation and reliance, mean that any sixth-form programme is likely to have a distinct sense of purpose and progression greater than that of the main school. Nevertheless, a sharp recent increase in the level of dissatisfaction with A level has highlighted its weaknesses in terms of preparing students effectively for progression – its relative lack of breadth, its unwieldiness and inflexibility in terms of modes of assessment, and its failure to nurture skills, knowledge and values developed through cross-curricular and extra-curricular means, in a coherent and integrated scheme of study.

The IBDP offers a kind of shape, coherence and sense of purpose that is quite different from, and more substantial than, that offered by A level; the six-subject structure, compulsory extended essay, cross-curricular Theory of Knowledge (TOK) course and extra-curricular Creativity, Action, Service (CAS) unit, which together make up the IBDP, form the vehicle for its explicit fostering of a network of skills, knowledge and values, the potential benefits of which for students' progression have recently been publicised as a result of the increasing popularity of the IBDP in the UK, and the inspiration that it and other baccalaureate systems clearly provided for Tomlinson's 14–19 Reform Working Group.

The ways in which IBDP students experience the breadth, coherence and ethos of the programme, and are shaped afterwards by its workings, can be seen clearly in the testimonies of my ex-students, whose comments I have interpolated in the following exploration of the way the IBDP works with a number of cross-curricular themes, such as the acquisition of study skills and the development of cultural awareness.

Study, organisation and communication skills: Learning independently and in groups

Success in the IBDP is dependent to a considerable extent on students' ability to organise themselves and their time, and to show awareness of the structure of the IBDP as a whole and responsibility for the completion of all its elements. Whilst similar obligations are naturally part of any students' experience of study, and the need to balance the demands of a large number of commitments in a wide range of subjects is, of course, a feature of the GCSE course, the demands that the IBDP places on students in this regard – through the breadth and depth of its curriculum, and through the combination of curricular, cross-curricular and extra-curricular emphases – are far greater than those at GCSE and A level. Many students remember this as one of the most challenging aspects of the IBDP, and one of the experiences for which they are most grateful when they progress to university and employment.

> Doing the IBDP was an extremely valuable exercise in time management; studying many different subjects to a high level taught me to prioritise and to use the little time I had to do the work effectively. I learnt to research topics quickly and efficiently – a very helpful technique to have learnt before getting to university.
>
> Student B

> I look back on the IBDP as the time of my life when I worked harder than ever before or since, although to what extent that is retrospective myth-making I am unsure. Perhaps it accustomed me to hard work so that subsequent efforts have felt less difficult. Certainly it forced time management skills, including prioritisation, upon me. These were undoubtedly useful skills at university.
>
> Student F

> I have always believed that the IBDP was excellent preparation for university. I had little difficulty organising my university study since I actually found it to require less organisational aptitude than the IBDP.
>
> Student H

Closely connected with such skills is the ability to study effectively – both independently and as part of a team. In these respects, the IBDP offers a number of valuable experiences, which are not a standard feature of the experience of A-level students. The most well known of these is the extended essay, through which independent learning skills are particularly challenged, and which teachers and students of all subjects can use as a standard point of reference in monitoring the overall development of a student's writing and research skills. The regular one-to-one contact students have with their essay tutors is particularly important as a bridge between class learning and independent learning. Because of the way the extended essay combines curricular, extra-curricular and cross-curricular status, it can provide a powerful focus both for the drawing-together of a student's learning and experience, and in the development of a student's specialist interests, and its benefits are, again, often cited by those who have gone on to university.

I feel that the IBDP was more like a university course than a pre-university course as it encouraged self-motivated study, though with more guidance than at university. It was therefore a very good preparation for what was to follow.

Student B

At university, I never missed a deadline, and, whilst others were struggling with the workload, I did not really notice it. The extended essay played a great part in this as I was already used to writing long essays. I don't think I would have been as well prepared in this respect if I had opted for A levels.

Student C

The IBDP allowed me to build on skills for independent learning, without constant supervision and direction from teachers. This has been of crucial importance during my subsequent education, as it has often been the case that I have been set tasks with no indication of where to go for information or what books or journals should be used.

Student G

There is also an emphasis on teamwork, social learning, and oral skills through the compulsory science research project, the oral assessments in English and languages and the exploratory atmosphere of TOK classes; the nurturing of oral and social skills in these subjects certainly amounts to a far greater commitment to this mode of learning and communication than A level has made. In addition, students often comment on the richness of class discussion throughout the IBDP, attributable perhaps to a number of factors, including the strength of IBDP group identity. Although all IBDP students follow individual programmes, the emphasis on teamwork and discussion, the overlap between students' programmes, and the extent of the compulsory elements mean that these students' social coherence tends to be strong. Indeed, it is the balance and variety of learning and assessment methods that the IBDP overall ensures for its students that might be argued to be one of its most beneficial aspects, through its careful structuring of individual elements, and apportioning of varied and appropriate assessment methods for each part of each element.

What was particularly valuable about the TOK course was that there was relatively little emphasis placed on written work and assessment. Lessons were a forum where students felt very free to contribute to discussion and explore all kinds of questions. These classes were valuable training in contributing to discussion.

Student D

The IBDP encourages independent thinking. It was very unlike my brief [sixth-form college] experience. There was little learning from textbooks. There was, instead, a lot of group discussion and encouragement of personal response, which helped me develop strong critical-thinking and communication skills.

Student E

I believe the [science] project was very helpful as an introduction to group presentation skills ... This project certainly offered the opportunity to prepare and present in a relatively formal way.

Student G

It was expected that as students of the IBDP we would set high standards for ourselves while still working to create a supportive environment, and communicating informally about current tasks is something that I now encourage my students to do as much as possible.

Student I

Finally, the IBDP provides a solution to the problem of 'key skills', with which A level has been wrestling. In contrast to A level, the IBDP ensures that all students study English (if English is their first language) and mathematics. For those who opt for one or both of them as a subsidiary 'standard-level' subject, rather than one of their main 'higher-level' subjects, this compulsory feature of the course provides them with a lifeline to skills that they need in their other subjects, even when they prove particularly challenging for them (as is often the case in mathematics); and many find that, here, they have an advantage over A-level students in later work and study.

I am glad that I continued studying a wide range of subjects, particularly mathematics and languages. During the later years of my degree when I was conducting research projects, I found it easier to refresh my knowledge of maths than my colleagues who had not done any since they were 16.

Student A

Although some of the specialist knowledge (maths, Russian, physics) that I learned specifically to pass my exams has subsequently disappeared, I think that my knowledge and approach to life and study has been broader-based than it would have been without the IBDP ... It means that I am able to treat statistical nonsense like government demanding schools to be 'above average' with the contempt it deserves.

Student F

Critical-thinking skills and application of knowledge: Breadth, depth and coherence

Clearly, the breadth of the IBDP is one of its chief distinguishing factors, one that an increasing number feel that the post-compulsory sector should provide, and one strongly appreciated by its students, many of whom choose to take the IBDP because of it, and continue to benefit from the groundwork it lays for them when they have moved on.

Taking a range of subjects also made me a more useful employee. In my first [job], I was working in publishing lists over a broad range of subjects – history, international relations, philosophy, politics and sociology. My IBDP training meant I was unfazed by this, and had a decent amount of basic knowledge about many of these subjects.

Student E

At another level, the IBDP added value to my interactions with society from which both sides have benefited. I am able to recognise the pleasure that others can find in specialisation in their chosen fields, and have a real respect for those ... in areas which are not my own, but about which I am not completely ignorant either.

Student F

Whereas most students feel that the value of this breadth lies in the solid grounding it gives, many eventually find that a greater value of breadth is the way in which it enables links to be made between subjects, and a coherent overview of learning to emerge – especially when, as in the IBDP, subject choices are structured in such a way that all students study subjects in all the main areas of learning – languages, mathematics, sciences, humanities and arts. They also often report the profound effect this has on their subsequent thinking.

Because the IBDP covers a wide range of subjects, study skills must cover this spectrum of ways of thinking and working ... I believe this is an aspect of the IBDP that has had the most impact on my post-sixth-form life, since I continue to follow a multidisciplinary path because I enjoy utilising the different ways of thinking and approaching subjects that the IBDP helped me to acquire.

Student G

The emphasis placed on experiencing the IBDP as a holistic learning programme encouraged me to think about academic subjects in terms of their connectedness rather than as discrete and bounded areas of study, something that has served me well in my current research.

Student I

The TOK course is undoubtedly the major element in the cross-curricular coherence of the IBDP, and another element of the programme that students frequently cite with gratitude in terms of its contribution to their progression, because of its impact on conceptual understanding, critical-thinking skills and metacognitive awareness; almost all the students in my survey testified to its influence on their future lives.

I can clearly remember thinking, whilst taking a module called 'History and criticism' at university, that the TOK and social anthropology courses, and also the literature courses I had studied in the IBDP, had developed my critical thinking and ability to think around a subject. Whilst I had no problem understanding the influence of different paradigms on composers or the complicated writing of philosophers about music and its function in the society in which it was written, to mention just two elements of the course, my classmates struggled. The way that the IBDP opens your mind to thinking about every aspect of a subject was not something that those who had done A levels in my class were used to applying to music.

Student B

TOK played its role as the cohesion or 'core course' of the IBDP well, for me … From what I know of A level, there is no equivalent [of TOK]. General studies could not perform the same function because students are not following such a structured course with the basic components in common.

Student D

TOK taught me that nothing is as simple as it seems, and everything can be questioned … It is surprising how often subjects we touched on in TOK have re-emerged in seemingly unrelated subjects later on in my education.

Student G

The development of thinking skills in the IBDP is certainly not confined to TOK, however, and there is little evidence, in my experience, to suggest that the breadth of the course leads to a shortage of depth in individual subjects. One of the most interesting features of the IBDP is the way in which it tends to promote a style of learning that encourages students to synthesise knowledge and apply the general to the specific, both within and between subjects – the kind of transferable skills that *Curriculum 2000* was aiming towards in its notion of 'synopticity'. Peterson is quite explicit about the way the IBDP curriculum is informed by such an approach – a deliberate move away from what he calls the 'encyclopaedism' of continental European education, and the half-hearted 'bolt-on' general studies approach adopted in the UK (1987: 38–9). In English, for instance, comprehensive but atomistic knowledge of individual classic texts, such as A-level English literature promotes, is replaced by a broad and comparative study of genres, themes and cultures, as well as a solid training in close reading of short texts – and similar approaches are used in other IBDP subjects. Thus, whilst some detail may be dispensed with, depth is maintained and often increased, in comparison with A level. Again, the analytical training offered by the IBDP is a common theme in students' reflections on progression.

Critical skills which were valuable at university were developed by the thematic history syllabus. A subject such as 'War – its causes, practices and effects' demanded that a student synthesised knowledge in a way that the study of distinct historical events does not. I cannot say if this differs from A-level teaching, but I can identify it as an important way that the IBDP course taught me to organise my thinking about separate but related events, subjects and disciplines.

Student D

[The IBDP] was brilliant training for my literature degree, which was all about individual interpretation and learning to construct an argument. Both the IBDP and my university degree after it provided very good training for my job. As an editor in a publishing house I am having to respond to books and manuscripts on a personal level every day. I need to be able to trust my own responses and be able to express these articulately and reasonably to colleagues and authors. I would single out this emphasis the IBDP places on independent thinking as the most valuable element of the course and the most important thing I took away from it. It has aided me in my career but also in my life outside my work, helping me to make some controversial decisions.

Student E

As a young lecturer responsible for UCAS admissions and a lot of first-year teaching, I do get the impression that A-level students have a real problem with thinking critically … Many do find it difficult to raise their thinking to university level and to operate at the analytical and conceptual levels … I have not taught any IBDP students yet, so again a comparison is difficult, but it certainly seems to me that the IBDP's emphasis on discussion, thought and variety of approach, and the degree of reflexivity and personal responsibility that is implicit … would be an advantage.

Student F

From conversations with friends who took A-level English literature, I have found that the major difference is that they studied far fewer texts and genres than I did for the IBDP. Although the popular perception is that the A-level course is more in-depth, I do not think there is really evidence for this. I felt that we had studied texts in depth, and that we had a better background in literary analysis from having studied so many different genres, and sometimes more than one text within genres, so that we had a better grasp of how English literature has developed. Furthermore, the world literature texts gave us a great advantage over A-level students in their introduction to diverse cultural and political issues.

Student H

Internationalism: Understanding society, culture and language

Whilst it is for its breadth and integrated nature that the IBDP has become particu-larly well known, my own view is that, at a time when intercultural understanding

students, and it is interesting to note that one student in my survey maintained strong active links with both organisations at university (where she was president of her university's Amnesty International group) and since.

> Volunteering at Oxfam ... gave me invaluable work experience, but also taught me a lot about injustice in the world, and reinforced my views about certain issues such as fair trade. As a result, I have become a member of the Oxfam Urgent Action letter writing campaign, which continues to be an important part of my life.
>
> Student G

In concrete terms, as is clear from Table 8.1, the progression of the students in my survey has been highly successful. Several students – already quoted – commented on the fact that they felt somewhat disappointed by their experience at university after the IBDP. Perhaps the most plaintive of these was Student C:

> When I went to university, I have to admit that it was a real anti-climax, both because I didn't feel stretched academically and because the people with whom I had to live did not have as high standards as those I spent the IBDP years with. In a sense you could argue that socially and academically I was spoiled by the IBDP. Those two years were certainly the richest in terms of friendships and study.

Nevertheless, good university degrees and successful academic or business careers have followed for all of them, and most have commented specifically on the ways in which their IBDP experience prepared them effectively for study and employment. There is often a sense of these students weighing their experience against that of the A-level students they have subsequently studied and worked with, and realising that the IBDP might have helped them to achieve more than they might otherwise have done. It is a difficult claim to support in any substantial way, but I would certainly say that the general level of their achievement, as a group, looks optimal for every student in this group, whether exceptionally able (as some were) or just able (as all were).

Perhaps it is not fanciful to suggest that without the IBDP, some of these students might not have got as far as they have; certainly, their responses give an overwhelming impression of students who were thoroughly embraced and motivated by the structure and ethos that the IBDP offered them, as well as by their individual studies. Such a picture is borne out by my experience with dozens of other IBDP students. The majority of our students are academically able, some exceptionally able, and some not so able – but at all levels, I have experienced a high incidence of students reaching absolutely optimal levels of achievement and motivation for their ability.

We must remember, of course, that A levels produce many outstanding students, and that the elaborate provisions of the IBDP are not a prerequisite for good teaching or learning, or for the development of breadth of knowledge, study skills and sociocultural awareness. We must also be wary of the uncritical belief that all

IBDP students consequently become model citizens, who lead blameless and self-less lives entirely informed by a sense of moral, cultural and social justice. The last word here goes to Student F:

> I think I felt that [the IBDP] offered me an advantage in terms of critical thinking and expressing my opinions, but to what degree this was good teaching, my own innate abilities and the students I was fortunate enough to study with, rather than the IBDP itself, I am not sure … I could spout a load of stuff about the IBDP improving my range of cultural reference, making me more tolerant of different attitudes and nationalities and introducing me to new ideas. But then I was never the sort of person to go round hitting people at random with a brick or abusing ethnic minorities … Am I a good or bad citizen? How much does the IBDP have to answer for anyway? I have to say that I am not sure the IBDP gave me a greater sense of social responsibility …
>
> I didn't spend all the very limited free time available to me during the IBDP helping old people, rescuing drowning kids, or cleaning up the streets. But I don't think I should have done. When you're 16–18, that stuff feels like a terrible imposition, and I can't believe that resentment is a good basis for citizenship. On the other hand, I probably did do some volunteering that I wouldn't otherwise have done, and I guess that makes you more aware of how shitty some socially necessary jobs are. But if it just persuades you to work hard enough and fight hard enough to make sure that you can pay someone else to do those jobs, has it really made you a better citizen? I'm not sure. Maybe [my teachers] can remember whether cynicism was a trait that the IBDP developed or whether I was always like this?

I would like to think that without the IBDP, with its explicit ethos and overt promotion of values, this student's lively scepticism and his ability to view things from outside the framework would not have had as much exercise as they did. However, his comment is an important reminder that subscription to the IBDP's ethos of social awareness, however enthusiastic, may ultimately be complacent, and that the IBDP arguably remains, in many important respects, a traditionalist curriculum with an old-fashioned liberal humanist foundation.

Conclusion

This book appears as a result of the recent growth of interest in the IBDP as a possible model for the reform of 14–19 education in England. Whilst issues of assessment have been the catalyst for this reform, issues of opportunity and progression are clearly more profound and significant. This chapter has attempted to show how the integrated model of education promoted by the IBDP is actually experienced by students of the programme in ways that can give them clear advantages over A-level students, not least in terms of the strong influence exerted on their self-perceptions, achievements and contributions to society in later life. It is a pity, then, that a recent report by the Qualifications and Curriculum Authority (QCA) on post-16 education – a comparison between A level and the IBDP – limits itself to an almost exclusively quantitative and assessment-focused approach, which, although it clearly indicates that the IBDP is broadly comparable with A level in terms of academic achievement in individual subjects, fails to engage with the ethos and content of the IBDP as a whole. As the report itself says:

> How does one compare a very specific, designed programme of study (including non-assessed elements such as service to the community) with a clear philosophy, to individual examinations having no overall philosophy beyond the aims and rationale in each subject? (2003: 6).

Whilst there are undoubtedly good reasons why the IBDP is not considered an appropriate model for a comprehensive 14–19 system, it would indeed be a shame if we were not able to take into account the kind of experiences that my ex-students have written about so passionately. If we did, we should surely devise a system that, rather than having 'no overall philosophy beyond the aims and rationale in each subject', provided a broad, integrated and inspirational curriculum, which enabled all post-16 students to progress to future study, employment and citizenship with the kind of skills, knowledge and awareness that the IBDP is designed to engender.

References

Hill, I (2003) 'The International Baccalaureate' in G Phillips and T Pound (eds) *The Baccalaureate: A Model for Curriculum Reform*, Routledge, London.

IBO (International Baccalaureate Organisation) (2003) *Perceptions of the International Baccalaureate Diploma Programme*, IBO, Geneva.

Peterson, A (1972) *The International Baccalaureate: An Experiment in International Education*, Harrap, London.

Peterson, A (1987) *Schools Across Frontiers: The Story of the International Baccalaureate and the United World Colleges*, Open Court, La Salle, Illinois.

QCA (Qualifications and Curriculum Authority) (2003) *Report on the Comparability between GCE and International Baccalaureate Examinations*, QCA, London.

Index

7512 C19